DATE DUE

DEMCO 38-296

SUFFERING
AND THE
REMEDY OF ART

R

SUFFERING AND THE REMEDY OF ART

HAROLD SCHWEIZER

STATE UNIVERSITY OF NEW YORK PRESS

Published by
State University of New York Press, Albany

For information, address the State University of New York Press,
State University Plaza, Albany, NY 12246

Production by David Ford and Christine Lynch
Marketing by Nancy Farrell

Library of Congress Cataloging-in-Publication Data

Schweizer, Harold, 1950–
    Suffering and the remedy of art / Harold Schweizer.
        p.   cm.
    Includes bibliographical references and index.
    ISBN 0–7914–3263–7 (hc : alk. paper). — ISBN 0–7914–3264–5 (pbk. :
alk. paper)
    1. Suffering in literature.   2. Suffering in art.   I. Title.
PN56.S742S38   1996
809'.93353—dc20   96-16289
                                                                CIP

10   9   8   7   6   5   4   3   2   1

For my parents, Eleonore and Edmund Schweizer-Jäger

CONTENTS

III. SUFFERING AND THE REMEDY OF ART

ACKNOWLEDGMENTS

Since my interest in the subject of this book goes back some years, I owe thanks to various people and institutions who, knowingly or not, have helped me in conceiving the project and in bringing it to conclusion.

My colleagues at Bucknell, Greg Clingham, Kathleen Creed-Page, Pauline Fletcher, and John Rickard have been very supportive at various stages. I am grateful to Michael Payne who put aside his own work to read and comment on my work whenever I asked him. Myrna Treston helped with kind encouragement, good suggestions, and with the permissions. I would also like to thank my graduate assistant, Elizabeth Sahm Kelly, for further help with the permissions and with proofreading.

Thanks to my students in the 1993 spring theory seminar and to my students in Tours, France for forgiving my perpetual drifting to this subject. I owe much gratitude also to my students in the 1995 spring seminar on literature and suffering, particularly to Jennifer Beck, and to Nicole Shenk who helped with some early research; and finally to my students in the Theory of Tragedy seminar who prompted me to make last revisions; all were instrumental in refining my thinking. Some former graduate students have faithfully supported me with their continued interest and friendship: Cynthia Cronrath, Holly Henry, and Richard Kahn.

I am much indebted to Angela Cozea for her generous reception of my paper in Graz, Austria and her subsequent helpful suggestions; Irving Feldman for his comments on chapter nine when I prepared to present it as a paper; John Felstiner for his spontaneous response to my work on Celan; Tess Gallagher for her many kindnesses, her staunch friendship, and her spirited readings of several chapters; M. A. R. Habib for his very detailed and insightful comments; Andrew McNeillie for his kindness and encouragement; and Alicia Ostriker for her generous and instructive critique.

During my sabbatical leave, part of which was spent in Switzerland, we were greatly cared for and supported by Janet and Werner Eberli, Claudia and Freddy Grob, Emmi and Paul Iten, Blanche and

Hans Kündig, Bruce Lawder and Gabrielle Ruedin, Thomas Honegger and Viviane Müller, and the Schindlers who let us use their beautiful house in Wappenswil. Martin Heusser kindly invited me to give a very early version on the chapter on photography at the University of Zurich. I thank them all from my heart.

Belated thanks are due to the American Council of Learned Societies for a past fellowship; it was then, though I didn't know it, when I first began to think of this project. And it would have been altogether impossible to write this book without Bucknell's generous award of the NEH Chair in the Humanities 1993–1996, and a sabbatical leave during 1993–1994.

Finally, I am grateful to my wife Lynne for her tremendous support of this project, not only for her close and critical reading of the manuscript and her incisive editorial advice, but also for her encouragement to take the time I needed to write this book.

Several chapters or parts thereof have their beginnings in books and journals: versions of the essays on Nietzsche, Freud, and Donoghue have appeared in *The Bucknell Lectures in Literary Theory* published by Basil Blackwell, Oxford. In that context, I would like to thank Peter Brooks, Denis Donoghue, and J. Hillis Miller for their generous input into that work. I am gratefully indebted to Suzanne Poirier, editor of *Literature and Medicine*, and her editorial assistants Jennifer Cohen and Marguerite Valance, for their insightful suggestions and editorial help with Chapter 1, "To Give Suffering a Language," which was published in *Literature and Medicine*, October 1995. It is here reprinted with minor changes by permission of the Johns Hopkins University Press. A shorter version of "Lyric Suffering in Auden and Feldman" was published in *ELN* (31:2, Dec. 1993). The chapter on Raymond Carver is reprinted with some revisions from *Profils Américains*, ed. Claudine Verlay (Université Paul Valéry, Montpellier III). I thank the publishers of those earlier versions for their generosity.

PERMISSIONS

Grateful acknowledgment is made to the publishers who have given permission to use quotations from the following works:

Excerpts from "Matthew Arnold" and "In Time of War XVII," from *The English Auden: Poems, Essays and Dramatic Writings 1927–*

1939 by W. H. Auden, edited by Edward Mendelson. Reprinted by permission of Faber and Faber Limited.

"Musée des Beaux Arts" and extract from "The Composer," from *Collected Poems* by W. H. Auden, edited by Edward Mendelson. Reprinted by permission of Faber and Faber Limited.

"Musée des Beaux Arts" from *W. H. Auden: Collected Poems* by W. H. Auden. © 1940 and renewed 1968 by W. H. Auden. Reprinted by permission of Random House Inc.

Seventeenth sonnet of "In Time of War," from *W. H. Auden: Collected Poems* by W. H. Auden. © 1945 by W. H. Auden. Reprinted by permission of Random House Inc.

"Matthew Arnold" and nine lines of "The Composer," from *The Collected Poetry of W. H. Auden* by W. H. Auden. © 1940 and renewed 1968 by W. H. Auden. Reprinted by permission of Random House Inc.

Excerpt from "Confessional," from *In the Western Night: Collected Poems 1965–1990* by Frank Bidart. © 1990 by Frank Bidart. Reprinted by permission of Farrar, Straus and Giroux Inc.

Landscape with the Fall of Icarus by Pieter Brueghel the Elder, reprinted by permission of Musées royaux des Beaux-Arts de Belgique.

Excerpts from "Blackberry Pie," from *Where I'm Calling From* by Raymond Carver. © 1988. Reprinted by permission of Grove/Atlantic Inc.

Excerpts from *Where Water Comes Together With Other Water.* © 1984 by Tess Gallagher. Reprinted by permission of Tess Gallagher and International Creative Management Inc.

Excerpt from "Niedrigwasser," from *Sprachgitter* by Paul Celan, by permission of S. Fischer Verlag.

Excerpts from "Dein Vom Wachen," "Schieferäugige," "Ein Dröhnen," and "Mit den Verfolgten," taken from Paul Celan, *Atemwende*, © Suhrkamp Verlag Frankfurt am Main 1967, and translations of "Abglanzbeladen" and "In den Dunkelschlägen," and excerpts from "Wo ich mich vergass" and "Merkblätter-Schmerz," taken from Paul Celan, *Lichtzwang*, © Suhrkamp Verlag Frankfurt am Main 1970.

Excerpts from Paul Celan, "Speech on the Occasion of Receiving the Literature Prize of the Free Hanseatic City of Bremen," in Paul Celan, *Collected Prose*, translated by Rosemarie Waldrop. © 1986. Reprinted by permission of The Sheep Meadow Press.

Excerpts from "Pledged to the persecuted," "Solve," "A rumbling," "The Straitening," "To stand," "I can still see you," "Alchemical," from *Poems of Paul Celan*, translated by Michael Hamburger, © 1972, 1980, 1988, 1995 by Michael Hamburger. Reprinted by permission of Persea

Books, by permission of Anvil Press Poetry Ltd. (1965), and by permission of Michael Hamburger.

From "Der Meridian" by Paul Celan, by permission of Eric Celan.

Excerpt from "East Coker," *Four Quartets*, © 1943 by T. S. Eliot and renewed 1971 by Esme Valerie Eliot. Reprinted by permission of Harcourt Brace and Company.

Excerpt from "East Coker," from *Collected Poems 1909–1962* by T. S. Eliot. Reprinted by permission of Faber and Faber Limited.

Excerpts from *Teach Me, Dear Sister* (Viking Penguin Inc., 1983) and *All of Us Here* (Viking Penguin Inc., 1986) by permission of Irving Feldman.

Excerpts from "Death of the Horses by Fire" and "Bonfire." © 1987 by Tess Gallagher. Reprinted from *Amplitude* with the permission of Graywolf Press, Saint Paul, Minnesota.

"Moon Crossing Bridge" and excerpts from "Yes," "Wake," "Corpse Cradle," "Reading the Waterfall," "Black Pudding," "Embers," "Paradise," "Deaf Poem," "Spacious Encounter," "Anniversary," "Knotted Letter," "I Don't Know You," and "Near All That Is Lost." © 1992 by Tess Gallagher. Reprinted from *Moon Crossing Bridge* by permission of Graywolf Press, Saint Paul, Minnesota.

Napalm Victim, South Vietnam (1967) by P. J. Griffiths, by permission of Magnum Photos, New York.

"Paul Celan: A Grave and Mysterious Sentence," from *Wild Gratitude* by Edward Hirsch. © 1985 by Edward Hirsch. Reprinted by permission of Alfred A. Knopf Inc.

Excerpt from "The Double Axe," from *The Double Axe and Other Poems* by Robinson Jeffers. © 1977 by Liveright Publishing Corporation. Reprinted by permission of the publisher.

Excerpts from "Apology for Bad Dreams," "Delusion of Saints," "A Little Scraping," "Subjected Earth," "Give your Heart to the Hawks," "An Artist," "Boats in a Fog," "Margrave," "At the Birth of an Age," "Thurso's Landing," "Still the Mind Smiles," "The Tower Beyond Tragedy," and "Soliloquy" reprinted from *The Collected Poetry of Robinson Jeffers*, volumes One (1920–1928) and Two (1928–1938), edited by Tim Hunt, with the permission of the publishers, Stanford University Press. © 1938 by Donnan Jeffers and Garth Jeffers; © 1995 by the Board of Trustees of the Leland Stanford Junior University.

Excerpts from Robinson Jeffers, *Cawdor/Medea*. © 1946, 1956 by Robinson Jeffers. Reprinted by permission of New Directions Publishing Corporation.

"Epilogue" and excerpts from "Departure," "Unwanted," "Lives," "We Took our Paradise," "To Mother," "Robert T. S. Lowell," Home," "Doomsday Book," "Ulysses and Circe," "Notice," "Shifting Colors," from *Day by Day* by Robert Lowell. © 1977 by Robert Lowell. Reprinted by permission of Farrar, Straus and Giroux Inc., and by permission of Faber and Faber Limited.

Sipa Photo Agency and *Newsweek* for the reproduction of the photograph used for the *Newsweek* cover of May 10, 1993.

Excerpts from *The Father* by Sharon Olds. © 1992 by Sharon Olds. Reprinted by permission of Alfred A. Knopf Inc.

Excerpt from *The Dead and the Living* by Sharon Olds. © 1983 by Sharon Olds. Reprinted by permission of Alfred A. Knopf Inc.

Excerpt from "Paralytic," from *The Collected Poems of Sylvia Plath* by Sylvia Plath. © 1963 by Ted Hughes. Copyright renewed. Reprinted by permission of Harper Collins Publishers Inc.

Excerpts from "Daddy," "Years," "Getting There," and "Edge," from *Ariel* by Sylvia Plath. © 1963 by Ted Hughes. Copyright renewed. Reprinted by permission of Harper Collins Publishers, Inc.

Excerpts from "Paralytic," "Daddy," "Years," "Getting There," and "Edge," from *Ariel* by Sylvia Plath. Reprinted by permission of Faber and Faber Limited.

From *Antigone* in *Sophocles I*, edited by Grene and Lattimore. Reprinted by permission of The University of Chicago Press.

Excerpt from "The Pure Good of Theory," from *The Collected Poems of Wallace Stevens* by Wallace Stevens. Reprinted by permission of Faber and Faber Limited.

Excerpt from "The Pure Good of Theory," from *Collected Poems* by Wallace Stevens. © 1954 by Wallace Stevens. Reprinted by permission of Alfred A. Knopf Inc.

INTRODUCTION

Art is primarily the consciousness of unhappiness,
not its compensation.

—Maurice Blanchot, *The Space of Literature*

. . . it is now virtually in art alone that suffering
can still find its own voice, its consolation,
without immediately being betrayed by it.

—Theodor Adorno, *Aesthetics and Politics*

At a time when postmodern taste directs us towards the play of signifiers and the pleasures of the text, this book is unfashionably serious. Arthur Schopenhauer aptly wrote, "Life is deeply steeped in suffering, and cannot escape from it; our entrance into it takes place amid tears, at bottom its course is always tragic, and its end is even more so."[1] What then is the purpose of art? While Schopenhauer thought of art as a temporary suspension of the tragedy of existence,[2] I would here like to offer variations or alternatives, not always optimistic ones, to a redemptive theory of art. My proposition is complicated by the very fact that its reference—suffering—although universal is nevertheless an elusive reality. How or what art can redeem or remedy, is difficult to determine. While suffering is a universal human predicament, it also remains the most unsharable, incommunicable mystery, the very epitome of secrecy and particularity. And while art may probe most deeply into the mysteries of suffering, it also remains distant and aloof from it. Poetry, as Shelley wrote in his "Defence of Poetry," is "as the form and the splendor of unfaded beauty to the secrets of anatomy and corruption."[3]

Suffering and the Remedy of Art is about wounds that will not close despite the sutures, scarring, and bandaging, the patchwork and layering of literary language. Literary language reveals the secret of suffering only by keeping it—but thereby, I suggest, it legitimizes the experience of suffering itself. By "keeping the secret of suffering," I mean to

1

suggest that art is in some fundamental way analogous to suffering.[4] Referring to a tradition of the aesthetic spanning from Kant through Schopenhauer to the New Critics and beyond, I propose that art is as autonomous, gratuitous, and irreducible to analysis as suffering. Both art and suffering can be diagnosed, and neither can be understood; both are purposeless and gratuitous. In these analogies art echoes Schopenhauer's similar concept of music:

> . . . music does not express this or that particular and definite pleasure, this or that affliction, pain, sorrow, horror, gaiety, merriment or peace of mind, but joy, pain, sorrow, horror, gaiety, merriment, peace of mind *themselves*, to a certain extent in the abstract, their essential nature. . . .[5]

While Schopenhauer's qualification "to a certain extent in the abstract" offers apologies for the implied mysticism of his claim, I maintain here similarly and with similar apologies and qualifications that art may be *essentially*, or ontologically, related to suffering. Both have an existence in and by themselves, and through both we perceive orders larger than our cognitive concepts. But neither art nor suffering attain such autonomy without estrangement and alienation from their social and historical contexts. Thus, neither art nor suffering—and here I depart from the tradition referred to above—permit us to become pure, disinterested subjects of knowing in their presence. The analogous "essential nature" of art and suffering assigns art a gravity, and us a moral responsibility. Both the gravity of art and our moral responsibilty are too easily abrogated in the aesthetic traditions by the ideology of disinterested objectivity.

In the experience of suffering the ideology of objectivity, the claims of reason and knowledge, are called into question. Philosophical distinctions of body and spirit, sensation and intellect, the universal and the particular, the physical and the metaphysical, no longer apply. The very law of identity is in crisis. If suffering is the site of the crisis of meaning and understanding, art, I claim, is an analogical site. By virtue of its irreducibility to meaning or explanation, by its very refusal to function according to the laws of reason and logic, art acquires an opaque materiality like the body in pain. Like the suffering body, the meaning of art is in its non-referential autonomous dimension, its own subjective temporality and irreducible particularity.[6]

Like suffering, art returns to sounds and sense prior to language or meaning, so as to remind itself each time anew of the origins it has in common with human existence itself. Yet, even if artistic representation is fundamentally attuned to the incommensurability of its cause, all art must lastly compromise the incomprehensible by transforming the formless into form and the unsharable truth of suffering into bearable fictions. Even Theodor Adorno admits, after a time of particular urgency, that "it may have been wrong to say that after Auschwitz you could no longer write poems."[7] Art, he adds elsewhere, "may be the only remaining medium of truth in an age of incomprehensible terror and suffering."[8]

The paradoxical impossibility and simultaneous necessity to represent, to communicate, to speak of suffering is, I assume, generic to any work of art. Much of this book is thus concerned with the paradox of "the remedy of art"—a term I derive from Nietzsche,[9] who would caution against a literal understanding of "remedy." Rather, the remedy of art resembles in its motives and movements, its coverings and closures, the dressing of wounds it can hide but not heal. Or, one might say, art is a remedy only in the sense in which it binds up to make visible.

The incognito of suffering remains throughout this book the paradoxical point of departure for my forays into works and texts ranging from philosophy to photography, from poetry to prose, from Job to Jeffers, or from Antigone to Auden. I look for the Schopenhauerian "suffering of existence" in very particular instances and experiences of physical and mental wounds and diseases, in misery, pain, and death endured by characters as they appear in these pages: a little girl in a burn ward, a boy wounded in the Bosnian war, a nameless Vietnamese woman, Job, Antigone, a survivor of the Holocaust, a wife bereft of her husband, a daughter bereft of her father, a brother of his brother, a woman, a man. The elegists and mourners whose mostly lyrical responses to suffering I record individualize and dehistoricize the concept of suffering so that suffering can be seen as the solitary, individual experience that it always is.[10] Although this book may amount to a redemptive narrative, which I will confess below, and although it begins and ends in a deliberate fashion, the arguments are always confined within the individual chapters. Their common theme, in the broadest sense, is the problematic relationship between suffering and language. The concern is always how this problem is worked out in the individual instance.

The autonomy of each chapter is meant to suggest that experiences of suffering are always incomparable. No one's pain can serve as an example for another's. In each instance one must begin again and enter the scene of suffering on its own terms: the radically individual nature of suffering is prior or past to any theory or set of generalizations. While these assumptions are elaborated in the first chapter, where I discuss the case of a severely burned little girl, some contingencies in the encounter of suffering with language are also established in that same first chapter: we must give suffering a language and we can learn to listen to suffering. A literary hermeneutic might be particularly suited for such a listening because it validates the "essential nature" that suffering and art have in common. The inexhaustable mysteries of suffering and art harbor a desire for closure, but their closures require a hermeneutics of suspicion, for both suffering and art necessitate endless attention.

I have included a discussion of photography following the first chapter because photography articulates with exemplary clarity the question about the relationship between suffering and representation. In the two traumatic photographs that I discuss in the second chapter, the very visibility of suffering is in question. Although a photograph promises what Robert Lowell has called "verbatim description," there is, it seems, no such unmediated language: the disclosure of suffering in photography is cancelled by our gaze.

The third chapter articulates my tragic predispositions and theoretical affiliations. It offers in two brief theoretical reflections a theory of language as simultaneous concealment and revelation, a bandaging and uncovering. In each section of this chapter the organizing principle of the linguistic structure is a pre-linguistic wound. Nietzsche's Schopenhauerian notion of "an eternal suffering" or Freud's proposition of an originary Oedipal trauma each structures language as a dialectical contest between the forces of forgetting and remembering, between repression and recovery. Nietzsche's metaphor, "the remedy of art," permits a temporary consciousness of the linguistic or poetic nature of language itself. If metaphor may stand as representative of the poetic claims of language, then poetry offers treatment for suffering in the form of fictionality or forgetfulness, but not healing. The illness that has called for "the remedy of art" lies dormant in the syntax of the poetic formula. Freud's talking cure resembles Nietzsche's remedy of art. Both address the question of how one binds up suffering in language. Both also show how necessary and how interminable is the process of binding up and that the narrative texture of this metaphoric bandaging is always insufficient, leaving gaps and openings. The only remedy for suffering, as Freud's endless revisions and his concept of transference suggest, is interminable further interpretation. Taken together, the first three chapters deal with the difficult, often paradoxical, relationship between the truth of suffering and our theories about it.

By "Tragic Suffering," in the second part of this book, I mean to suggest that the tragic is a particular form of "the remedy of art," perhaps one that implies an institutionalized forgetting of its own metaphoricity. In my readings of *Job*, *Antigone*, and *King Lear*, I try to show that all three characters must overcome or refute the genre of "tragedy" and its implications of form, meaning, and representability of suffering.

In Job, the "tragic" might be in the notion of a divine sanction of Job's suffering, or in the concept of its extensions into the authoritative canonical book, both of which—the idea of God (or God as idea) and the idea of the book—Job must refute in order to authenticate his suffering. Eventually, it is in the loss of either divine or bookish authority, that Job's suffering is to be located—if one could conceive of such location.

Antigone's suffering is expressed as her "pious duty," which I read as a displacement of her suffering onto the gods. Their names are invoked as representatives of the secrecy of her suffering. The play thus becomes a tragedy of specular intrusion and illusion from which Antigone hastens to escape to her tomb, which I understand as the exemplary site of textual opacity and the tableau of Antigone's interiority. Similarly to Antigone's suicide, I read Cordelia's death in *King Lear* as that tragedy's final gesture of refusal to account for the cause of Lear's suffering. If love is its cause, as I argue, it is as unaccountable, as gratuitous and immeasurable as Cordelia's death.

In the third part of this study, which reiterates the title of this book, I turn to modern literary responses to suffering to examine how art can be a remedy or how suffering can be authenticated—given the aesthetic, textual, and ethical dilemmas worked out in the first two sections. The notion of the "modern" is itself the subject of a transitional chapter on Matthew Arnold, where I discuss Arnold's association of the tragic with a classical aesthetic and of the painful with a modern form of unrepresentable or irredeemable suffering. The chapters that follow examine the implications of the painful from various perspectives, taking their examples mainly, but not exclusively, from the lyric, whose autonomy echoes the autonomy of suffering and whose monologic form is the form of modern tragedy.

Robinson Jeffers' poetry seems to me the most explicit example of Arnold's modern painful predicament. In Jeffers' poetry suffering appears as an incontestable bodily reality, the most reductive and irrefutable certainty from whence Jeffers undertakes a materialist conception of decentered human value. Human suffering, being always implied in and obliterated by a universal principle of suffering, finds expression only as the endurance of its own ontologic paradox. The effects of the decentering of the value of human suffering are rendered with succinct irony in W. H. Auden's poem, "Musée des Beaux Arts," the focus of the next chapter. Subjecting Auden's poem to Irving Feldman's critical/poetic response, I try to draw aesthetic and moral inferences from Auden's modernist interpretation of suffering, where the cries of the sufferer are muted and turned inward, and where suffering becomes the allegory of an intimate, unvalorizable subjectivity.

In Paul Celan's poems, language and suffering mirror each other. Celan's language, to my mind, is the most terrifying example of the language of suffering. Through the figure of translation, I attempt to show how Celan's poetry brings to speech the silence of those murdered, exiled, or violated by the Holocaust, and how Celan's language of choice, German, might be read as a form of translation by which the fate of the Jews becomes the destiny of his verse. The following chapter on Sylvia Plath and Robert Lowell moves to the intimate lyrical site and consciousness of an unrelieved, unredeemed suffering. Here I ask how the the so-called confessional lyric might invest itself with hope in aesthetic representation and how in these instances the remedy of art will not suffice.

Sharon Olds' elegies about her father's terminal illness propose in the next chapter a view of suffering and death as irredeemable matter, while Tess Gallagher's elegies on the death of her husband attempt to assign the poem a spiritual power launched against the totality of death. If Olds' and Gallagher's modern elegies raise the question how one mourns, the two poets offer radically different poetic and stylistic answers. Annie Dillard's book, *Holy the Firm,* fuses the two entities—matter and spirit—that structured my discussion of Olds and Gallagher. In this chapter, I seek to analyze the moral and aesthetic ramifications of Dillard's narrative of suffering and sainthood. In the penultimate chapter, in a close reading of a particular story of Raymond Carver's, written shortly before his death, I trace that writer's desire to recover from his/story by way of a lyrical transformation of time. The last chapter opens by responding to a recent book which denounces the culture of redemption, and to which I respond by showing how Denis Donoghue's autobiography, *Warrenpoint,* reconstitutes the value of remembering—as an example of the value of art—against life in time which has been called "dismemberment."

Although my references in this book are eclectic and noncanonical, the thematic connections between the chapters imply—against my original intentions—an overall redemptive narrative. My original attempt to identify suffering as radically different from the aesthetic, as irreducibly beyond language, has proven impossible. Although suffering, in Maire Jaanus's words, "tears the symbols off the subject and reduces him to pure unintelligible interiority, the realm of the grinding organic processes," I find in the structure of works of art a structure of analogy and empathy, and in the hermeneutical task a form of comprehension. But neither art nor literary interpretation can or should be understood as redemptive or curative in any simple or straightforward way. The purpose of this book is to suggest that a listening to pain and suffering may profit from a literary hearing and vice versa. It is not only that literature tells of suffering but that suffering may tell us something about the nature of literature.

NOTES

1. Arthur Schopenhauer, *The World as Will and Representation* (1818), trans. E. F. J. Payne, 2 vols. (New York: Dover Publications, 1969), 2: 635–36.

2. Ibid., 1:196 and also 2:368: "Now as all suffering proceeds from the will that constitutes the real self, all possibility of suffering is abolished simultaneously with the withdrawal of this side of consciousness." See ibid., 2:371. "With the disappearance of willing from consciousness, the individuality is really abolished also, and with it its suffering and sorrow."

3. Percy Bysshe Shelley, "A Defence of Poetry," in *Romantic Poetry and Prose*, ed. Harold Bloom and Lionel Trilling (New York: Oxford University Press, 1973), 758.

4. See Theodor Adorno, *Aesthetic Theory* (1970), trans. C. Lenhardt (London: Routledge and Kegan Paul, 1984). ". . . what detracts from the gravity of art is the fact that aesthetic autonomy as the image of suffering remains fundamentally uninvolved in suffering, the source of its gravity" (57).

5. Schopenhauer, *The World as Will and Representation*, 1:261.

6. For these and other observations I am much indebted to Professor Rafey Habib, Rutgers University.

7. Theodor Adorno, *Negative Dialectics* (1966), trans. E. B. Ashton (New York: The Seabury Press, 1973), 362.

8. Adorno, *Aesthetic Theory*, 27. See Shoshana Felman, "Education and Crisis, or the Vicissitudes of Teaching," in *Trauma: Explorations in Memory*, ed. Cathy Caruth (Baltimore: Johns Hopkins University Press, 1995), 39–40.

9. See chapter three.

10. In this respect, the present study differs conceptually from Cathy Caruth's announcement in *Trauma*: "The attempt to gain access to a traumatic history . . . is also the project of listening beyond the pathology of individual suffering . . ." (156). See also *Daedalus* 125 (winter 1996), an issue dedicated to "Social Suffering."

1

SUFFERING IN TRUTH AND THEORY

To Give Suffering
a Language

Literature and Medicine

The resident doctor said,
"We are not deep in ideas,
imagination or enthusiasm—
how can we help you?"
I asked,
"These days of
only poems and depression—
what can I do with them?
Will they help me to notice
what I cannot bear to look at?"

—Robert Lowell, *Day by Day*

Rational cognition has one critical limit
which is its inability to cope with suffering.
—Theodor Adorno, *Aesthetic Theory*

In his book *The Illness Narratives*, Arthur Kleinman admits that "Clinical and behavioral science research . . . possess no category to describe suffering, no routine way of recording this most thickly human dimension of patients' and families' stories of experiencing illness. Symptom scales and survey questionnaires and behavioral checklists quantify functional impairment and disability, rendering quality of life fungible."

But medical categories, he adds, are woefully insufficient to account for the intimate and inward experience of illness: ". . . about suffering they are silent. The thinned-out image of patients and families that perforce must emerge from such research is scientifically replicable but ontologically invalid; it has statistical, not epistemological, significance; it is a dangerous distortion."[1] Unlike the "practitioners who are turned out of medical school as naive realists," Kleinman's aim is to delay the naming of the illness, so as to "legitimiz[e] the patient's illness experience—authorizing that experience, auditing it empathically."[2] What one hears in the patient's story is "a changing system of meanings"[3] that necessitates at a later stage a disentangling of its various narrative strata: "symptom symbols, culturally marked disorder, personal and interpersonal significance, and patient and family explanatory models."[4]

These "four types of meanings" in a patient's narrative are not too different from the complex layers that constitute the "thickness of surface" with "infinitely receding depths" that have been attributed to Sophoclean tragedy.[5] In Kleinman's book, thickness and depth are pervading metaphors to describe the complexity of illness narratives. Their complexity, Kleinman notes, necessitates a fine-tuned reconstruction, analysis, and deconstruction. The clinician-turned-anthropologist, or literary critic, now discovers in the layered textuality of the patient's illness narrative the four types of meaning mentioned above. Each of these meanings in turn "thickens the account and deepens the clinician's understanding of the experience of suffering."[6]

Although illness narratives evidently have a literary dimension, Kleinman's pragmatic concerns prohibit the "excessive speculation" of which he accuses psychoanalysts and cultural analysts. Instead, he advocates that "we should be willing to stop at that point where validity is uncertain."[7] If such self-imposed limitations are justified by the urgency of Kleinman's pragmatism,[8] a literary analysis of illness narratives insists that precisely the point where validity is uncertain *should* warrant excessive speculation. A therapeutic analysis—one that stops where validity is uncertain and forbids excessive speculation—forecloses articulation of just those anonymous bodily processes that constitute the sufferer's most intimate experience of pain. Concealed in the many-layered linguistic, social, and psychological complexities of illness narratives and their elaborate interpretations still lies, unheard and speechless, the mute materiality of suffering itself.

But if suffering is in the unbearable, silent body rather than in the sharable, disembodied language of its narratives, how then can suffering speak? How can one hear the unspeakable? How can one listen without assuming one has understood? Indeed, how can one *begin* to understand?

What inclines a *literary* inquiry toward such questions is the very literature it has sought and failed to analyze.[9] For literary inquiry attempts to analyze what is lastly irreducible to analysis. Precisely because of this paradox a literary inquiry might help the physician to acknowledge or witness—not to diagnose or to explain—the solitary, secret body in pain. Perhaps the very language of the aesthetic, a language without any meaning other than its own occurrence, might echo the mysterious occurrence of suffering. Perhaps the mystery of art has its origins in the secrecy of suffering, the keeping of which is the purpose of the work of art.

"Reason can subsume suffering under concepts," as the German philosopher Theodor Adorno notes, "it can furnish means to alleviate suffering; but it can never express suffering in the medium of experience, for to do so would be irrational by reason's own standards. Therefore, even when it is understood, suffering remains mute and inconsequential. . . ."[10] Adorno's remedy for such a crisis of understanding is art, the irrationality of which alone could account for the irrationality of suffering. Although different in terminology, Elaine Scarry's observations in her book *The Body in Pain* are similar to Adorno's. Scarry points out in a well-known phrase that ". . . for the person in pain, so incontestably and unnegotiably present is it that 'having pain' may come to be thought as the most vibrant example of what it is 'to have certainty,' while for the other person it is so elusive that 'hearing about pain,' may exist as the primary model of what it is 'to have doubt.'"[11] Particularly in the context of chronic illness, examples of such doubt must be numerous: "practitioners trained to think of 'real' disease entities, with natural histories and precise outcomes, find chronic illness messy and threatening," Kleinman writes. "They have been taught to regard with suspicion patients' illness narratives and causal beliefs. The form of those narratives and explanations may indicate a morbid process; the content may lead them astray."[12] In medical and clinical languages the doubt of "the other person" cannot remain unconfirmed but must be proven legitimate. Often this means proving that the sufferer does not suffer.

Like the sufferer's narrative, "literature," as Maurice Blanchot writes, "professes to be important while at the same time considering itself an object of doubt."[13] Its dual nature recalls the dual aspects of suffering, the certainty of the sufferer and the doubt of the other person.

Like the patient's illness narrative, literature leads the reader astray. And like the practitioner of medicine, the reader of literature reads with suspicion. Thus, literary critics and medical practitioners have in common the pursuit of an elusive reality beneath the layered complexity of their respective illness narratives. Just as the meaning of literature is not to yield a particular meaning or message, so suffering, in its intimate materiality and enigmatic randomness, remains mute and inconsequential.

How then can the irrationality of art serve the physician? What can the medical practitioner learn from art when it continually foils our attempts to appropriate the inexplicable, when it thwarts our desire to make sense out of secrecy? We can learn something about the violence of our hermeneutic, that is to say, about the breathless expediency with which we convert mystery into meaning, suffering into disease, and pain into pathology. One of the most ancient warnings against such hermeneutical haste in the face of suffering can be found in the book of Job. It opens with an exemplary scene of empathy and solidarity. Upon seeing that Job's "grief was very great," his friends "sat down with him upon the ground for seven nights and none spake a word. . . ."[14] Although their silence speaks well of their initial respect and sympathy, soon enough their impatience becomes audible—"who can withhold himself from speaking?"—and their reductive rationality proverbial: "Lo we have searched it, so it is; hear it, and know thou it for good."[15]

In light of my contentions against instrumental reason, my own appropriations here of a particular case of severe suffering, taken from the Preface of Arthur Kleinman's *Illness Narratives,* must necessarily appear as inconsistent. To minimize the inconsistencies of my argument, I must resist, in as much as possible, my own explanatory desires. I must attempt—and this is the impossible task of the present argument—to enhance our understanding of suffering by letting it appear as the unexplained.

If I recommend this approach as an initial stage in the acknowledgment of the irreducible secrecy of suffering, I also want to acknowledge the necessity of Kleinman's pragmatic concerns. There is extensive and convincing evidence in his book that illness narratives and their interpretations do indeed facilitate therapeutic treatment. Thus, for the purposes of the present argument, I turn to Kleinman's Preface to locate the phenomenon of suffering at a moment precisely *before* the practical interventions of interpretation, diagnosis, and therapy. By lengthening a very brief story of a burn patient that Kleinman tells in his Preface, I draw attention to a moment *before* (or indeed frequently beyond) therapeutic treatment, which is a fundamental existential moment that the sufferer often bears unbearably long and alone.

ARTHUR KLEINMAN'S CASE OF THE LITTLE GIRL

> Nothing hurts her like the extravagance
> of questions, because to ask is to come near,
> to be humbled at the clotted nucleus.
>
> —Tess Gallagher, *Moon Crossing Bridge*

The Illness Narratives opens with a story about a seven-year old girl who had been badly burned over most of her body. Kleinman's task as a clinical student, he reports, was to hold the girl's "uninjured hand, as much to reassure and calm her as to enable the surgical resident to quickly pull away the dead, infected tissue. . . ." After many futile attempts to establish some connection with the girl, Kleinman tells of a sudden communicative breakthrough: "angered at my own ignorance and impotence, and uncertain what to do besides clutching the small hand," he suddenly finds himself "at wit's end." The very presence of pain now makes possible a deeper motivating force. The former therapeutic strategies that were to distract the little girl by talking about her home, family, or school, anything other than her suffering, now fall away and the medical student's loss of words paradoxically permits a therapeutic breakthrough: "I found myself asking her to tell me how she tolerated it, what the feeling was like of being so badly burned. . . ." It is as if the sight of the painful process of debridement had yielded to a vision of pain itself. For such unbearable revelation one needs an equally revelatory language. Such a language, stripped of its rhetoric and having passed through ignorance and uncertainty to wit's end, now evokes the girl's response. She answers in "terms direct and simple," while lifting towards the student "a face so disfigured, it was difficult to read the expression." Although themselves almost devoid of figuration, the girl's direct and simple terms—all the more poignant for their literalness—begin to refigure her face, to reconstruct that which is difficult to read, to humanize, to put a human face on the terrible accident that has befallen her.

Above all, Kleinman's story demonstrates the urgent necessity to give the sufferer a language—a necessity that underlies perhaps the foundation of literature itself.[16] Such a language, as Kleinman's example illustrates, is born out of the strain and failure of rhetoric or method, so that precisely in their inefficacy the sufferer's pain can be revealed. Then, both patient and physician must attempt to speak nevertheless, and simply, as if one were learning to speak again, as if one were to apply the first layers of a covering on an open wound.

The difficulty of reading what is illegibly inscribed in the disfigurements of suffering is now mitigated by the reconstructive efforts of a language spoken as if the patient and physician were speaking for the first time. These linguistic efforts must face their own difficulty in the paradox of the word pitched against the wordless, material reality of suffering—a reality so real, a certainty so calamitous, that any word added to it seems only to subtract from it.

Not many patients can speak with the primordial authority of the little girl in Kleinman's story. It is a story that describes the encounter with suffering as an arduous and painful retreat back to the beginnings of language,[17] where science and medicine must yield to ontological and epistemological questions—precisely those questions, as Kleinman points out, about which medical categories are silent.[18] For before we quantify the intimate inward pain in symptom scales and survey questionnaires and behavioral checklists, we must sit down upon the ground, so to speak, for seven nights and ask: How is it for this person to suffer? How can we share her suffering?

"Pain comes unsharably into our midst," Elaine Scarry writes, "as at once that which cannot be denied and that which cannot be confirmed."[19] Here at wit's end, at the point of a veritable epistemological crisis, is the moment of artistic, hermeneutical, or narrative beginning, the beginning of reading and writing. Here the author or the reader begins the book, each subsequent reader and writer asking Kleinman's exemplary literary question, "tell me, what is it like?" But one does not, as Kleinman's story intimates, arrive at this question easily or directly, without having passed through ignorance, impotence, and uncertainty. Indeed, one cannot arrive at wit's end without resistance; for the failure of resistance *is* wit's end.[20]

One must thus want to learn what one does not want to learn, and it must be difficult to arrive at the question one had sought to avoid all along. Other questions and other stories demand to be asked and told first. None of them were truly meant and intended, indeed all but sought to distract from the question that was meant. Yet just these repetitions of what was not meant always imply the possibility of a true encounter. And it is precisely the possibility of such an encounter reached through repeated and faulty approaches that makes speaking to the sufferer analogous to literary interpretation. Eventually, to deserve to ask what I have called the exemplary literary question, "what is it like?" requires the admission of the limits of understanding. It requires many "futile attempts" so that these limits are not prematurely assumed. Indeed, only in the very futility of asking can the claims of the sufferer begin to be heard.

If such a process of futile attempts is echoed in T. S. Eliot's *Four Quartets*:

> In order to arrive at what you do not know
> You must go by a way which is the way of ignorance. . . .
> And what you do not know is the only thing you know . . .

—one can only begin to write because one is willing to encounter that which will be unknown. And as the encounter with the unknown leads to a crisis of understanding, that very crisis holds the possibility of a recovery of the original motivation to write. Thus, Eliot concludes, "And so each venture is a new beginning, a raid on the inarticulate / With shabby equipment always deteriorating. . . ."[21]

To encounter the other in her pain and to tell her story is therefore not simply a matter of asking the right question. Rather, each asking (each writing and each interpretation) is an effort to attain the state of mind that the French philosopher Jean-François Lyotard has called "the suffering of thinking." For Lyotard, suffering is the very condition of thinking insofar as the experience of bodily ascesis demands of the mind ". . . an emptying that is required if the mind is to think." This is not a willed or intentional "emptying" but a mental—perhaps even spiritual— receptivity, as becomes clear when Lyotard points out that

> this obviously has nothing to do with *tabula rasa*, with what Descartes (vainly) wanted to be a starting from scratch on the part of knowing thought—a starting that paradoxically can only be a starting all over again. In what we call thinking the mind isn't "directed" but suspended. . . .
> . . .

> It is thought itself resolving to be irresolute, deciding to
> be patient, wanting not to want, wanting, precisely, not to
> produce a meaning in place of what *must* be signified.[22]

Lyotard's imperative *must* is audible when Kleinman does not tell us
what the girl answered, only *that* she answered and "in terms direct and
simple." In their directness and simplicity, her voice and words create an
order over the chaos of her pain. Her speaking is made possible by
Kleinman's question. She speaks in the space of a mutuality created by
his question. But rather than to him, she speaks to and of the other she
has become through her suffering. By the very act of speaking she thus
gives herself a meaning in the very absence of meaning.

Or to say the same differently: In the discretely descriptive terms
by which Kleinman recounts the child's response we can hear the desire
of the medical student's question. The question is not so much, *What* is
it like? or *How* do you feel? as, Can you still *speak*? Can you still affirm
in the absence of meaning an order of words? The desire is not that the
little girl would give an account exactly of *how* she tolerated it, or of
what the feeling was like—even if one *could* give expression to such suffering. Rather, the desire of the question is that she would speak and
thus affirm the possibility of speaking, so that at this moment speaking
itself would remake her world.

Although she speaks, the girl's speaking is liberated from having to
perform in any referential context. What she says cannot be and need
not be, indeed it must not be, verified. But in order to speak, suffering
must be heard. Kleinman's story is the account of the difficulty of attain-
ing that hearing.

There is no better exemplification of such "hearing" than what the
Jewish poet Paul Celan calls "not exactly listening":

> Or better: someone who hears, listens, and looks . . . and
> then does not know what was said. But who would have
> heard the speaker, who would have "seen him speak," who
> would have perceived language and Gestalt, and at the same
> time . . . breath, that is to say, direction and fate.[23]

Although the medical student's impatience and ignorance led him to a
point at wit's end where he did not exactly listen, now he does see her
speak: "She stopped, quite surprised, and looked at me. . . ." In her bodily gestures the little girl already articulates the "breath," "direction and
fate," which she then goes on to ennunciate.

In spite of her "terms direct and simple," it is a fate that remains ir reducible to fact.[24] The meaning of the girl's speaking is not in *what* sh says, or in the particular answer she gives, but in the affirmation of lan guage in the presence of pain, which may be the affirmation of th human in the very dehumanizing corporeality of suffering.

Finally, Kleinman writes, ". . . whatever effect I had on her, her e fect on me was greater. She taught me . . . that it is possible to talk wi patients, even those who are most distressed, about the actual experien of illness, and that witnessing and helping to order that experience can of therapeutic value." He has been taught a lesson in the aesthetic. For talk about suffering, he has learned, is neither to distract the patient r to diagnose her illness nor to prescribe a solution; it is not in the order something but in the idea of order itself in which the girl seeks to be made or (literally) re-membered. And it is not in remembering *someth* (her life or her face) but in the act of re-membering as such that speaking finally resembles a form of art. Art, like the girl's speaking, i imitation and remaking, a mimesis and poesis.

"Poetry claims its right to exist just as do occurrences," as Go wrote.[25] I would suggest similarly that the relevance of art for suffe is in its radical ontologic analogy. Like suffering, art has neither r ence, nor object, nor utility. There is only the secret, unaccountabl currence itself. Yet, to understand suffering as analogous to art give fering a language in which the very secrecy of suffering and its def of instrumental reason can be transformed into an ontology. The p which is the linguistic event of something unforeseeable and unnece something of phenomenal or ontological rather than of ethical valu comes an occurrence like suffering over which the poet or patient is erly no longer an author and the reader or doctor no master. If suf then cannot be authorized or mastered, it can yet be told—told a tells stories, sings songs, paints pictures, or recites poetry.

The little girl answers because the speaking of the medical stud longer seeks to distance himself from her pain. And while the pa thus permitted to speak and to appear in her language, and wh fering has been permitted to speak, the medical student learns to While the girl speaks in order to reaffirm language and in this la her self, the medical student listens in order to hear nothing l speaking. He listens not to explain but to understand, not to di but to witness and to help. And if helping proceeds from witnes must listen, like the poet or her interpreter, only for the place

the language comes from. Paraphrasing Stanley Cavell's notion of acknowledgment as ethically prior to knowledge, Gerald Bruns notes: "It is what happens in hermeneutical experience, where understanding is an achievement not of objective consciousness but of openness and answerability, where openness means exposure."[26] Or, as Maurice Blanchot puts it: "Attention is the reception of what escapes attention, an opening upon the unexpected, a waiting that is the unawaited of all waiting."[27]

If initially the job of "the neophyte clinical student was to hold her uninjured hand . . ." and if the same student was ". . . uncertain what to do besides clutching the small hand . . ." now the little girl speaks, and "while she spoke, she grasped my hand harder. . . ." Imperceptibly the tables have turned. Having thus learned the order of therapeutic treatment, the medical student has also learned the aesthetic—"a knowledge without desire," as Schopenhauer called it. He can let go of her hands and open them to receive hers.

As one attends to the aesthetic, one attends to suffering: not so that one would explain suffering—for no one can explain it—but so that one would understand without giving understanding an object, so that suffering can become the occasion of an endless act of comprehension.

NOTES

1. Arthur Kleinman, MD, *The Illness Narratives: Suffering, Healing and the Human Condition* (New York: Basic Books, 1988), 27.

2. In the context of chronical illness, such a legitimization of the patient's experience of suffering "is a key task," Kleinman adds "but one that is particularly difficult to do with the regularity and consistency and sheer perseverance that chronicity necessitates." Ibid., 17.

3. Kleinman, *Illness Narratives,* 17–18.

4. Ibid., 233.

5. Adriane Poole states, "Both play and character [Antigone] have a typically Sophoclean thickness of surface which suggests infinitely receeding depths." See *Tragedy: Shakespeare and The Greek Example* (Oxford: Basil Blackwell, 1987), 185.

6. Kleinman, *Illness Narratives,* 233.

7. Ibid., 74.

8. Among four categories where such validity is at stake—"correspondence to reality, coherence, usefulness in the context of a person's problem, and

aesthetic value"—Kleinman claims that "For the clinician the third is what counts" (*Illness Narratives*, 74).

9. An excellent account of what I mean by "failed to analyze" is given by Gerald L. Bruns, "On the Tragedy of Hermeneutical Experience," in *Hermeneutics Ancient and Modern* (New Haven: Yale University Press, 1992), 179–94.

10. Theodor Adorno, *Aesthetic Theory*, trans. C. Lenhardt (London: Routledge, 1984), 27.

11. Elaine Scarry, *The Body in Pain: The Making and Unmaking of the World* (New York: Oxford University Press, 1985), 4.

12. Kleinman, *Illness Narratives*, 17.

13. Maurice Blanchot, *The Gaze of Orpheus and Other Literary Essays*, trans. Lydia Davis (Barrytown, N.Y.: Station Hill, 1981), 22.

14. The Book of Job (KJV), 2:13.

15. Ibid., 4:2, and 5:27.

16. Cf. Arthur Schopenhauer, *The World as Will and Representation* (1818), trans. E. F. J. Payne, 2 vols. (New York: Dover Publications, 1966): "If our life were without end and free from pain, it would possibly not occur to anyone to ask why the world exists, and why it does so in precisely this way, but everything would be purely as a matter of course" (2:161). Richard Sewall makes a similar point quoting Aeschylus' "'Wisdom comes alone through suffering'" and Dostoevsky: "'Suffering is the sole origin of consciousness.'" See *The Vision of Tragedy* (New Haven: Yale University Press, 1980), 180. David Bakan assigns pain a central significance in respect to culture, social institutions, and religion: "In the thought of a number of classical social theorists—Bentham, Adam Smith, and others—pain is a given and constitutes the basis for explaining the complex interactions of men and their arrangements." See *Disease, Pain, and Sacrifice* (Chicago: The University of Chicago Press, 1968), 58. Keats interprets Aeschylus's proverbial phrase (above) into, "Sorrow is wisdom," and "Until we are sick, we understand not" Quoted in Hermione de Almeida, *Romantic Medicine and John Keats* (Oxford: Oxford University Press, 1991), 307. Theodor Adorno claims that all forms of social action are fundamentally against suffering. See *Negative Dialectics* (1966), trans. E. B. Ashton (New York: Seabury Press, 1973), 203. Elaine Scarry points out that "pain and the imagination are each other's missing intentional counterpart, and . . . they together provide a framing identity of man-as-creator. . . ." See *The Body in Pain*, 169.

17. Jacques Derrida quotes Artaud's similar concept, "'speech before words.'" Artaud sees in the birth of words after speech a tragic sequence. See *Writing and Difference* (1967), trans. Alan Bass (Chicago: University of Chicago Press, 1978), 240. This moment is for Maurice Blanchot the eminently literary moment: "The language of literature is a search for this moment that precedes literature." Or: "Literature says: 'I no longer present, I am; I do not signify, I present.'" See *The Gaze of Orpheus*, 46, 47.

18. Kleinman, *Illness Narratives*, 27.

19. Scarry, *The Body in Pain*, 4.

20. See Bruns, *Hermeneutics*: ". . . the hermeneutical experience always entails an 'epistemological crisis' that calls for the reinterpretation of our situation, or ourselves, a critical dismantling of what had been decided" (184). And, paraphrasing Stanley Cavell: ". . . hermeneutical experience always entails the event of exposure that belongs to tragedy" (*Hermeneutics*, 187).

21. T. S. Eliot, *The Complete Poems and Plays* (London: Faber and Faber, 1969), 181, 182.

22. Jean-François Lyotard, *The Inhuman: Reflections on Time* (1988), trans. Geoffrey Bennington and Rachel Bowlby (Stanford: Stanford University Press, 1991), 18–19. Lyotard's "irresolute thought" resembles here very much Hans-Georg Gadamer's notion of "openness in which experience is acquired." See *Truth and Method* (1960), trans. Joel Weinsheimer and Donald G. Marshall (New York: Crossroad, 1989), 352.

23. Paul Celan, *Gesammelte Werke*, 5 vols (Frankfurt: Suhrkamp, 1983), my translation. The original German reads as follows: "*Aber es gibt, wenn von Kunst die Rede ist, auch immer wieder jemand, der zugegen ist und . . . nicht richtig hinhört. Genauer: jemand, der hört und lauscht und schaut . . . und dann nicht weiss, wovon die Rede war. Der aber den Sprechenden hört, der ihn 'sprechen sieht', der Sprache wahrgenommen hat und Gestalt, und zugleich auch . . . Atem, das heisst Richtung und Schicksal*" (3: 188). See Paul Celan, *Collected Prose*, trans. Rosmarie Waldrop (Riverdale, N.Y.: The Sheep Meadow Press, 1990), 39.

24. "What is recognized is reality as other, not as the same: reality as that which is more Fate than Fact" (Bruns, *Hermeneutics*, 186).

25. "*Das Gedichtete behauptet sein Recht, wie das Geschehene.*" Quoted by Leonard Olschner, "Anamnesis: Paul Celan's Translations of Poetry," *Studies in Twentieth-Century Literature* 12 (summer, 1988): 194.

26. Bruns, *Hermeneutics*, 186.

27. Maurice Blanchot, *The Infinite Conversation*, trans. Susan Hanson (Minneapolis: University of Minnesota Press, 1993), 121.

2

Coverings / Apertures:
The Invisibility of
Suffering

Barthes on Photography

> I wanted to explore it, not as a question
> but as a wound . . .
> —Roland Barthes, *Camera Lucida*

My reflections on two traumatic photographs, a cover of *Newsweek* and a war photograph by P. J. Griffiths, both of which show faces partly or wholly invisible, bandaged eyes and heads, call into question the eye as instrument of knowledge. Can one take a photograph of suffering? Can one represent suffering on the cover of a news magazine? What are the aesthetic and moral implications? I shall contextualize these questions with Roland Barthes' early essay "The Photographic Message" (1961) and his last book, *Camera Lucida*, published shortly before his death in 1980.

"The press photograph is a message," reads the opening statement of "The Photographic Message." The message transmits "the literal reality" or "it is its perfect *analogon* . . ."; the photograph "is exclusively constituted and occupied by a 'denoted' message, a message which totally exhausts its mode of existence." But in spite of its "analogical plentitude," the photograph invites description, a "second-order message" which alters its denotative, analogical plentitude, signifying "something different from what is shown." From this dialectic between photographic denotation and connotation, Barthes then derives the concept of a "photographic paradox," consisting of the "co-existence of two messages, the one without a code (the photographic analogue), the other with a code (the 'art,' or the treatment, or the 'writing,' or the rhetoric, of the photograph)."[1]

Photographs, Barthes claims, must be read like texts because their decipherment depends on the reader's knowledge of a connotative code within which the photograph acquires its meaning and effect. For Barthes, then, a photograph may read "as though it were a matter of a real language, intelligible only if one has learned the signs." ". . . [T]he reading closely depends on my culture," it depends "on my knowledge of the world, and it is probable that a good press photograph . . . makes ready play with the supposed knowledge of its readers. . . ."[2]

Since "connotation extends a long way" Barthes asks, "Is this to say that a pure denotation, a *this-side of language*, is impossible?" Initially, the traumatic photograph, under which category Barthes lists "fires, shipwrecks, catastrophes, violent deaths," seems to assure precisely this: that pure denotation *is* possible. Trauma suspends language, blocks meaning, prevents connotation. The traumatic photograph is "the photograph about which there is nothing to say; the shock-photo is by structure insignificant: no value, no knowledge, at the limit no verbal categorization can have hold on the process instituting the signification."[3] But even as he ponders the possibility of a purely denotative photography, Barthes has already included even the traumatic photograph in the extensions of connotation:

> Certainly situations which are normally traumatic can be seized in a process of photographic signification but then precisely they are indicated via a rhetorical code which distances, sublimates and pacifies them. Truly traumatic photographs are rare.[4]

The only allowance for the appearance of the purely denotative, traumatic photograph is made in Barthes' proposal that "the more direct the trauma, the more difficult is connotation; or again, the mythological effect of a photograph is inversely proportional to its traumatic effect."[5]

Indeed, would not a purely denotative photographic trauma undermine the genre of Barthes' "good press photograph," dedicated as it must be to information and exposition? Or would not such trauma, if it were purely denotative, uncoded, unreadable, incite political (or military) action precisely *because* there is nothing to say? Barthes' answer to these questions is implicit in the closing paragraph of "The Photographic Message" where he assigns the press photograph a connotative function of social integration and reassurance. The "very subtlety" of the press photograph's connotative message constitutes "the forms our society uses to ensure its peace of mind. . . ."[6]

When in *Camera Lucida* Barthes returns to the subject of photography under notably more personal circumstances than in the former essay, he reopens the question of the photographic trauma by employing a binary logic that recalls the connotation/denotation dialectic in "The Photographic Message."[7] In his interview for *Le Matin*, Barthes explains:

> One must define one's terms whenever one writes a work of analytical reflection, and I chose two Latin words that simplified things. *Studium* is the general, cultural, and civilized interest one has in a photograph. It's what corresponds to the photographer's work: he tries to please our *studium*, our . . . taste, in a way. Thus, all photos of reality in general have a sense of *studium*.
>
> But I noticed that certain photographs touched me more sharply than their general interest warranted, through details that captivated me, surprised and awakened me in rather enigmatic fashion. I called that element the *punctum*, because it's a kind of point, a sting, that touches me sharply.[8]

Studium enables a reading of the cultural connotations of the picture; it is the form through which, as Barthes writes in *Camera Lucida*, our "polite interest" is awakened or which "mobilizes a half desire, a demivolition"; we like but never love the *studium* of the photograph. By contrast, *punctum* breaks, stings, pricks or cuts the *studium* so that in that detail or moment of rupture—Barthes speaks of wounds and bruises—the code of the *studium* is in question, the intention of the photographer no longer grasps the narrative of the photograph, and the language of the critic can no longer explain or describe.[9] While it seems that *punctum* and *studium* enter into a dialectical relationship similar to connotation and denotation, Barthes' encounter with the Wintergarten

Photograph in *Camera Lucida*, depicting his mother and her brother as children, reveals the radically undialectical nature of *studium* and *punctum*, and suggests the unassimilable otherness of traumatic photography—or of the trauma of photography:

> I am alone with it, in front of it. The circle is closed, there is no escape. I suffer, motionless. Cruel, sterile deficiency: I cannot *transform* my grief, I cannot let my gaze drift; no culture will help me utter this suffering which I experience entirely on the level of the image's finitude (this is why, despite its codes, I cannot *read* a photograph): the Photograph—my Photograph—is without culture: when it is painful, nothing in it can transform grief into mourning. And if dialectic is that thought which masters the corruptible and converts the negation of death into the power to work, the photograph is undialectical: it is denatured theater where death cannot "be contemplated," reflected and interiorized; or again: the dead theater of Death, the foreclosure of the Tragic, excludes all purification, all *catharsis*.[10]

Barthes' refusal to supply a picture of his mother, whose recent death he mourns in *Camera Lucida*, intimates the unsharably personal nature of the *punctum*. But his refusal also highlights, by implication, the terrible moral and aesthetic paradoxes by which we encounter traumatic press photographs, such as the *Newsweek* cover, or Griffiths' picture of a Vietnam napalm victim. Is it possible, in the public realm, in the glare of hyper visibility, to perform a reading in the "realm of mourning"[11] in which Barthes writes his *Camera Lucida*? Or will the genre and public nature of those photographs render the intimacy of suffering invisible? Can the press photograph, as Barthes concludes in "The Photographic Message," achieve no pure denotation? How rare are truly traumatic photographs?

THE *NEWSWEEK* COVER OF MAY 10, 1993

> As much as they create sympathy,
> photographs cut sympathy . . .
>
> —Susan Sontag, *On Photography*

The May 10, 1993 issue of *Newsweek*, showing the bloody face of a Bosnian boy blinded by Serbian artillery, facilitates a discussion of these issues not only because the genre of the cover of a news magazine dramatizes or amplifies any discussion about photography, but also because three weeks after the appearance of that issue of *Newsweek*, the editorial reports that the cover "provoked an unusually strong reaction from our readers."

We might think of the shocking quality of this picture as our initial inability to verbalize our perception. But if we keep looking, if we don't turn the page, the large headline, BOSNIA, and the wistful political speculations above—"The U.S. Economy: A Shadow Recovery" and below—"Clinton Gets Tough—at Last—Will Air Power Be Enough?"—already overlay our visual perception with a connotative economic, historical, political, and militaristic context—even if such connotations, rather than reassuring us, betray some doubt about their own rhetoric. At the same time, the apparent necessity of these headlines, dramatizing and interpreting the suffering of the boy, also cast into doubt the rhetorical force of his wounds. Into such a contest of rhetorical discourses—all discourses of doubt—the correspondents of *Newsweek* sent their letters.

The "overwhelming majority," the editors report, judged the picture as "too disturbing to put on a family magazine"; they would have wished, as one reader puts it, that "a responsible magazine . . . refrain from bringing such a repulsive image to my dining-room table." Another reader demanded "an end" to suffering, yet another "was repulsed to the point of nausea." One wished to remind the editors that they should "Please remember that your readers live in homes, we have children." And yet another complained that "graphic pictures of the atrocities should not be staring out at the general public. . . ."[12]

In their turn, the editors of *Newsweek* respond that they "did not make the choice lightly and took very seriously the prospect that [the picture] might offend some readers." They weigh the political consequences and point out that Secretary of State Warren Christopher carried the picture to Moscow to use it to plead for allied intervention. At the end of their response, the editors close by mentioning the "happy result" of the media exposure: the boy's flight, subsidized by a wealthy Croatian-American couple, to California, where "after an unsuccessful operation to save his eyesight, doctors are working to rebuild his face and restore him to otherwise normal health." The editorial response implies much about the function of the genre of the cover and the principles of selection implicit in the publication of journalistic photography.

In journalistic photography, the *punctum* is always already neutralized by the *studium* of the journalistic genre. In the case of the

The cover of *Newsweek*,
May 10, 1993
(Sipa)

Newsweek cover, such neutralization is offered by the dilution of the picture in headlines and commentary, or by its distribution to an indiscriminate public where the burden of the trauma is shared worldwide—even if this absurdly lightens the burden to insignificance. Both the textual and the public realm dilute the *punctum*, spread out the trauma to a thin film of pseudo-knowledge on which the profound is squarely visible, the intimate is general. The wounds of Sead Bekrik are displaced as soon as they are displayed. To publish the wounds of Sead Bekrik is thus to sublate the sublime into the endlessly disseminating, synthesizing power of language, which language precedes the picture in its journalistic genre so that the subversive power of the picture is always already foreclosed.

In the readers' responses to the *Newsweek* cover we note an inability or refusal to read the picture in these linguistic or cultural terms. These readers insist on seeing the picture as such, properly not knowing how to read what they see because the visual rhetorical premises[13] implicit in the magazine cover are momentarily ruptured. For these readers, or rather for these viewers, the picture lingers as picture in the lag between the *punctum* and the *studium,* between their shock and the connotative assurances the cover vainly attempts, between the truth of suffering and the fiction that the cover fails to establish in the place of suffering. These viewers' inability to read the cover as cover might be caused by its dramatic, urgent framing, which both visually and generically (a title page is always urgent) "conceal[s] the textuality of the photograph itself—substituting passive receptivity for active (critical) *reading.*"[14] In questioning the editors' intentions, the readers thus complain about the absence of a readable text. For them, the photograph remains *punctum* and its rupturing, wounding quality conjures up protective instincts: "Please remember that your readers live in homes, we have children."

Although Barthes points out that "News photographs are very often unary" and that the unary photograph, because of its unproblematic relationship with reality, has no *punctum,* this seems in the present case questionable.[15] What exact quality it is in the photograph that ruptures its generic and cultural encoding, one can only guess. Perhaps the *punctum* is in the position in which the boy is photographed, with his arms folded behind his head as if comfortably at rest. Yet again, if the boy's restful posture momentarily disorganizes our presuppositions about pictures showing wounds and suffering, we manage to hastily organize this disorganization either by noting its necessity—the boy is probably carried on a stretcher—or by unconsciously associating his position with a Christlike, sacrificial pose.[16]

If we draw closer, we notice the second *punctum*: the detail of the torn and bloody flesh partly—and therefore all the more suggestively—shown underneath the bandage. It is likely, I suppose, in this latter uncivilized, uncoded detail that the picture's literal relation to reality becomes (too) explicit and where the mediations of the *studium* are acutely missing. If the *studium* is missing, if it should be present to conceal and heal what we cannot read or understand, we recognize that the bandaging of wounds is not only a medical but an eminently cultural activity, suggesting a fundamental analogy between medicine and writing.

In the issue of May 31, the editors of *Newsweek* seek to nurse, to bind up, to redress the injuries that the cover of May 10 caused its viewers. If those viewers had only seen but failed to read the picture, the editorial explanation now provides for them a second opportunity to read and to cover their gaze. In closing with a report on the doctors' efforts to rebuild the boy's face and restore him to normal health, the editorial offers a redemptive or curative narrative, whose political and ethical analogies have remained—and may now remain—elusive. For both accounts, that of Warren Christopher's diplomatic employment of the picture, as well as the account of the boy's flight to California, offer aesthetic closure. They offer precisely that cultural context, those narrative connotations, or those layers of textual binding up by which now the picture need no longer be seen but can be read—even if the editorial accounts of the fate of Sead Bekrik report at the same time a partial failure (the doctors could not restore his eyesight) in which his wounds remain, as in the picture, partly visible.[17]

But then again such failure and such partial visibility of remaining injuries, such partial openness of this editorial narrative, may already have been sublated and bound up in the rhythm and rhetoric of the narrative closure resembling a fairy tale ending: "And as for Sead Bekrik, the 12-year-old boy in the picture, the media exposure had a happy result. . . ." Such a sublation of failure in closure, indeed such a closure of failure, is what now produces a neutralizing effect, making the picture readable, *lisible* not *scriptible* to use Barthes' terms, remedying the violence of wounds by the violence of closure.[18] The Secretary of State's journey to Moscow and the boy's flight to California thus each offer a moral or narrative resolution to the photograph's resistance to meaning.[19]

However, for that much greater majority of readers of *Newsweek* who did not express their outrage at the rupturing qualities of the picture, and who evidently did not need such resolutions, the photograph's power to incite a momentary crisis of meaning must have almost instantly generated meanings for that crisis itself. For that majority of readers, the effect of the photograph might initially have been similar to the explosion of the bomb. And if the rhetorical violence of the cover is felt precisely in such hyperbolic similarity, the similarity, in turn, serves as a remedy for the shock produced by the cover. Shells and bombs, like magazine covers, strike indiscriminately. Being blinded by a bomb is no choice, but nor is seeing a magazine cover. What the similarity demonstrates is the breathless expedience by which perception is pacified and crisis of meaning converted into meaning. Thus, our shock is redemptive, it is in the illusion that we, too, have been struck, and if only rhetorically for that all the more innocently and unexpectedly.[20]

The moralistic implication in these remarks could be articulated by saying that radical objectivity, such as is rendered particularly in the unsparing disclosure of wounds and injuries, is always also, as Barthes observes, a gesture of innocence,[21] which sublimates in turn a natural affinity to victims of trauma and suffering. If suffering is a fact beyond choice, an event, journalistic photography presents itself in a comparable phenomenology. For both in photographs, as in wounds, the inevitable is accomplished; therefore both the sufferer and the photographer are innocent. Both are presented with facts whose violent objectivity is beyond question precisely because it is imposed, not desired: it happens. Both wounds and photographs therefore serve as exemplary instances of legal evidence and epistemological proof. Even if photographs are constitutionally of the past, as Sontag and Barthes have pointed out, journalistic photography adds that it is always a past about which nothing could be done. Of course, these notions of the innocence of the photographer and of the viewer, and of their therefore natural sympathy with the victim in the photograph, cannot pretend to be taken at face value. They are precisely the terms by which the ideology of the photograph encourages our passivity and represses our ethical responsibilities.[22]

These repressions are instantaneous. If the injuries caused by the *punctum* of the cover does not *turn into* but already *is* a *studium*, our innocence has been proven without suffering or participation. By having seen the cover we have already acted upon it, even if such acting demands only our momentary presence, a presence which in the case of the spectator of the image is by proxy of the photographer at the scene. In the same representative, indirect and yet instantaneous way we are morally implicated in the "happy result" of Sead Bekrik's flight to California simply by virtue of the existence of the front page. If this amounts to an accidental ethics, such then would be the code of connotation by which, as Barthes writes, our society ensures its peace of mind.[23] The rhetoric of this code of connotations which furnishes proof both of our innocence and of our objectivity is deeply inscribed in the genre of the cover.

What is further inscribed in that genre—and which has been implicit in the "momentary" presence required for the structures of repression to take hold—is the temporal aspect of our gaze. For in turning the page, in not having to sustain our gaze for long, the title page permits what Victor Burgin has called "our imaginary command of the look"[24] before a longer look might question our gaze.

It hardly needs mentioning that not only innocence and objectivity are epistemologically related, but also that both predicate spatial, visual distance as their means of operation. If the Old Masters, as W. H. Auden declared, were always right about suffering, we are always informed about it. To inform, as the editors of *Newsweek* predictably explain in their response, is one of the purposes of photojournalism. But the distance implied by information is also a moral distance. Such a distance defines, by its very name, the genre of television, which I take to be an endlessly metonymic chain of magazine covers where the lost past is converted into an incommensurable space between us.

If it is true, as Dorothee Sölle points out, that there is no suffering that is another's—"*Es gibt kein Leid, das fremdes Leid ist*"[25]—and if one could reinforce this by saying there is no suffering if it is not ours, then magazine covers and television demand our continual, and eventually habitual, moral absence from suffering. If Sölle's moral imperative fails to address us in the cover of *Newsweek*, we have become estranged from ourselves because we do not recognize ourselves in another's suffering. The *Newsweek* cover is thus finally only a mirror that shows us ourselves unseen *as* the other. Our gaze is monologic, our mode of participation voyeuristic.

Even if we cannot close our eyes to avoid what Levinas has called "the avidity proper to the gaze,"[26] Stanley Cavell suggests that it is only ". . . when we keep ourselves in the dark . . . that we convert the other into a character and make the world a stage for him."[27] While the genre of theater draws attention to such objectification in order precisely to overcome it—even if theater (as Cavell suggests) may well become tragedy because the other remains estranged, victim to our distance—our public gaze never articulates the tragedy of these representational conditions.[28] *"Das Licht der Öffentlichkeit verdunkelt alles,"* the light of publicity obscures everything, as Hannah Arendt commented in remarkably similar political circumstances.[29] To which Theodor Adorno—again in somewhat comparable historical context—adds that under such circumstances "art may be the only remaining medium of truth. . . ."; the increasing darkening of the world demanding as its adequate representative the irrationality of art.[30] The charge, of course, that one would in these terms level against the cover of *Newsweek* is that it is not self-conscious theater, or self-conscious representation, or avant garde art, or that it does not make its form a more explicit form of misinformation, that it is not informed about information, does not spell out the compromises of its own representational claims.

If Sead Bekrik's suffering has representative value, this also implies that, apart from such representative value, individual suffering is insufficient to produce any such political incentive as urged in the subheading. The shadowy possibility of an economic recovery promised above might produce more convincing reason for Clinton to get tough and for air power to be used. Moreover, if only its representational claims assign value to individual suffering, perhaps such value is itself only tenuous if we regard the unreality of public identity which should assign it. For in addressing everyone, the picture addresses always someone else, and if the claim implicit in the boy's suffering is always addressed to the other, we can remain unaddressed.

Without its various rhetorical layers and closures, the picture of the boy lying on a stretcher would keep wounding the narrative of his and of our lives. If the moment of puncture or rupture is the essence of the moment of the photograph, it is in this moment of crisis of meaning when the force of signification, the claim of the sufferer, could have been felt. All of this implies, of course, the truth of Barthes' observation that truly traumatic photographs are rare—if indeed they exist at all in the genre of the press photograph. But what is also implied by the incommensurability of suffering and culture, of *punctum* and *studium* is that the covering, bandaging, and binding up of the trauma by the rhetoric of the cover cannot morally address or represent the suffering which it depicts.

The *Newsweek* picture and the editorial commentary—as they labor to rebuild the boy's face and restore him to otherwise normal health—also duplicate the failure of the doctors in that they cannot restore our eyesight either.

P. J. GRIFFITHS' PHOTOGRAPH

> Our eyes detain us at the *forms*.
>
> —Friedrich Nietzsche, *Philosophy and Truth*

P. J. Griffiths' photograph is, as he intended, not a magazine photograph, or journalistic novelty, but a record of "'what actually happened there.'"[31] Even if the staging and iconographic codes of the two pictures appear to some extent similar, the difference between a journalistic and a documentary photograph is decisive. Griffiths' picture appears appropriately not on magazine covers but in documentary or aesthetic contexts, such as *Eyes of Time* or *British Photography*,[32] where the photograph is viewed not by the public but by the individual on its own aesthetic terms without the fierce solicitations of politics and history. It is the structure of this photograph itself rather than its political ramifications or public appeal that must articulate its rhetorical or aesthetic value. Here then, I suggest, the total absence of any headline or commentary, except for the laconic caption, "Napalm Victim, South Vietnam" (1967) and the mostly illegible label wired to the wrist of this person, produce the incommensurable photographic paradox, the undialectical photograph, the photograph one cannot read. And if these statements cannot, admittedly, amount to a demonstrable theory, one finds oneself here in a somewhat comparable private encounter, alone with it, in front of it, as Barthes is before the Wintergarden Photograph.

The absence of any immediate interpretive commentary intimates an ontologic and ethical priority of Griffiths' subject. Despite its clear historical connotations, the photograph recovers to some extent an individuality and intimacy, however veiled. Like the *Newsweek* picture, Griffiths' photograph literalizes the notion of photography as concealing a depth which remains inaccessible to the eye. Both photographs highlight, thematically as well as structurally, the paradox of a blindness visible and of a visibility that renders blind. Neither picture can reveal

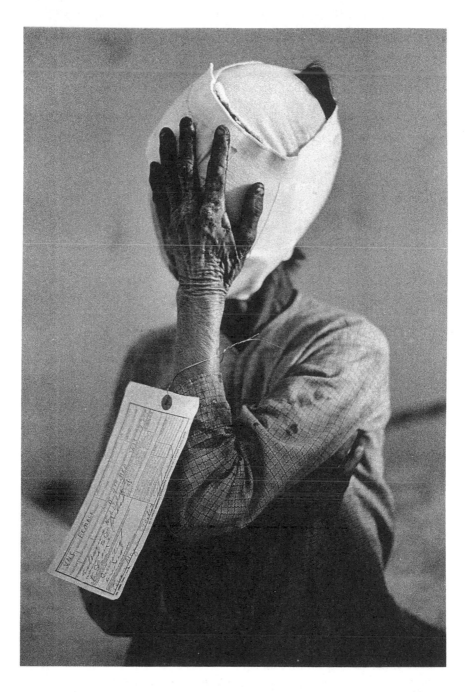

Philip Jones Griffiths.
Napalm victim, Vietnam, 1967
(Magnum)

suffering to the eye. If the issue of the paradox of seeing structures much of the visual rhetoric of Griffiths' picture, as it does of the *Newsweek* cover, here the connotative discourse of language appears visibly suspended while the *Newsweek* cover, as we have seen, impatiently seeks to establish cultural connotations. If the *Newsweek* picture (eventually or instantaneously) erases the *punctum*, Griffiths' photograph acquires it gradually; it eventually haunts our memory in the way Barthes suggests that ". . . the *punctum* should be revealed only after the fact, when the photograph is no longer in front of me."[33]

Such a latency of *punctum* is perhaps in the sufferer's pose of stunned surprise. While *Newsweek* presents the sufferer in a temporary aperture of a larger dramatically developing narrative—it is significant therefore to note that the *Newsweek* picture is a fragment of a video that had appeared on CNN—Griffiths' photograph has a static, pensive intensity. The *Newsweek* picture suggests movement in time and space, and therefore a cathartic narrative by virtue of its cinematographic context but also by virtue of the publicity implicit in the photojournalistic genre, while the person in Griffiths' picture, standing or sitting upright, rests in an intense, lonely equilibrium partly established by her left arm supporting her right arm. Her mode of existence seems fulfilled within the photographic; it is, in Barthes' words, "a message which totally exhausts its mode of existence," an example of the photograph that suggests an "analogical plentitude . . . so great that the description of the photograph is literally impossible. . . ."[34] The *Newsweek* picture, by comparison, is a photograph only by default—a snapshot, part of a larger moving picture, "drawn towards other views," as Barthes would say.[35] While in Griffiths' photograph a person poses, as it were, before the camera, in the *Newsweek* picture the boy (merely) passes before it.[36] Griffiths' photograph can be considered the epitome of Barthes' observation that photography "is without future (this is its pathos, its melancholy). . . . Motionless, the Photograph flows back from presentation to retention."[37]

If the "pose" of the person in Griffiths' picture reminds us of portraiture, the irony of the allusion to portraiture produces a *punctum*. Not only is it questionable whether the person in this picture either knows that she is photographed or whether she wants to pose for a photograph, but the whole photograph questions itself as photograph. For this person's facelessness is the terrible instance of the presentation of the unrepresentable, a portrait that is not a portrait, a portrayal of something that cannot be portrayed.

What the picture does show is a figure locked in the clash of antinomies: fate and face, urgency and immobility, visibility and blindness. In any conceptual categories—visual, historical, psychological, social, geographic—this sufferer is rendered incomprehensible. Separate from temporal and spatial concerns, absent from the world, she waits. Time and place are incidental, here and nowhere at once; the caption neither adds nor subtracts. This then, is suffering as such: its incognito, its invisibility, its a-temporality.

In the *Newsweek* cover, by contrast, time and place are of the utmost importance; they are what the picture is all about. There suffering has a temporal, historical significance and the remedies offered by the *Newsweek* cover are likewise temporal and historical. In spite of its historical reference, Griffiths' picture is timeless, or a-temporal. While the sufferer in the *Newsweek* picture is both spatially and psychologically, so to speak, rushed to another site, the sufferer in Griffiths' picture remains where she is. What the *Newsweek* cover depicts is frightening, yet our fear is readily pacified precisely by the picture's historical connotations, while Griffiths' photograph has a haunting effect. The *Newsweek* cover evokes our fear, Griffiths' picture evokes our pity. The *Newsweek* cover shocks but does not surprise; Griffiths' picture surprises but does not shock.

Such remarks, testing the possibility of seeing Griffiths' picture as signifying only by photographic, aesthetic means rather than by linguistic or cultural connotations, cannot omit mentioning the label on the subject's wrist—not least because its size seems disproportionate. If we strain (therefore) to decipher the label we learn from such efforts only that the subject is female. Otherwise indecipherable, the label spells out that such officiously referential writing may be a violent misnaming, not only for reasons well depicted in its hyperbolic bureaucracy, but also because it generates the gaze of fascination which may operate in the name of thwarted decipherment.

For, this piece of writing, this oversized label, which so ostentatiously wants to send the woman on her way, just as our reading of the label would have wished to do, this writing and reading might have had the potential to lift the unbearable suspension of time and space in the aesthetic of the photograph. A readable label might have indicated the degrees of the woman's burns, the surface percentage of her wound, where she should be sent for treatment, what the treatment should be. Such references or connotations would scatter and dilute the lyrical intensity of the picture. Yet, in the undecipherability of the label the picture jealously guards all means of opening its visual aesthetic to a redemptive narrative.

Evidently, such a narrative could neither remedy nor explain nor prevent such suffering. But nor can the photographic lyric—and it is perhaps those impossibilities that we can see. What we can see in Griffiths' picture is a lonely, unrelieved anonymity, the unsharable secrecy of suffering. Its static, lyrical a-temporality. An invisibility. The hand and the bandages prohibit all mutual confidence between the photographer and the subject which the near frontal view might otherwise have signified. Indeed, Griffiths' photograph is the prohibition of photography, the indictment of the camera. The bandage and the hand, finally, become the emblems of an aesthetic of traumatic photography, which, as it unfolds to show, becomes a binding up, a covering.

If the formlessness of suffering appropriately requires for its representation an aesthetics of the sublime, such an aesthetic, as Lyotard points out in his essay "Representation, Presentation, Unpresentable," cannot be offered by photography. Its aesthetic and ideological constraints prohibit photography from "overturn[ing] the supposed 'givens' of the visible so as to make visible the fact that the visual field hides and requires invisibilities, that it does not simply belong to the eye (of the prince) but to the (wandering) mind."[38]

In their allegorical covering and bandaging of eyes the *Newsweek* cover and Griffiths' photograph make *these* very issues visible. The two pictures illustrate Susan Sontag's notion of photography by showing what cannot be seen, or by bandaging what is seen and thereby making the princely eye suspect and the mind wander.[39] These photographs can thus only complete themselves by inviting us, as Susan Sontag observes in her book *On Photography* to "'. . . think—or rather feel, intuit—what is beyond it, what the reality must be like if it looks this way.'"[40]

NOTES

1. Roland Barthes, "The Photographic Message," in *Image, Music, Text*, trans. Stephen Heath (New York: The Noonday Press, 1977), 15–19.

2. Ibid., 28, 29.

3. Ibid., 30–31.

4. Ibid., 30–31. The assumption of the photographers' presence at the scene already subjects the trauma to language, the denotative immediacy of

photographic perception to overdetermined, textual connotation. Even the photographer's presence is thus always already a form of representation, defined as it is by visual perspective and some form of framing and aesthetic deliberation. For a more explicit treatment of these issues see Victor Burgin, "Looking at Photographs," in *Thinking Photography*, ed. Victor Burgin (London, Macmillan, 1982): "To the point-of-view, the system of representation adds the *frame* . . . through the agency of the frame the world is organized into a coherence which it actually lacks, into a parable of tableaux, a succession of 'decisive moments'" (146).

5. Barthes, "The Photographic Message," 31.

6. Ibid., 31.

7. See Martin Jay, *Downcast Eyes: The Denigration of Vision in Twentieth-Century French Thought* (Berkeley: University of California Press, 1993), 450–52.

8. "From Taste to Ecstasy," in Roland Barthes, *The Grain of the Voice: Interviews 1962–1980*, trans. Linda Coverdale (Berkeley: University of California Press, 1985), 352.

9. Roland Barthes, *Camera Lucida: Reflections on Photography* (1980), trans. Richard Howard (New York: Hill and Wang, 1981), 26–27.

10. Ibid., 90.

11. Ibid., 91.

12. *Newsweek*, May 31, 1993.

13. See Umberto Eco, "Critique of the Image," in *Thinking Photography*, 38.

14. Burgin, "Looking at Photographs," 146.

15. Barthes, *Camera Lucida*, 40–41.

16. For this latter association I am indebted to William Holzberger.

17. Such partial visibility and gradual covering of wounds by text is also illustrated by the layout of the editorial page in the May 31 issue in which the readers' letters are published.

18. See Jay, *Dowcast Eyes*: "A photograph's 'studium' produced only the limited pleasure of recognition, comparable to that of the 'readerly' text he had described in *S/Z*" (453).

19. See Barthes, "Rhetoric of the Image" in *Image, Music, Text*, 32.

20. Barthes, "The Photographic Message," 19.

21. Barthes, "Rhetoric of the Image," 42.

22. See Burgin, "Photographic Practice and Art Theory," in *Thinking Photography*, 45–46.

23. Barthes, "The Photographic Message," 31.

24. Burgin, "Looking at Photographs," 152.

25. Dorothee Sölle, *Leiden* (Freiburg: Herder/Spektrum, 1993), 210.

26. Emmanuel Levinas, *Totality and Infinity* (1961), trans. Alphonso Lingis (Pittsburgh: Duquesne University Press, 1969), 50.

27. Stanley Cavell, *Disowning Knowledge: In Six Plays of Shakespeare* (Cambridge: Cambridge University Press, 1987), 104.

28. Barthes sees the connection between theater and photography through their intermediary: Death. See *Camera Lucida*, 31.

29. Hannah Arendt, *Men in Dark Times* (Harmondsworth: Penguin, 1973), 9.

30. Theodor Adorno, *Aesthetic Theory*, trans. C. Lenhardt (London: Routledge and Kegan Paul, 1984), 27.

31. Quoted in Marianne Fulton, *Eyes of Time: Photojournalism in America* (New York: Little, Brown, 1988), 212.

32. Mark Haworth-Booth, "Where We Come From: Aspects of Postwar British Photography," in *British Photography: Toward a Bigger Picture* (New York: Farrar, Straus and Giroux, 1988), 4.

33. Barthes, *Camera Lucida*, 53.

34. Barthes, "The Photographic Message," 18.

35. Barthes, *Camera Lucida*, 89.

36. See ibid., 78.

37. Ibid., 90.

38. Jean-François Lyotard, *The Inhuman*, trans. Geoffrey Benington and Rachel Bowlby (Stanford: Stanford University Press, 1991), 125; see also 105–7 or 135–43.

39. Susan Sontag states, ". . . the photographic view is to show that it is hidden." See *On Photography* (New York: Farrar, Straus and Giroux, 1977), 121.

40. Sontag, *On Photography*, 23.

3

SUFFERING
AS METAPHOR

NIETZSCHE'S "REMEDY OF ART"

> *. . . ce que montre Nietzsche c'est que la philosophie,*
> *depuis Socrate, par sa propre voie, celle des concepts,*
> *possède le même vouloir que la tragédie: guérir le*
> *regard blessé en maîtrisant les contradictions . . .*
>
> —Sarah Kofman, *Mélancholie de l'art*[1]

> . . . the high and excellent Tragedy, that openeth
> the greatest wounds, and sheweth forth the
> Ulcers that are covered with Tissue . . .
>
> —Sir Philip Sidney, *An Apologie for Poetrie*

> . . . to stop courageously at the surface,
> the fold, the skin, to adore appearance,
> to believe in forms, tones, words,
> in the whole Olympus of appearance. Those
> Greeks were superficial—*out of profundity.*
>
> —Friedrich Nietzsche, *The Gay Science*

In the famous dialectical contest between Dionysos and Apollo, in Nietzsche's *Birth of Tragedy*, ". . . the original Oneness, the ground of Being, ever suffering and contradictory time and again has need of rapt vision and delightful illusion to redeem itself."[2] Since "we ourselves," as Nietzsche goes on, "are the very stuff of such illusion," I shall here try to examine how consistently illusion perpetuates itself in the very process of inquiry and understanding. The first occasion for such a demonstration is a short paragraph in *The Birth of Tragedy* which can be taken as an exemplary passage illustrating the issue, raised by Kleinman, whether speculation should have limits and whether one should stop where validity is in question. Beyond those limits, which are in medical circumstances sometimes (but not always) reasonably prescribed, there is, as Nietzsche will show, only the remedy of art. The remedy of art is not, as we shall see, a remedy for suffering but a demonstration that in order to suffer we need the remedy of art. Indeed, human suffering— Nietzsche thinks of Schopenhauerian universal suffering as ground of existence—is beyond remedy and precisely *this* truth, if it is to be bearable, necessitates the remedy of art. "As an aesthetic phenomenon existence is still *bearable* for us," Nietzsche writes in *The Gay Science*, "and art furnishes us with eyes and hands and above all the good conscience to be *able* to turn ourselves into such phenomenon."[3]

Since this chapter addresses a second issue, that of translation, I should add that I encountered the passage in question in two different translations. Each translation became, in turn, a different form of appearance, each demonstrating to some degree how, as Nietzsche would say, the truth is conveyed as metaphor, carried into, or made up as, illusion. Since each translation is therefore constitutionally unreliable, each points up that the original text must also be a translation. The very concept of "the remedy of art" is itself an assumption grounded in no more primordial a reality than another text, Schopenhauer's philosophy, from which Nietzsche derives the notion of an eternal futile striving and suffering as the ground of existence.[4] Our notions then are always translations without an original, carried out, as it were, in a foreign language, a language foreign to its cause. "For between two absolutely different spheres," as Nietzsche writes in "On Truth and Lies in a Nonmoral Sense," ". . . there is no causality, no correctness, and no expression; there is, at most, an *aesthetic* relation: I mean, a suggestive transference, a stammering translation into a completely foreign tongue."[5]

In his essay "Ariadne's Thread: Repetition and the Narrative Line," where our passage is quoted as well, J. Hillis Miller quotes a story told by Walter Pater of a "'strenuous, self-possessed, much honored monastic student'" whose twelfth volume of a mathematical treatise suddenly emits "'a violent beam, a blaze, a new light, revealing . . . a hundred truths unguessed at before, yet a curse, as it turned out, to its receiver, in dividing hopelessly against itself the well-ordered kingdom of his thought.'"[6] Like Miller or Pater's novice, Nietzsche subscribes to "*wissenschaftlichkeit,*" only to carry it to a point where method becomes metaphor:

> ... *die Peripherie des Kreises der Wissenschaft hat unendlich viele Punkte, und während noch gar nicht abzusehen ist, wie jemals der Kreis völlig ausgemessen werden könnte, so trifft doch der edle und begabte Mensch, noch vor der Mitte seines Daseins und unvermeidlich, auf solche Grenzpunkte der Peripherie, wo er in das Unaufhellbare starrt. Wenn er hier zu seinem Schrecken sieht, wie die Logik sich an diesen Grenzen um sich selbst ringelt und endlich sich in den Schwanz beisst, da bricht die neue Form der Erkenntnis durch, die tragische Erkenntnis, die um nur ertragen zu werden, als Schutz und Heilmittel die Kunst braucht.*[7]

In Francis Golffing's translation of Nietzsche's *Geburt der Tragödie* we read that

> ... the periphery of science has an infinite number of points. Every noble and gifted man has, before reaching the midpoint of his career, come up against some point of the periphery that defied his understanding, quite apart from the fact that we have no way of knowing how the area of the circle is ever to be fully charted. When the inquirer, having pushed to the circumference, realizes how logic in that place curls about itself and bites its own tail, he is struck with a new kind of perception: a tragic perception, which requires, to make it tolerable, the remedy of art.[8]

That this tragic perception not only requires the remedy of art, but also unmasks the pretentions of science is explicitly stated in *The Gay Science* where Nietzsche confesses his "*ultimate gratitude to art.*—If we had not welcomed the arts and invented the kind of cult of the untrue, then the general untruth and menadaciousness that now comes to us through science—the realization that delusion and error are conditions of human knowledge and sensation—would be utterly unbearable."[9] How then can "the remedy of art" be both another untruth as well as a remedy against it?

The remedy, we have read and reread and read yet again one page from the end of the book, is the veil of Apollo, "those countless illusions of fair semblance which any moment make life worth living and whet our appetite for the next moment."[10] Of that repeated moment in Nietzsche's *Birth of Tragedy*, when the veil of Apollo spreads over the tragic perception, we have yet another veil, the veil of Walter Kaufmann's translation, which renders Nietzsche's *"als Schutz und Heilmittel die Kunst"* into "art as a protection and remedy."[11] The difference between Kaufmann's and Golffing's translations is decisive: Golffing's "remedy of art" is a metaphor substituted for Nietzsche's simile *"als Schutz und Heilmittel die Kunst"* that is, art *as* remedy. It is in that subtle difference that Nietzsche's tragic stance appears and where the question if art can be both lie and remedy is answered.

The simile negates the metaphor: art is not identifiable with remedy but only identifiable in its likeness to—but then also in its unlikeness to—remedy. Nietzsche's *"tragische Erkenntnis,"* then, is a perception that is tragic precisely because, while being tempted by the possibility of the metaphoric equation of art and remedy, the tragic realization calls attention to that equation as a deception. Art is "as a remedy," as Kaufmann translates, which is to say, not in essence a remedy. The simile persuades us momentarily to believe that art is remedy. But the simile *as* simile, just as art *as* remedy, betrays the hope in remedy; it invokes but simultaneously revokes the equation. The metaphor is silent about such a deception; it deceives better, it forgets its epistemology, it does not hold us up. While in the simile—"art *as* remedy"—logic bites its own tail, in the metaphor—"the remedy of art"—logic forgets its own metaphoricity. In the simile, art consoles but it only consoles *as* art: not "art *is* remedy" but "art *as* remedy." "Art *is* remedy" is an empty promise, a forgetting, perhaps a necessary forgetting.

Nietzsche's notion of "the forgetting of metaphor," as Sarah Kofman observes, resembles Freud's notion of repression: both terms "stand opposed to a linear conception of time and . . . imply a conflict between a play of forces."[12] This is explicit when Kofman writes:

> Thus the forgetting of metaphor does not occur at a specific point in time—after a certain time. . . . It is originary, the necessary correlate of metaphorical activity itself: man has always already forgotten that he is an "artist from the beginning," and that he remains one in all his activities.[13]

Although "man has always already forgotten" and there is "only appearance, from which no bridge leads to the true reality, the heart of the world,"[14] the forgetfulness of metaphor—like the language of the unconscious—now and then allows for "a brief moment" of insight into "the struggle, the pain, the destruction of appearances."[15] Otherwise, any attempt to bridge, to traverse, or to translate the true reality, or the heart of the world, (excepting those "who communicate with things almost entirely through unconscious musical relations"),[16] inevitably carries across its own destruction. The word *metaphor* from the Greek *metaphora,* to transfer, to carry across, does not keep its promise. "Language promises, but what it promises is itself," as Miller writes in *The Ethics of Reading.*[17] The gap between the suffering of existence and appearance cannot be traversed, while Golffing's metaphor steps over it as if nothing were there.

But indeed nothing is there except the illusions by which "nothing" becomes momentarily "something." By comparison to an absolute "nothing," even Nietzsche's concept of nonrepresentational, originary music makes rhetorical compromises. Although music should be exempt from the illusions of representation, because it "symbolizes a sphere which is both earlier than appearance and beyond it,"[18] it still "refers" and "symbolizes" and is thus always already different from the "primordial contradiction and pain" which it would seek *to be.* Sarah Kofman is right therefore to emphasize the metaphoricity of music itself when she writes, ". . . Nietzsche calls the will, *metaphorically,* the music or melody of the world." (Italics mine)[19]

Thus the "remedy of art" is a catachresis, "the violent, forced, or abusive use of a term from another realm to name something which has no 'proper' name."[20] For just what is it that art remedies? We do not known. The "remedy of art" is a deferment of a fundamental meaninglessness, a nihilistic *Ungrund* rather than an existential *Abgrund,* because "to name the abyss," as Miller explains, "is to cover it, to make a fiction or icon of it, a likeness that is no likeness."[21] Elsewhere Miller writes, "without the production of some schema, some 'icon,' there can be no glimpse of the abyss, no vertigo of the underlying nothingness. Any such schema, however, both opens the chasm, creates it or reveals it, and at the same time fills it up, covers it over by naming it, gives the groundless a ground, the bottomless a bottom"[22]—and the ground, Miller should add, a groundlessness—if he wanted to deconstruct his own production of schema.

Golffing's metaphor denies this perception of the duplicity of the ground/less; his metaphor is itself—as it should be—a remedy of art, an art that is always also the remedy of forgetting, incidentally exemplified in Golffing's forgetting to translate the *"Schrecken,"* the horror, the vertigo which occurs in Nietzsche's text, when the tragic realization breaks through. In his discussion of *The Birth of Tragedy*, Paul de Man mentions various dramatizations—and Nietzsche's noble and gifted man may be one—by which "the possibility of this bridge, of this translation (Nietzsche speaks of 'übersetzen' and 'überbrücken') [is] performed in the metaphorical narrative by means of which Dionysos can enter into a world of appearances and still somehow remain Dionysos."[23] But de Man's "somehow" indicates that Dionysos must compromise his identity just as Apollo must compromise his insight. It is thus impossible to know whether art protects us either from the terrible truth or from the terror of its absence. Neither can we say whether the horror we experience in either case is an authentic experience or a traditional dramatization of this very predicament. Even the horror of the tragic realization may be a metaphor. There is no philosophic ground for horror, just as there may be no reason for consolation. Neither is there any reason to distinguish between the existential *Abgrund* and the nihilistic *Ungrund;* our redemptive misreadings cover them all. "Language knows that its kingdom is day and not the intimacy of the unrevealed," as Maurice Blanchot notes, ". . . something must be left out."[24]

The noble and gifted man's "tragic perception" therefore cannot be verified other than as necessity that calls for the remedy of art. That necessity in turn structures metaphoricity itself by which art can perform as remedy for something that can never be verified other than as the necessity for metaphor, and by which necessity in endless repetition truth can remain, as Lacoue-Labarthe puts it, a "wound still open in the tissue of philosophy, a wound that does not heal and that reopens constantly under the hand that would close it."[25]

A post-structural position grounded on Nietzsche's, a work without a ground so to speak, is thus like Nietzsche's work, post-philosophic or pre-Socratic. Philosophy, for Nietzsche, is a theory of metaphor and narrative: it is all inclusive, including the philosopher as a teller of tales whose sheer rhetorical necessities allow only the construction of a flying bridge and a hasty crossing before the abyss swallows that bridge as well.

What then can be said (in conclusion) if the metaphoric veil seems to obstruct all but final statements? Perhaps when Derrida points out that "[m]etaphoricity is the logic of contamination and the contamination of logic,"[26] the metaphoricity of *this* statement depends on our acceptance of the concept of "contamination" as a ground which can still support a statement about it. If it can, Derrida's metaphor repeats and confirms Nietzsche's own Schopenhauerian notion that at bottom, structuring metaphoricity itself, there is something like a primal metaphor of wounds and suffering, *das Ewig-Leidende und Widerspruchsvolle*,[27] which causes the phenomenon of metaphor itself.

Or, perhaps more practically: To substitute metaphor by concept, as Kofman has shown, amounts to "an effacement of the personality,"[28] an effacement, reduction, or repression of the subject as constituted as a non-unitary, polymorphous entity. The concept fixes and generalizes—Nietzsche calls it a killing, mummifying, and preserving. If the forgetting of metaphor engenders the concept or if the concept sustains repression, the experience of suffering can be understood as a form of involuntary return to a primal necessity, a preconceptual, pre-Socratic state—perhaps Freud's primal scene, or perhaps that "scorching moment of hesitation" which is for Julia Kristeva "the supreme and sole interest of literature."[29] Such a state, scene, or moment, as both Nietzsche and Freud understood, and as the terms tragedy or transference suggest, lies beyond the periphery of science, beyond wit's end, beyond understanding. It is there where we need the remedy of art.

And finally: when Susan Sontag in her book *Illness as Metaphor* recommends that "the most truthful way of regarding illness—and the healthiest way of being ill—is one most purified of, most resistant to, metaphoric thinking,"[30] her advice is audibly Socratic, based on the very notion of the ontologic priority of concept over metaphor, of health over illness. One might ask whether the violence done to the sick person by reducing her illness experience to a concept or a disease is not a form of repression of the far more polyphonous, indeterminate experience of suffering itself, and whether Nietzsche's attempt to reinstate a pre-Socratic philosophy, and the priority of metaphor over concept, might not have promised a less reductive art of remedy.

FREUD'S NARRATIVE CURE

> Those blessed structures, plot and rhyme—
> why are they no help to me now
> I want to make
> something imagined, not recalled?
>
> —Robert Lowell, *Day by Day*

> Only our momentary and accidental knowledge makes
> something rounded and changeless of the past.
>
> —Georg Lukács, *Soul and Form*

> We must not forget that the patient's illness,
> which we have undertaken to analyse,
> is not something rounded off and become rigid
> but that it is still growing and developing
> like a living organism.
>
> —Sigmund Freud, "Transference"

In the eighteenth of his *Introductory Lectures on Psycho-Analysis*, Freud confesses to some difficulty in surmounting the patient's resistance to psychoanalysis. "We came upon discoveries in this connection for which we were at first unprepared."[31] The editor points out, in a footnote, that the issue of this lecture will be returned to in Freud's lecture on transference. There, the same question is asked again:

> What must we do in order to replace what is unconscious in our patients by what is conscious? There was a time when I thought this was a very simple matter: all that was necessary was for us to discover this unconscious material and communicate it to the patient.

The task, Freud admits, is complicated by the "removal of the resistance which maintains the repression."[32] Then, however, follow almost euphoric ennumerations of past successful treatments of hysteria, anxiety states, obsessional neurosis, in all of which "our expectation is fulfilled . . . we really succeeded in accomplishing our task. . . ." And a little further on: "We have succeeded in reviving the old conflict which led to repression. . . ."[33] Yet what has been waiting behind these deceptive formulae of a redemptive hermeneutic are Freud's unexpected discoveries, announced in the earlier lecture on "Transference." "There are . . ." he now admits, "other forms of illness in which, in spite of the conditions being the same, our therapeutic procedure is never successful." When the patients are paranoics, melancholics, sufferers from dementia praecox, "we are faced . . . by a fact which we do not understand and which therefore leads us to doubt whether we have really understood all the determinants of our possible success with the other neuroses."[34]

Scarcely five years later, in the opening paragraph of the third chapter of *Beyond the Pleasure Principle* (1920), Freud returns to this moment of doubt, announcing that "twenty-five years of intense work" had made him realize that psychoanalysis was more than hermeneutics. The patient, asked "to confirm the analyst's construction," never attained a conviction of the truth of any account of his repressions. Rather than remembering the unconscious "as something belonging to the past" *(ein Stück der Vergangenheit)*, the patient was forced to repeat the unconscious in his present experiences. Freud's *"Stück der Vergangenheit"* is the lost object of an art of interpretation, a *Deutungskunst*, thwarted by the suddenly complicated phenomenon of "present experiences." Not only is the past no longer "one piece," to which one may return at will, but the patient who would have pleased the doctor *(wie der Arzt es lieber sähe)*, if he had remembered himself in the process, is thus cast into a state of perpetual dismemberment.[35]

While formerly Freud's psychoanalytic method had modelled itself on a more straightforward art of interpretation, that of Sherlock Holmes' logic of deduction, where a secret cause determines the outcome of a crime, for Freud, as François Lyotard points out, analysis is no longer "subject to knowledge but to 'technique,' art. The result is not the definition of a past element. On the contrary, it presupposes that the past itself is the actor or agent that gives to the mind the elements with which the scene will be constructed."[36] Thus, rather than the conventional notion of a truthful narrative, Freudian psychoanalysis advocates the idea of narrative itself, not fact but fiction, or not "what was" but "what might be," as Aristotle famously defined the difference between history and poetry, even to the extent that what might be, as Freud concedes, may be pure hallucination.

To mention Aristotle in the context of a curative narrative recalls Freud's enormous debt to tragedy—where, as Lukács observes, the past is a dangerous threat.[37] Or, as Hannah Arendt points out, like psychoanalysis, the form of tragedy allows the protagonist to become "knowledgeable by re-experiencing what has been done in the way of suffering, and in this *pathos*, in resuffering the past, the network of individual acts is transformed into an event, a significant whole."[38] Lyotard states this explicitly:

> In both Sophocles's tragedy and Freud's analysis, Oedipus, or the patient, tries to bring to consciousness, to discover the "reason" or the "cause" of the trouble s/he suffers and has suffered all his or her life. S/he wants to remember, to gather up the dismembered temporality that has not been mastered. Childhood is the name borne by this lost time. So King Oedipus starts searching for the cause of the evil, a sin that would be at the origin of the plague the city is suffering. The patient on the couch appears to be involved in an entirely similar enquiry. Like in a detective novel, the case is examined, witnesses called, information gathered. And so what I would call a second order plot is woven, which deploys its own story above the plot in which its destiny is fulfilled, and whose aim is to remedy that destiny. . . .[39]

Evidently Freud's case histories are rival tragedies, transformations of suffering into an aesthetic "significant whole" or into allegory, "a second order plot . . . which deploys its own story," but which story must always bear within itself the consciousness of its own tragic destiny: "the enquiry into the origins of destiny is itself part of that destiny," as Lyotard notes.[40] Such a destiny announces itself when in spite of the fictionality of the constructions, the narratives must present themselves with the same rhetorical certainty and with the same necessity with which the trauma initially occurred.

When Peter Brooks speaks of the "power" of narrative constructions, "to persuade us that things must have happened this way . . ."[41] one could ask oneself if not much of the power and conviction which is initially suffered in the trauma itself becomes thus a model of rhetorical power. The original trauma must be reinscribed in an aesthetic which substitutes for the past in the same way in which Nietzsche's "it was" is reinscribed into "thus I willed it." In Freud's language, the narrative cure is a "special place," "an artificial illness," "the realm of the 'as if,'" "a special kind of present," a "symbolic replay of the past"—all terms which are initially introduced in the essay on "Transference" as "a new edition of the old disorder" or "a new artificial neurosis": ". . . we are no longer concerned with the patient's earlier illness but with a newly created and transformed neurosis which has taken the former's place."[42]

Such metaphorical or textual conceptions of psychoanalysis have led Peter Brooks to admit in his book *Psychoanalysis and Storytelling* that Freudian psychoanalysis is not really different from literature. Neither is ground to the other, and their positions of authority are interchangeable. The lack of a distinction between the literal and the figurative therefore prohibits judgment of any truth value; rather, truth now takes place in the unverifiable twilight of Freud's transferential *Zwischenreich*. Brooks' assertions that "things must have happened this way," or ". . . we must consider all narrative truth to be 'true' in so far as it carries conviction, while at the same time asserting that if it carries conviction it must in some sense be true . . ."[43] announce, perilously, the absence of a ground of truth, and the necessarily circular epistemology of a narrative cure. The cure itself seems therfore not to be immune from becoming itself the mental disorder which it seeks to cure. Hence, the interchangeable roles of analyst and analysand or of reader and text.

The word for this process of interchange is the transference, perhaps the most fundamental of Freud's discoveries both for psychoanalysis and for the study of literature. It implies that the cure of mental illness, like the construction of a work of art, or like the interpretation of either, takes place neither in the present nor in the past, neither in the patient nor in the analyst, neither in the text nor in the reader. Its authority lies in its exchange, which is to admit also the indeterminacy of what constitutes that authority. The truth, like the authority of the analyst's constructions, is thus a self-conscious, interminable textual "edition" of the past, a story always under revision, always in transition between reader and text or between analyst and patient. Freud's interminable revisions of his past constructions may be the precursors of such a concept of narrative health. Proceeding by addition rather than by substitution, Freud's texts exemplify the status of health as endless story. Thus, only in its dynamic interaction, in its dialogic form, or as Peter Brooks claims—and this implies as well Freud's endless returns to his own texts—when the analyst "enters into the logic of [the patient's] symptoms"[44] can the cure attain its coherence, force, and completion—although the claim for completion, for the terminable analysis that is also implied here, must appear in question. This ought to be all the more so if it is largely the literary, that is to say, the interactive, transmissible, or scriptible nature of narrative, not the establishment of fact, that constitutes truth and health.

Narrative closure then, like aesthetic coherence and completion, is not in itself the cure, even if it harbors the promise of an eventual retrospective revelation of the meaning of suffering. The desire for the aesthetic seems to have its motivation in the patient's fundamental need to counteract his dismemberment with at least a symbolic form of presence—even if that presence can only be in language, the presence of an other. The therapeutic quality of the transference resides thus precisely in the same qualities that make a literary text literary. For like the literary text, which (as Hans-Georg Gadamer has observed) recovers the lost voice of writing by requiring an "always new, ideal speaking,"[45] psychoanalysis, in the last analysis, reconfirms the presence of the suffering patient, reveals her—in her state of dismemberment—as the subject of a story, through which telling the patient might become "a significant whole."

Arendt's word "significant," which she equates with the word "event," would in a Feudian context have to mean "signifying," for the patient, like his acts, are as "whole" only as the story itself. The story allows the subject, as Julia Kristeva puts it, "to live a second life, a life of forms and meaning, somewhat exalted or artificial in the eyes of outsiders, but which is the sole requisite for the subject's survival."[46] Such a fictional, nonfactual, or aesthetic theory of the narrative cure guarantees the patient what Kristeva, in an unusual appropriation of redemptive vocabulary, calls "forgiveness": "So that the unconscious might inscribe itself in a new narrative that will not be the eternal return of the death drive in the cycle of crime and punishment it must pass through the love of forgiveness, be transferred to the love of forgiveness."[47]

While the past retains traces of indecipherable writing, psychoanalysis is the recovery of that writing through an always new, ideal speaking. If the past is an irreparable fact, the present can be a revisable fiction. Thus, the analysand recreates himself as a fictional character in an interminable story which, as Brooks points out, "will never really be told. It can only be constructed, in the most conjectural manner."[48] However, if it is "only" in the most conjectural manner, and in nothing more determinate than in a manner of conjecture that the difference of the present experience can be affirmed against the past, if mental health cannot be established as fact, if the past is incurable, evidently psychoanalysis can offer no cure. Yet what narrative conjectures and the discourse of otherness can promise is treatment, a word that might intimate the interminability of psychoanalysis.

I am not sure, finally, that such an either "situational" or "fictional" or "accidental" ontology suffices to affirm our frail postmodern notion of subjectivity. But in the absence of firmer, more determinate values, Freud's narrative theory implies the importance of present (and this means interminable) social interactions. These now must replace both the final cure (as well as its religious or ideological analogues) as well as the truth of the past. The Freudian subject, Malcolm Bowie suggests, "is no longer a substance endowed with qualities, or a fixed shape possessing dimensions . . . it is a series of events within language, a procession of turns, tropes, and inflections."[49] Freud's notions of subjectivity thus stress the enormous significance of keeping alive a humanistic tradition, or its narratives; they appear to be our only ways of being well.

NOTES

1. . . . what Nietzsche shows is that philosophy, in its own style, which is that of the concept, has the same desire as tragedy: to heal the wounded gaze by mastering the contradictions . . . (my translation).

2. Friedrich Nietzsche, *The Birth of Tragedy* and *The Genealogy of Morals* (1872), trans. Francis Golffing (New York: Doubleday, 1956), 32.

3. Friedrich Nietzsche, *The Gay Science* (1887), trans. Walter Kaufmann (New York: Vintage Books, 1974), 107.

4. This is perhaps an unexpected logical extension of Schopenhauer's own existential view that ". . . on closer consideration, we shall find here [in the will-to-live] also that it is rather a blind urge, an impulse wholly without ground or motive." Arthur Schopenhauer, *The World as Will and Representation* (1818), trans. E. F. J. Payne, 2 vols. (New York: Dover Publications, 1969), 2:357.

5. Friedrich Nietzsche, "On Truth and Lies in a Nonmoral Sense" in *Philosophy and Truth: Selections from Nietzsche's Notebooks of the early 1870's*, trans. Daniel Breazeale (Atlantic Highlands, N.J.: Humanities Press, 1979), 86.

6. J. Hillis Miller, "Ariadne's Thread: Repetition and the Narrative Line," *Critical Inquiry* 3, (autumn, 1976): 59–60.

7. Friedrich Nietzsche, *Die Geburt der Tragödie*, in *Werke*, vol. 1, ed. Karl Schlechta (Frankfurt: Ullstein Materialien, 1980), 86–87.

8. Nietzsche, *The Birth of Tragedy*, trans. Golffing, 95.

9. Nietzsche, *The Gay Science*, 107.

10. Nietzsche, *The Birth of Tragedy*, trans. Golffing, 145.

11. Friedrich Nietzsche, *The Birth of Tragedy and The Case of Wagner*, trans. Walter Kaufmann (New York: Vintage Books, 1967), 98.

12. Sarah Kofman, *Nietzsche and Metaphor* (1983), trans. Duncan Large (Stanford: Stanford University Press, 1993), 157n.

13. Ibid., 25. Later on Kofman states similarly: "The concept plays a privileged role in the forgetting of metaphor, in that it hides the metaphorical character of the process of generalization by founding it on an essential generality: the concept vouches for the 'untruth' and 'treacherousness' of metaphor, ensuring their stability whilst at the same time maintaining a forgetfulness of the genesis of the process, along with every other genesis. One might say, to speak with Freud, that the concept plays the role of the force of anticathexis which sustains repression" (*Nietzsche and Metaphor*, 35).

14. Nietzsche, *Die Geburt der Tragödie*, 119 (my translation).

15. Nietzsche, *The Birth of Tragedy*, trans. Golffing, 102.

16. Ibid., 127.

17. J. Hillis Miller, *The Ethics of Reading* (New York: Columbia University Press, 1987), 35.

18. Nietzsche, *The Birth of Tragedy*, trans. Golffing, 46. For his references to music as the most immediate of mimetic art Nietzsche is indebted to Schopenhauer who writes similarly: ". . . music is as *immediate* an objectification and copy of the whole will [to life] as the world itself is, indeed as the Ideas are. . . . Therefore music is by no means like the other arts, namely, a copy of the Ideas, but a *copy of the will itself*, the objectivity of which are the Ideas. For this reason the effect of music is so very much more powerful and penetrating than is that of the other arts, for these others speak only of the shadow, but music of the essence." See Schopenhauer, *The World as Will and Representation*, 1:257.

19. Kofman, *Nietzsche and Metaphor*, 8 (italics mine).

20. Miller, "Ariadne's Thread," 72.

21. J. Hillis Miller, *The Linguistic Moment: From Wordsworth to Stevens* (Princeton: Princeton University Press, 1985), 419.

22. J. Hillis Miller, "Stevens Rock and Criticism as Cure," *The Georgia Review* 30 (spring–summer 1976):12.

23. Paul de Man, *Allegories of Reading* (New Haven: Yale University Press, 1979), 101.

24. Maurice Blanchot, *The Gaze of Orpheus and other Literary Essays*, trans. Lydia Davis (Barrytown, N.Y.: Station Hill, 1981), 45.

25. Philippe Lacoue-Labarthe, *Typography: Mimesis, Philosophy, Politics*, ed. Christopher Fynsk (Cambridge: Harvard University Press, 1989), 213. See also Peter Szondi: "*Aber tragisch ist auch nur der Untergang von etwas, das nicht untergehen darf, nach dessen Entfernen die Wunde sich nicht schliesst*" *Werke* (Frankfurt: Suhrkamp, 1978), 209.

26. Jacques Derrida, *Dissemination* (1972), trans. Barbara Johnson (Chicago: University of Chicago Press, 1981), 149.

27. Nietzsche, *Die Geburt der Tragödie*, 32.

28. Kofman, *Nietzsche and Metaphor*, 22.

29. Julia Kristeva, *Powers of Horror: An Essay on Abjection* (1980), trans. Leon S. Roudiez (New York: Columbia University Press, 1982), 155.

30. Susan Sontag, *Illness as Metaphor* (New York: Vintage Books, 1979), 3.

31. Sigmund Freud, *Introductory Lectures on Psycho-Analysis* The Standard Edition, trans. and ed. James Strachey (New York: Norton, 1966), 348.

32. Ibid., 543.

33. Ibid., 545.

34. Ibid., 546.

35. Sigmund Freud, *Beyond the Pleasure Principle* (1920), The Standard Edition, trans. and ed. James Strachey (New York: Norton, 1961), 18. See *Jenseits des Lustprinzips*, in *Psychologie des Unbewussten*, Studienausgabe, Bd. 3 (Frankfurt: Fischer, 1982), 228.

36. Jean-François Lyotard, *The Inhuman: Reflections on Time* (1988), trans. Geoffrey Bennigton and Rachel Bowlby (Stanford: Stanford University Press, 1991), 31.

37. Georg Lukács, *Soul and Form* (1911), trans. Anna Bostock (Cambridge: MIT Press, 1974), 159.

38. Hannah Arendt, "On Humanity in Dark Times: Thought about Lessing," trans. Clara and Richard Winston, in *Men in Dark Times* (Harmondsworth: Penguin, 1973), 28.

39. Lyotard, *The Inhuman*, 27.

40. Ibid., 27.

41. Peter Brooks, *Psychoanalysis and Storytelling* (Oxford: Basil Blackwell, 1994), 59.

42. Freud, *Introductory Lectures on Psycho-Analysis*, 553.

43. Brooks, *Psychoanalysis and Storytelling*, 60.

44. Ibid., 69.

45. Hans-Georg Gadamer, "Text und Interpretation," in *Wahrheit und Methode*, vol. 2 (Ergänzungen) (Tübingen: J. C. B. Mohr, 1986), 353.

46. Kristeva, *Black Sun: Depression and Melancholia* (1987), trans. Leon S. Roudiez (New York: Columbia University Press, 1989), 207–8.

47. Ibid., 204.

48. Brooks, *Psychoanalysis and Storytelling*, 94.

49. Malcolm Bowie, *Lacan* (Cambridge: Harvard University Press, 1991), 76.

and terror (Mark 16:8). And Job puts his hand upon his mouth, saying "therefore have I uttered that I understood not; things too wonderful for me, which I knew not" (42:3). Then follows the epilogue—with distance and assurance: "And it was so . . ." (42:7). Though temporarily absorbed in the divine restitution of his estate and family, Job's silence and his profound spiritual gesture of abjection and repentance remain. As the book of Job moves from silence to silence, speaking to the fact that in the face of suffering one cannot remain silent, it is not only framed by silence but—as Blake's depictions of Job's wife at Job's side suggest—also accompanied by silence.

Job's wife is assigned only one verse: "Dost thou still retain thine integrity? curse God, and die" (2:9). Although her sentence may well reflect her own suffering at the loss of her children and her home and livelihood, she is not heard from again. In his essay on the book of Esther, Richard Howard reports the disappearance of Vashti, who is to Howard's "obstinate hypothesis one of those haunting, secret figures in literature, like Lot's wife, who make one decisive negative gesture, who violate a commandment and then vanish forever, leaving only a symbolic transgression for a memorial."[2] Job's wife shares the fates of Vashti and Lot's wife.

"The world in which these [Biblical] events transpired," writes Emmanuel Levinas

would not have been structured as it was—and it still is and always will be—but for the secret presence to the verge of invisibility, of these mothers, these wives and daughters, but for their silent footsteps in the depth and opaqueness of reality, depicting the dimensions of interiority and making the world habitable.[3]

Levinas' structural dependency of male Biblical agents on silent presence seems particularly applicable to the book of Job. Job's Job's dialectical other, the doubt that allows his certainty, the silence within which he articulates his complaint. Her curse Job's blessings, her silence forces him to speak, her illegitimacy his authority.

Among all these possibilities remains the impossibility of her —that, too, is a kind of silence. While Job's running sores bitable evidence, she has no boils and blisters. His very makes all the difference, authorizing his language, his

TRAGIC SUFFERING

II

4

JOB
OR THE
MEANINGLESSNESS
OF SUFFERING

JOB'S SILENCE

I will lay mine hand up

Upon seeing the suffering of Job the three frien
lifted up their voice and wept . . ." and "[s]c
upon the ground seven days and seven nigh
unto him: for they saw that his grief was
their silence they give him their presence
tance in speaking. At the end of the be
his silence is the site of God's presence
ing of the ear: but now mine eye se
hors himself and repents in dust
what Julia Kristeva (in a differe
stillness of destiny."[1]

The poetic dialogues e
Mark with the women ru

L
female
wife is J
margin o
calls forth
macy mark

But an
own sufferin
count as indu
bodily afflictic

very strife with God. For physical suffering has the authority of truth: "Do ye imagine to reprove words, and the speeches of one that is desperate . . . ?" Job asks his friends (6:26), for his right to speak and to be heard is imprinted in his skin:

> My flesh is clothed with worms and clods of dust; my skin is broken, and become loathsome. (7:5)

And a little further on:

> Therefore I will not refrain my mouth; I will speak in the anguish of my spirit; I will complain in the bitterness of my soul. (7:11)

Such language, such right and authority—so semiotically bestowed upon Job in visible signs of the wrong he suffers—are withheld from her. If Job will see God in his flesh (19:26), in his wife's body He is all but invisible. If God will be present in Job's wounds, in her body He remains absent.

Invisible and unrepresented, her suffering can be doubted, of which doubt her silence is the confirmation, whereas Job's suffering cannot be doubted: his losses are enumerated in detail and his suffering is elaborated in endless rounds of speech. While Job's suffering is articulated on his skin, she is given no sign, no rash, no running sore to speak and legitimize her losses and her grief. Without wounds, her suffering is not legitimized. She must be silent.[4] Silent, she is the embodiment of doubt, which Elaine Scarry likens to "a small tear in the page, a tiny fold in an almost invisible shred of tissue in the heart, the dropping of a single stitch in the endless rounds of a woven cloth."[5] It is around this small tear that Job weaves his complaint. Her sentence is the first stitch of this elaborate texture, the almost invisible conceptual beginning that will structure his discourse. Job is an exception then to Scarry's rule by which "Physical suffering destroys language. . . ." Rather, Job's suffering bestows upon him that "moral rightness (in the Old Testament as in most other human contexts) [which] tends to lie with the most articulate."[6]

But eventually Job will put his hand upon his mouth. After God's speech out of the whirlwind, he sees the incommensurability of language and suffering. For by speaking of his suffering, the concluding chapters of the book of Job suggest, Job is like one who speaks about God and must therefore (as Kierkegaard would say) always be in the wrong. Was his wife right? Can one be right about God, or about suffering, only in silence? "If I had called, and he had answered me," Job says early on, "yet would I not believe that he had harkened unto my voice. For he breaketh me with a tempest, and multiplieth my wounds without cause (9:16–17). Or is Job's silence at the end of the book the moral speechlessness of which Walter Benjamin says that "in tragedy, pagan man becomes aware that he is better than his gods, but this realization renders him speechless?"[7] Is Job a pagan tragedy? Or is Job's silence a movement beyond religion to God, beyond language into some inconceivable divine presence?

JOB SPEAKING

> Though I speak, my grief is not asswaged . . .
>
> —Job

> To know God without knowing man's misery
> is dangerous, just as it is dangerous to know
> one's misery without knowing God.
>
> —Maurice Blanchot, *The Infinite Conversation*

Job earns his tragic status from his refusal to suffer in silence. "He does not rest in his own suffering," comments Richard Sewall, quoting Eliot who wrote in *The Family Reunion* that "To rest in our own suffering / Is evasion of suffering. We must learn to suffer more."[8] Job, the exemplary sufferer, has learned it all; the prologue makes sure that no one can accuse Job of not having suffered enough: affliction after affliction, loss after loss, pain after pain is imposed upon him. Job, Kierkegaard writes, is "the voice of the suffering, the cry of the grief-stricken, the shriek of the terrified," and thus he is "a relief to all who bore their torment in silence, a faithful witness to all the affliction and laceration there can be in a heart, an unfailing spokesman who dared to lament 'in bitterness of soul' and to strive with God."[9] For God touches "all that he hath" except his life so that Job may earn the right and authority to speak on behalf of all who have suffered and of any suffering imaginable. "He has become Everyman, grieving for all human misery. He suffers not only his own personal pain but the pain of all the poor and despised," as Stephen Mitchell writes.[10]

Appropriately, his expressions of suffering are encyclopedic, encompassing all expressions of suffering, leaving out no response: fear: ". . . the thing which I greatly feared is come upon me, and that which I was afraid of is come unto me" (3:25); desire for death: "Even that it would please God to destroy me; that he would let loose his hand, and cut me off!" (6:9); self-disgust: "My flesh is clothed with worms and clods of dust; my skin is broken, and become loathsome" (7:5); cynicism: "I have sinned; what shall I do unto thee, O thou preserver of men?" (7:20); blasphemy: "he will laugh at the trial of the innocent" (9:23); despair: "Have pity upon me, have pity upon me, O ye my friends; for the hand of God hath touched me" (19:21). And though he has veritably made his bed in darkness (17:13), he retains an extraordinary hope: "And though after my skin worms destroy this body, yet in my flesh shall I see God" (19:26)—even if this prophetic allusion to bodily resurrection also implies Artaud's more worldly interpretation: *"c'est par la peau qu'on fera rentrer la métaphysique dans les esprits"* (it is through the skin that metaphysics will return to the spirit).[11]

In the views of a number of commentators the very length and eloquence of Job's utterances amount to an answer to his suffering: his complaint transforms "the experience of mere pain and distress [in]to the experience of suffering,"[12] Sewall observes. For Sewall, therefore, "Suffering itself, as the Poet of Job defines it, has been made to yield knowledge. . . ."[13] But the knowledge that suffering has yielded is only a tautology: Job asks for the meaning of his suffering and his asking becomes its meaning. The "answer" to Job's suffering is the expression of suffering itself. "The answers," David Daiches asserts, "have force and meaning in virtue of their poetic expression, of the place they take in the myth or fable or situation presented, and of the effectiveness with which they project a mood. Job's solution is no answer if detached from its eloquent expression and paraphrased as a philosophical position."[14] In *The Art of Biblical Poetry*, Robert Alter points out in an similar vein "that the exploration of the problem of theodicy in the Book of Job and the 'answer' it proposes cannot be separated from the poetic vehicle of the book. . . ."[15] In *The Literary Guide to the Bible*, Alter even assigns the book's poetic expression subversive qualities—". . . the literary medium is not merely a means of 'conveying' doctrinal positions but an adventurous occasion for deepening doctrine through the play of literary resources, or perhaps even, at least here for leaping beyond doctrine."[16]

But if the literary medium is the "answer" to suffering, the real (perhaps unintended) subversive quality of poetic expression is that there can be no God external to it. For if the answer to suffering is always already given by its poetic expression, Job cannot expect an answer other than from the tragic dimensions, the varied expressions, the eloquence of his complaints. Thus, the poetic "answer" leaps beyond doctrine only by its aesthetic self-sufficiency. By that, in turn, it is equal to the councellors' answers, except that it offers itself in quotation marks. The poetic "answer" is a fiction that knows itself to be a fiction, outside of which there is neither falsity nor truth.

The implications of such a poetic theology are momentous. Can an "answer" to suffering be aesthetically just but morally wrong? Does Job's God only accept a "literary" attitude towards the mystery of suffering? Does He give only "aesthetic" answers? Does He take sides between poetry and religion? Or indeed, since the expressions of suffering seem sublimely self-sufficient, did the author(s) of the book of Job want to exclude God from the book of Job? Is God's absence visible in Job's wounds—wounds which neither theology nor philosophy can close? And if neither religious nor philosophic discourse *in* the book of Job can bind those wounds, can the book of Job? Can a poetic text accomplish what philosophy and theology cannot?

However, Job, it seems, cannot accept answers in quotation marks, nor the logic of a merely poetic justice—and in the end he is blessed for his refusal. Neither the poetic structure of the book as a whole can stand as an "answer" to Job's suffering nor, as we shall see, can the voice out of the whirlwind. For indeed, it would be to belittle Job's suffering (perhaps any suffering) if Job did not ask precisely whether there is an answer beyond the pathos of asking. "Though I speak, my grief is not asswaged . . ." (16:6), "I cry unto thee, and thou dost not hear me" (30:20). Such crying out might amount to the "passionate and insistent requestioning . . . for the sake of true consolation," distinguished by Johann Babtist Metz from "a typically intellectual cult of questioning, which would be the most distant from precisely those who suffer."[17] If Job's speaking is to reach beyond the pathos of its expression, it will challenge any self-enclosed system, its own poetic form as much as the friends' well-wrought platitudes.

The friends are there to remind Job, as they would have reminded any avant-garde poet, that theologically the book has already been closed, that Job's suffering is heterodox, and that by analogy the poet, in writing the book of Job, opens up a deuteronomic canon in open rebellion against what has been established as canonical and closed. "For enquire, I pray thee, of the former age. . . . Shall not they teach thee, and tell thee . . ." pleads Bildad (8:8,10). The contest between heterodoxy and tradition, between writing and The Holy Writ, between opening and closure, is symbolically enacted in the structure of the book: In framing the poetic dialogues, the frame story acts the symbolic part of the book as a structural authority; it defines the canonical text as a forbidding, closed entity torn open by Job's suffering. But in the necessity of aesthetic closure—for the book begins and ends with that necessity—is also implied the pathos of the desire to bind up wounds and to answer unanswerable questions. But there is ample evidence in the book that such closures cannot be imposed on suffering, that it cannot be contained, that is is outside the written, that the text cannot bind up Job's boils and blisters, nor his complaint. If the etymology of the word religion goes back to *religio*, "to bind up," religion is doomed from the very beginning.

The argument of the friends does not advance after the first cycle of dialogues, "the book could go on forever . . . ," Richard Jacobson argues.[18] "What ye know," Job says, "the same do I know also" (13:2) and his friends: "What knowest thou, that we know not?" (15:9) The inadequacy of each response in turn compels each friend to begin his speech with the sole purpose to end all speeches, to end particularly Job's "multitude of words" (11:2). When Eliphaz prophesies that "Thou shalt come to thy grave in a full age" (5:26), even such a benevolent prophecy cannot hide its impatience for what will take forty-two chapters and seventeen verses until Job will have "lived an[other] hundred and forty years" (42:16). Personified in Job and his friends, the book thus enacts, dialectically, the necessity of its own compositional length but also its interminability, even as it repeatedly comments on the temptation to shorten, to enclose, to curtail, to shut up Job's suffering and its infectious systemic impurity. At an early stage in the book, Eliphaz' impatience is eloquently concealed:

> Thou shalt come to thy grave in a full age,
>   like as a shock of corn cometh in in its season.
> Lo this, we have searched it, so it is; hear it,
>   and know thou it for thy good.
>
> (5:26–27)

But the friends do not consider their own discourse as subject to such a rhythm of patience and temporal necessity. They have already searched it—parodying all those who henceforth would re-search it, each search and research positing an impatient end to patient Job. Bildad will rejoin Job's first response to Eliphaz, and the impatience is palpable: "How long wilt thou speak these things? and how long shall the words of thy mouth be like a strong wind?" which the *New English Bible* translates less euphemistically as: "How long will you say such things, the long-winded ramblings of an old man?" (8:2)—and Zophar, in the same vein responding to Job's rejoinder to Bildad: "Should thy lies make men hold their peace?" (11:3)—or Bildad to Job: "How long will it be ere ye make an end of words?" (18:2). Midway between the covers of the book Job, too, becomes weary of the progress of this book, inquiring of his comforters, "How long will ye vex my soul, and break me in pieces with words?" (19:2). And later on: "Oh, that my words were now written! / Oh that they were printed in a book" (19:23) or "Oh . . . that mine adversary had written a book!" (31:35).

Yet, to prolong the desire for closure, resolution, or death—all of which the concept of "book" signifies—but also to defer such ends—this, too, is the book's function—there is Elihu, said to be "a later addition to the poetic text." Is his addition to the text to comment on the openness of mid-eastern or postmodern texts?[19] Leslie Fiedler suggests that Elihu is "an afterthought, a last desperate attempt on the part of the poet who gave the *Book of Job* its final form to defend orthodoxy against Job's subversive challenge, which that poet, like Elihu, apparently believed had not yet been satisfactorily confuted."[20] As such, that is, as "a later addition" or as an "afterthought," Elihu epitomizes the poet's (or the text's) ironic self-consciousness of length and deferred closure. In the irony of his impetuous and grandiloquent announcement, "I also will shew mine opinion. For I am full of matter. . . . Behold, my belly is as wine which hath no vent; it is ready to burst like new bottles" (32:17–19), Elihu signals a youthful, somewhat intoxicated critique of traditional theodicy. Moshe Greenberg proposes that Elihu is "the unconventional representation of youth outdoing age bespeak[ing] the author of the rest of the poem, whose hallmark is subversion of tradition."[21] What is added is youth to a book of old men—which Elihu is well aware of when he ironically defers to the old: "I am young and ye are very old . . ." (32:6)—what is promised simultaneously is closure and reopening, the end of old men's texts and textual rejuvenation: "Behold, I waited for your words; I gave ear to your reasons, whilst ye searched out what to say" (32:11).

The point, however, of this obsessive textual self-consciousness of length, closure, reopening, and revision is that while everyone "searched out what to say" the right speaking may remain elusive, so that such elusiveness becomes itself rhetorically functional in suggesting that Job's suffering—indeed all suffering—is always blasphemous, always unspeakable. If Eliphaz declared early on that "we have searched it, so it is . . . ," now each word in the poetic dialogues has become a search yielding nothing, a silence made audible. Each complaint and response is framed by the absence of truth and meaning. Each elusive meaning, each missing answer is the silence in which the sufferer's claims are heard—even if not to hear them is the very purpose of the friends' answers.

The ground of God's complaint and the indictment of the accuser remain beyond the scope of Job or of his friends, and, measured by the abundance of critial commentary on the book of Job, beyond the scope of his readers as well. The disorder, randomness, the confusion of voices, the incoherence of the dialogues, the uncertainty of authorship—all of which has been noted (and reconstructed) by numerous commentators—these, too, are to break Job's purposes and the thoughts of his heart. The absence, in other words, of a recognizable single authorial intention or theological telos mark the book of Job as a "countertheological, properly revolutionary" text, to borrow Barthes' words.[22] Job, then, is a book without an author, whose absence Barthes significantly likens to the absence of God, leaving the "meaning" of Job's suffering in the secular hands of the reader. Only (interminable) interpretation is its remedy,[23] as the sudden addition of the youthful Elihu suggests. His youth can only further suggest the irony of further interpretation, and yet his unannounced addition also implies the necessity of perpetual further revision and commentary. In its perpetual openness to revision, the book of Job thus behaves like a Freudian narrative construction awaiting a further corrective addition. Elihu is the personified antecedant of the interpretive addition, of the necessity for textual elaboration, textual interminability, of the urgency and impossibility of an answer or closure to suffering.

If *faute de mieux,* the burden of interpretation, of answer and response, shifts to the reader, for whom the friends become the ancestral voices, there can be no reading that is not in itself complicit with the friends' foreclosure and prejudice. Indeed, their prejudice of Job's plight is already anticipated by the very structure of the book of Job. For the folktale at the beginning of the book exemplifies the prejudice with which one begins to read. The story of the wager is the exemplary literary story in which one wants to put one's foreclosure to the test. And just as the wager is the epitome of the reader's motivation to read, God's question to Satan at the beginning of the book is one of the exemplary literary questions: "Hast thou considered my servant Job, that there is none like him in the earth . . ." (1:8), which reads like a blurb on the cover of a book, prejudging the outcome. Thus, our reading, very much in accordance with Barthes' notion of the countertheological nature of reading, is always with an interest comparable to Satan's "going to a fro in the earth . . ." (2:2)—his "going to and fro" mimicking the scanning of the eyes across the page (just as the cloven foot resembles the pen). Such (secular or satanic) reading is perhaps the only way of reading the open text which cannot be "pierced" but must endlessly be "traversed." The text that one cannot pierce, as Barthes points out, has no "ultimate meaning."[24]

GOD SPEAKING

> He whom we *crave* to hear
>
> SPOKE AT LAST—;
>
> spoke not through the VEIL
> of earth and sea and air . . .
>
> —Frank Bidart, *In the Western Night*

But then God responds to Job out of the whirlwind. Is God to close what has been open, to pierce what has been fruitlessly traversed? Is the author to put back into the mouth of God the text that had been illicitly in the hands of the reader? Are we readers no longer but speechless spectators? In what he admits might "sound either hazily mystical or effusively hyperbolic," Robert Alter writes: ". . . the culminating poem that God speaks out of the storm soars beyond everything that has preceded it in the book. . . . Through this pushing of poetic expression toward its own upper limits, the concluding speech helps us see the panorama of creation, as perhaps we could do only through poetry, with the eyes of God."[25]

Here is the opening of the second round of God's answer out of the whirlwind:

> Moreover the Lord answered Job, and said,
> Shall he that contendeth with the Almighty instruct him?
> he that reproveth God, let him answer it.
> Then Job answered the Lord, and said,
> Behold, I am vile; what shall I answer thee?
>
> (40:1–4)

If the voice of God from the whirlwind is to answer, the answer does not come. Although God's speeches are introduced as what "the Lord answered Job out of the whirlwind," the "answer" is a question: "...I will demand of thee, and answer thou me" (38:1,3). But these answers in turn cannot be given: "Where wast thou when I laid the foundations of the earth?" (38:4). Job's answer, finally is another rhetorical question: "what shall I answer thee?" (40:4), upon which the same circular dialogue begins again: "Then answered the Lord . . . I will demand of thee, and declare thou unto me" (40:6,7). The rhetoric of God's speech out of the whirlwind is rhetorical, a parody perhaps of Job's notion that he has abundantly *heard* of God "by the hearing of the ear." More likely, God's speaking is audible silence. God has not answered. Just as Job's questions have returned to himself, God's questions return to God. Just as only God is able to answer God's questions, Job's suffering is his own.

Although God has spoken, his sublime demonstration of autonomy and self-reference reveal him only as analogous to the solipsism of Job's body—as if that body in its suffering were a microcosm of God's cosmos through which exemplary instance the larger cosmos would have momentarily become visible.[26] When Luther translates *"Nur sein eigenes Fleisch macht ihm Schmerzen, und nur um ihn selbst trauert seine Seele"* (Only his own body is in pain, only for himself grieves his soul. 14.22, my translation), Job's suffering appears as self-referential and inscrutable as God's creation.[27] Like God's creation, whose foundations, dimensions, and cornerstones, and the fearful beasts in sea and land are inexplicable, the phenomenon of suffering is impervious to interrogation. Just as Job dare not question or instruct the Almighty, neither will his suffering yield any explanation. Suffering and God, in their inscrutability and their answerlessness, are the same. If God breaks Job with a tempest and multiplies his wounds without cause, "Why dost thou strive against him?" (33:13)

The God of the theophany is defined not by ethical or moral considerations such as justice or mercy, but solely by his creation. He is the one

> To cause it to rain on the earth . . .
> To satisfy the desolate and waste ground; and to cause the
>   bud of the tender herb to spring forth[.]
>
> (38:26–27)

and whose questions

> Hath rain a father? or who hath begotten the drops of
>   dew?
> Out of whose womb came the ice? and the hoary frost of
>   Heaven, who hath gendered it?
>
> (38:28–29)

. . . are all rhetorical. For He is father and mother of all, begetter and womb of good and evil, darkness and light, the principle of creation, the answer to all questions. If God is a depersonalized blind will to life, a solipsistic, self-sufficient creative principle, then perhaps the rain has no father, the dew no begetter.[28]

Even in Paul Ricoeur's redemptive reading of the theophany such notions of an amoral creative principle may be implicit:

> The God who addresses Job out of the tempest shows him
> Behemoth and Leviathan, the hippopotamus and the croco-
> dile, vestiges of the chaos that has been overcome, represent-
> ing a brutality dominated and measured by the creative act.
> Through these symbols he gives him to understand that all is
> order, measure, and beauty—inscrutable order, measure be-
> yond measure, terrible beauty.[29]

To which Robert Alter adds:

> This is neither an easy nor a direct answer to the question of
> why the good man should suffer, but the imposing vision of a
> harmonious order to which violence is nevertheless intrinsic
> and where destruction [as] part of creation is meant to con-
> front Job with the limits of his moral imagination. . . .[30]

Inscrutable order, terrible beauty, destruction as part of creation, all confirm what Antonin Artaud calls "*la nécessité cruelle de la création*" (the cruel necessity of creation). For Artaud who, like the author of Job assigns God a place in a whirlwind, God is nature—for like nature he cannot but create, "*il ne peut pas ne pas créer.*"[31]

The tautology of Job's suffering, then, is comparable to the more sublime tautology of a universal law of creation, both suffering and creation being inscrutable orders defying the moral imagination. God's very first question to Job—"Where wast thou when I laid the foundations of the earth?" (38:4)—points up the incomprehensible nature of that greater law. Job was absent at its foundation and its laws, like the laws to which he is subject in his suffering, remain therefore a mystery. The law of creation is the spectacle of creation. It is something that can only be seen rather than understood. Likewise, suffering is the unthinkable, that which can be seen only as spectacle.[32]

Thus, Job's seeing at the end of the book of Job is perhaps finally and *for the first time* without concept or judgment, without precedent, fault, or deception, without falsity or truth. It is perhaps a vision that excludes writing, a spectacle that excludes speculation. It is perhaps a vision that cannot be articulated, a thought that resists thought,[33] or a vision that *should* remain unarticulated.

The "shattering claim to a direct vision of God," which, as Northrop Frye observes, "the Bible, even in the New Testament, is usually very cautious about expressing,"[34] announces Job's last, perhaps ultimate loss, the loss of his language of speculation and its exchange for spectacle, the loss of knowledge, religion, philosophy. The vision of God now prohibits not only what has been said, the hearing of the ear, but what is sayable, and not only what has been thought but what is thinkable. Job is to relinquish, in an all embracing ultimate reality, his claims to right and reason and meaning and language.

Although the very length of the forty-two chapters offers a narrative form of suffering, and thereby the implications of meaning and purpose, Job's suffering does not know what it narrates other than its duration. The meaning of suffering is the cruel necessity of existence. Perhaps at this point in the book of Job, Job's suffering is an example of Hölderlin's "extreme limit of distress" where "'nothing [is] left but the conditions of time and space.'"[35]

JOB'S RESTITUTION

". . . if one knows God and knows one's misery," Maurice Blanchot comments on Pascal, "one knows that one can only know the remoteness of God, God manifest insofar as he is distant."[36] But what if the spectacle of God suspends *all* knowledge, even the knowledge of speculation, of remoteness and distance, implicit in Pascal's faith? And could it be that in that very suspension of knowledge God were to be present, even though not a presence that could be verified or communicated? For where if not in the breakdown of all modes of knowledge, in the failure of philosophy and religion, in the margins of silence, in the cries of the sufferer, would God be present? André Lacocque, who compares the whirlwind to Nebuchadnezzar's furnace, thinks that one would

> look for God's presence *outside* of it, and preferably in the aloofness and the motionlessness of the heavens. But *Yhwh* is Himself in the whirlwind, nowhere else. Job had shouted: "Where are you, God?" God now returns the question to Job: "I am here, in the midst of the tempest . . . but you, Job, are you still with Me?"[37]

Suffering, in light of this insightful paragraph, is assigned a sublime, metaphysical nature: in the presence of incommensurable pain is God. However, it is not only God who reveals Himself to Job in his suffering, subordinating Job's suffering to something incomprehensibly higher, but Job's *suffering* that reveals a God conceived in terms of a traumatic experience: as fire and storm.

If God reveals himself neither in hope nor healing, neither in discourse nor dialogue, neither in religion nor philosophy He may yet reveal Himself in the absence of meaning. Precisely there where one thought God to be absent, He might be present. For our thoughts of absence are but speculations, forms of knowledge and doubt. If so, the presence of God in Job's wounds marks God's absence not as negative of presence but as the unnameable, extra-dialectical, precognitive space through which God passes into and out of history. The wound is, as it were, a terrible sacred door.

Elaine Scarry notes that in the Old Testament, "The 'realness' of God" is visible "in the wounded human body." It is a God, she maintains, who has no material reality apart from the human body.[38] The incommensurability of suffering, its unyielding to questions, its incurability are the forms of God's appearance. These bear Him into time, although one cannot speak of appearance. One must speak of presence felt indubitably as absence, one must speak of suffering. In suffering God appears but, to us, only in the forms of absence: as a question lacking an answer, a hope lost, a healing delayed, a pain which remains when everything has gone.[39]

At a similar juncture in Paul Celan's poetry, at the point when everything has gone, Alvin Rosenfeld writes: ". . . with the demise of the creature, it is as if the Creator himself has been taken out of language, his life-giving Name negated. What remains [and Rosenfeld refers here particularly to one poem of Celan's entitled "Psalm"] is Jewish stubbornness—a lingering and defiant piety—expressed in the devotional yearnings of a bloodied remnant bending still faithfully toward the source of its original bloom."[40] Such a gesture of a bending towards original bloom is accomplished in Job's final restitution.

NOTES

1. Julia Kristeva, *Black Sun: Depression and Melancholia* (1987), trans. Leon S. Roudiez (New York: Columbia University Press, 1989), 229.

2. Richard Howard, "Apart: Hearing Secret Harmonies," in *Congregation: Contemporary Writers Read the Jewish Bible*, ed. David Rosenberg (New York: Harcourt Brace Jovanovich, 1987), 410.

3. Emmanuel Levinas, "Judaism and the Feminine Element," trans. Edith Wyschogrod, *Judaism* 18 (winter 1969):32.

4. Given the Deuteronomic proprietary laws, Job's wife has never owned any of the "seven thousand sheep, and three thousand camels, and five hundred yoke of oxen, and five hundred she asses, and a very great houshold" (1:3) all of which is in the name of Job. Indeed, his wife's legal non-entity makes not only her suffering, but even her death unnecessary. Unlike any other of Job's properties, she need not suffer loss or injury or death. Her suffering remains redundant and she is silently restored to Job's household at the end of the book.

Is there a correlation between the still persistent undervaluation of women's work, their lack of social status, and the unreality of their suffering? While these questions draw a larger, well documented context around female suffering and the law, the same questions also ironically confirm Levinas' observation that the silence of (Biblical) women "still is and always will be" structuring male experience. See Wendy Kaminer, *A Fearful Freedom: Women's Flight from Equality* (Reading, Mass.: Addison Wesley, 1990), 148; Martha Minnow, *Making all the Difference: Inclusion, Exclusion, and American Law* (Ithaca: Cornell University Press, 1990), 273; Deborah L. Rhode, *Justice and Gender* (Cambridge: Harvard University Press, 1989), 150; Judith A. Baer, "Nasty Law or Nice Ladies? Jurisprudence, Feminism and Gender Difference," *Women and Politics* 11 (1991); Lynne Henderson, "Law's Patriarchy," *Law and Society Review* 25 (1991).

Moreover, questions about the value of suffering are reflected in the ideology of the tragic—which is always a legal language—particularly in the issue of rank. In this tradition, as Raymond Williams points out, tragedy and accident, significant and insignificant suffering, depend on "a law or an order to which certain events are accidental and in which certain other events are significant. Yet wherever the law or order is partial (in the sense that only certain events are relevant to it) there is an actual alienation of some part of human experience." Raymond Williams, *Modern Tragedy* (Stanford: Stanford University Press, 1966), 49. Karl Jaspers who bases the distinction between tragedy and suffering on rank, writes: "*Das Tragische wird ein Vorzug Hochstehender,—die Anderen müssen sich begnügen im Unheil gleichgültig vernichtet zu werden*" (the tragic is a privilege of nobility—the others must be content to be annihilated with indifference). Karl Jaspers, "Über das Tragische," in *Was ist Philosophie?* (München: dtv, 1980), 386.

It seems possible, then, to conclude that Job's wife's suffering remains unheard, repudiated, unrepresentable, because it is always incapable of entering into the realm of the politically and economically significant. The suffering of Job's wife is invisible and exemplary of the accidental. Preventing her suffering from entering a legal (or linguistic) articulation is to prevent its valorization as real and authentic. Job's wife's words are words without (economic) substance.

5. Elaine Scarry, *The Body in Pain: The Making and Unmaking of the World* (New York: Oxford University Press, 1985), 198.

6. Ibid., 201.

7. Walter Benjamin, *Ursprung des deutschen Trauerspiels* (Frankfurt: Suhrkamp, 1982): "*in der Tragödie besinnt sich der heidnische Mensch, dass er besser ist als seine Götter, aber diese Erkenntnis verschlägt ihm die Sprache . . .*" (90, my translation).

8. Richard Sewall, *The Vision of Tragedy* (New Haven: Yale University Press, 1980), 18, 180.

9. Søren Kierkegaard, *Fear and Trembling / Repetition* (1843), trans. Hong and Hong (Princeton: Princeton University Press, 1983), 197.

10. *The Book of Job*, trans. and intro. by Steven Mitchell (San Francisco: North Point Press, 1987), xvi.

11. Antonin Artaud, *Le théâtre et son double* (Paris: Gallimard, 1964), 153.

12. Sewall, *The Vision of Tragedy*, 19.

13. Ibid., 21.

14. David Daiches, *Literary Essays* (Chicago: University of Chicago Press, l967), 207.

15. Robert Alter, *The Art of Biblical Poetry* (New York: Basic Books, 1985), 76.

16. *The Literary Guide to the Bible*, ed. Robert Alter and Frank Kermode (Cambridge: Harvard University Press, 1987), 15.

17. Johann Baptist Metz, "Suffering unto God," trans. J. Matthew Ashley, *Critical Inquiry* 20 (summer 1994): 622.

18. Richard Jacobson, "Satanic Semiotics, Jobian Jurisprudence," *Semeia* 24/25 (1979–80):67.

19. Alter points out that ". . . in the ancient Near East a 'book' remained for a long time a relatively open structure, so that later writers might seek to

amplify or highlight the meaning of the original text by introducing materials that reinforced or extended certain of the original emphases" (*The Art of Biblical Narrative*, 91).

20. Leslie Fiedler, "Job," in *Congregation: Contemporary Writers Read the Jewish Bible*, ed. David Rosenberg (New York: Harcourt Brace Jovanovich, 1987), 334.

21. "Job," in *The Literary Guide to the Bible*, 297.

22. Roland Barthes, "The Death of the Author," in *The Rustle of Language*, trans. Richard Howard (New York: Hill and Wang, 1986), 54.

23. See Paul Ricoeur, *Hermeneutics and the Human Sciences*, trans. and ed. John B. Thompson (Cambridge: Cambridge University Press, 1981), 201.

24. Barthes, "The Death of the Author," 54.

25. Alter, *The Art of Biblical Poetry*, 87.

26. Paul Ricoeur mentions Max Scheler's tragic knot through which "the blindness of order is transformed into the enmity of fate; the tragic is always personal, but it makes manifest a sort of cosmic sadness which reflects the hostile transcendence to which the hero is a prey." Paul Ricoeur, *The Symbolism of Evil* (1967), trans. Emerson Buchanan (New York: Beacon Press, 1969), 323.

27. In *The Art of Biblical Poetry*, Robert Alter shows how God's speech out of the whirlwind takes up Job's imagery from chapter three and offers in its expansion and inversion a response to Job's sense of painful constriction and inwardness (85–110).

28. See André Lacocque, "Job and the Symbolism of Evil," *Semeia* 24/25 (1979–80):37. Similarly, Stephen Mitchell asks in his introduction to *The Book of Job*: Does the rain have a father? The whole meaning is in the *lack* of an answer" (xxv).

29. Ricoeur, *The Symbolism of Evil*, 321.

30. Alter, *The Art of Biblical Poetry*, 106.

31. Artaud, *Le théâtre et son double*, 159.

32. See Ricoeur, *The Symbolism of Evil*: ". . . if the secret of tragic anthropology is theological, that theology of making blind is perhaps unavowable, unacceptable for *thought*" (212).

33. See ibid., 214. However, in his chapter on Job, Ricoeur will claim that the silence of Job "is not altogether the seal of meaninglessness. Neither is it altogether the zero degree of speech. Certain words are addressed to Job in exchange for his silence" (see *The Symbolism of Evil*, 321).

34. Northrop Frye, *The Great Code: The Bible and Literature* (London: Routledge and Kegan Paul, 1982), 197.

35. Jean-François Lyotard, *The Inhuman*, trans. Bennington and Bowlby (Stanford: Stanford University Press, 1991), 114.

36. Maurice Blanchot, *The Infinite Conversation* (1969), trans. Susan Hanson (Minneapolis, University of Minnesota Press, 1993), 104.

37. Lacocque, "Job and the Symbolism of Evil," 39.

38. Scarry, *The Body in Pain*, 200.

39. See for an excellent deconstruction of the presence-absence dialectic: Mark C. Taylor, "Denegating God," *Critical Inquiry* 20 (summer 1994): 592–610.

40. Alvin H. Rosenfeld, *A Double Dying: Reflections on Holocaust Literature* (Bloomington: Indiana University Press, 1980), 88.

5

ANTIGONE
OR THE SECRECY
OF SUFFERING

ANTIGONE'S SUFFERING

> . . . the depressed patient
> (that stranger withdrawn into his own wound) . . .
>
> —Julia Kristeva, *Black Sun*

Julia Kristeva opens her book on depression and melancholy, *Soleil Noir*, by admitting that her work is about an incommunicable pain, "*un gouffre de tristesse, douleur incommunicable*," an abyss of sorrow, an unspeakable pain, so severe that it makes us lose "*le gout de toute parole*," our very desire to speak. Suffering allows the sufferer an absence, as Kristeva notes, "from other people's meaning" and a simultaneous "supreme metaphysical lucidity."[1] Such absence, such metaphysical lucidity, and therefore such secrecy are epitomized by Antigone.

When the chorus suggests to her that perhaps she is paying her "father's pain"[2] (857), she responds, "You speak of my darkest thought. . . ." Although she connects this darkest thought with "my pitiful father's fame" and "the doom that haunts our house" (858–59), the exact causes of her suffering, indeed of her fierce determination to suffer, appear difficult to determine. They are insufficiently explained by the contest into which she so passionately enters with Creon. "It is not for him to keep me from my own," she announces, but it not clear what exactly "my own" refers to. Is it the dead? The house of Oedipus? Or is it her "father's suffering," from which she herself is "sprung," furtively mentioned in her first appearance? And there are further problems: although the play enacts the inescapability of a familial curse, and the tragedy is a model of a *Schicksalsdrama*, there is for Antigone no reversal of fortune, no recognition, no *peripeteia*. Nor is Antigone, it seems, just the heroic defender of a "pious duty," the defender of "the gods" against Creon's political pragmatism. These, I suggest, are but the chiffres for a secret motivation which fulfills itself in the welcome disguise of a moral necessity.[3] The play may thus become a version of Blanchot's avant garde literature, protesting against revelation, and whose language is "opacity" and "the flutter of closing wings."[4] All of which amounts in these pages to a hermeneutical proposition the truth of which cannot be textually confirmed: if Antigone *has* a secret, it must remain in the paradox that whatever revelations the play offers, these are the safest means of keeping her secret.

It is therefore difficult to diagnose Antigone's suffering. Is it external or internal, fated or self-appointed? Is it tragic or painful, Greek or modern? Does Antigone's suffering epitomize the difficulty of diagnosis, of assigning suffering a name and determinate cause? Creon refers to it in almost clinical terms as an innate madness, "that disease" (732), which he thinks Antigone suffered "from her birth" (562). Ismene attributes it to "a hot mind" (88), the chorus thinks she is "bitter . . . her father's child" (471), and Antigone herself refers to her suffering as a life of sorrows from which she hopes soon to escape: "Who lives in sorrows as many as mine / how shall he not be glad to gain his death?" (463–64). If "Death means the failure of representation," as Simon Richter points out,[5] the play will keep its secrets.

It seems a very long play for Creon—"Terrible tidings make for long delays," says the guard prophetically, and his narrative enacts allegorically all tragic narratives which must postpone their end so that they can achieve their cathartic effect:[6]

> And so a short trip turns itself to long.
> Finally, though, my coming here won out.
> If what I say is nothing, still I'll say it.
> For I come clutching to one single hope
>   that I can't suffer what is not my fate.
> (232–36)

Although in Creon's last words, "My fate has struck me down" (1342), the long play seems to have reached its closure, the question of the fatedness of suffering is left open. Creon's line is too easy. Since he is the only one condemned to survive, he may be left to ponder the question of suffering and responsibility yet a little longer than anyone else. Possibly one *can* suffer what is not fated. Creon would have no guilt, Antigone no character or nobility, if it were not so—and thus the nature of suffering remains in question, as it does in all tragedies. For Antigone, it has no clearly determinable beginning and its end is buried in her suicide. What did she have to hide? Perhaps the very haste with which she seeks to bring about her end intimates something about her suffering.

For Creon, as we have said, it is a long play. His recognition is delayed until he is ready to acknowledge his guilt. "Let me go, let me go. May death come quick . . ." (1329), he cries at the end, having himself become an unburied corpse, forced to survive the death of his son and his wife and of Antigone. For Antigone it is already over at the beginning as if she were to enact what Georg Lukács calls "the mystical timelessness of the tragic substance."[7] For Lukács, the tragic is only an instant which, since it has to be represented in time, is always misrepresented. Later, in his *Theory of the Novel*, Lukács assigns the tragic status to the "absolutely lonely man" whose voice is lyrical, monologic. In the dialogues of the dramatic action, to borrow Lukács' words, the "*incognito*" of Antigone's soul "becomes too pronounced. . . ."[8] Creon, who vows to "learn of any man the soul, / the mind, and the intent until he shows / his practise of the government and law" (175–77), is to convert the timeless into time; he is the disseminator of the lyrical into government and law. In his reign of terror, as Blanchot would say, "everything is public, and the most guilty person is the suspect—the person who has a secret, who keeps a thought, an intimacy to himself."[9] For Creon, the genre of the play is thus an ideal occasion for a presentation or *Vorstellung* into whose spotlight Antigone's tragic incognito is dragged to be viewed, pitied, and sentenced.

Creon's edict is an example of the Platonic obsession with the unconcealed, an obsession which must repress what will not come to light, and what will not make sense. All must live in the realm of Greek light and apollonian appearance. But Antigone, as Martha Nussbaum observes (echoing Kristeva's melancholic sufferer), "is strangely remote from the world."[10] For her, the light has always already gone out and she moves from the very beginning in the dionysian realm of her "darkest thought" (858). The play will call into question the validity of light, of reason, of the visible, of philosophy, or of the theater, whose literal meaning is "a place where one looks."[11] Being looked at, Antigone suffers like Christ, who was looked at by everyone on the cross, as Kristeva notes, "but in the tomb he hides from his enemies' eyes, and the saints alone see him in order to keep him company in an agony that is peace."[12] If Job's suffering was unthinkable and finally had to yield to spectacle rather than to speculation, here spectacle itself is unbearable. *Antigone* might be an invisible spectacle.[13]

Antigone has no interest in the play. What she knows at the end she already knows at the beginning. To Creon she says, "Why are you waiting? Nothing that you say / fits with my thought" (499–500), and to Ismene: "My life died long ago. / And that has made me fit to help the dead" (559–60). Her part is all haste, precipitous—except at the end when she hesitates, "shall I descend, before my course is run" (896). Here Eros (whose only voice is otherwise Haemon's) briefly wrestles with Thanatos to allow for Antigone's beautiful farewell:

> Unwept, no wedding-song, unfriended, now I go
> the road laid down for me.
> . . .
> O tomb, O marriage-chamber, hollowed out
> house that will watch forever, where I go.
> To my own people, who are mostly there;
> Persephone has taken them to her.
> Last of them all, ill-fated past the rest, shall I descend,
> before my course is run.
>
> (878–79, 891–96)

Creon's "course" is first delay. In Elizabeth Wykoff's translation, his question to Antigone, "You knew the order not to do this thing?" (447), can be read either as a legalistic establishment of facts or as an offer to Antigone to deny her crime.[14] The latter seems more likely if Antigone's subsequent, fearless admission should have maximum moral weight. Although Creon wants Antigone's admission "not at length but in a word" (446), she will eventually remind him, "Why are you waiting?" (499). Eventually, Creon, too, wishes to accelerate the action—"Now, no delay" (577)—but his final "overturned" decision, "I'll go at once" and . . . hurry to that place . . ." (1109), comes only after the tragedy is consummated. Fearing such reversal, such discovery, or self-discovery, fearing perhaps to be unburied (like Polyneices), brought back to her life of "many sorrows" (463), Antigone commits suicide. The haste with which she brings about her death—only delayed by her elegaic departure—reflects critically on her attitude towards the representation of her suffering, as if that representation were itself endured as a pain. Her suicide not only bears witness to an irreducible secrecy of her suffering, it is also the final triumph of her fierce determination to inwardness and privacy. It is an expression of her victory over her antagonist who had sworn that nothing can remain concealed, that all inward soul, the mind, and the intent of any man could serve the state.

Much of Antigone's enigma and charisma resides in the violence done to her by the temporal and visual form of her dramatic representation. As has often been noted, Creon's time on the stage by far exceeds that of Antigone.[15] He performs what Lukács calls "*das Vorbereitende*," the presentation, the preparatory part for a mystical metamorphosis from narrative (or performance) to the timeless substance of *what* is being narrated:

> the preparatory part is there only for the spectator's sake, it prepares the spectator's soul for the leap of the great transformation. The tragic character's soul ignores everything preparatory, and everything changes in a flash, everything suddenly becomes essential when the fateful word is spoken at last. Likewise, the character's composure (or serenity or rapture) in the face of death is heroic only in appearance, only in the ordinary language of psychology. The dying heroes of tragedy—as a young dramatist once put it—are dead a long time before they actually die.[16]

The narrative of life, the tragedy of Antigone, is merely a postponement. The tragic character, tragic because she must suffer this postponement and must suffer being represented, narrated, and revealed, is thus always already dead while always still alive. For Sophocles' *Antigone*, where the unburied presence of the dead Polyneices is the focus of the plot, such notions of death in life might therefore be of particular interest. Indeed, it becomes clear why Kierkegaard's imaginary lecture about *Antigone* is to the *Symparanekromenoi*, the moribund, the posthumous, those who speak *au delà du tombeau*, "the fellowship of buried lives"[17] who will be receptive to the idea that Antigone has always been a corpse.

KIERKEGAARD'S *ANTIGONE*

> There is nothing, perhaps, which
> ennobles a human being so much as keeping a secret.
>
> —Kierkegaard, *Either/Or*

So secret is Antigone's suffering to Kierkegaard that he can only claim knowledge of it through an illicit, erotic encounter whose confession and exploitation is the subject of his essay entitled "The Ancient Tragical Motif as Reflected in the Modern." Kierkegaard will follow the ancient tragedy to a point, he announces, but from there on "everything will be modern." The burial of Ployneices—visible cause and doom of Antigone—receives scant attention by Kierkegaard; his fate is passed over as an echo of Oedipus' sorrowful destiny, a fateful necessity: "Antigone cannot bear to have her brother's corpse flung away . . . it worries her that no tears should be shed . . . she almost thanks the gods because she is selected as this instrument." Kierkegaard's depiction of external tragic action echoes his description of classical tragedy in *Fear and Trembling* where "even the most tried of tragic heroes dances along in comparison with the knight of faith."[18] Likewise, in the Greek version of the tragedy, "Antigone lives as carefree as any other young Grecian maiden. . . ."

For the modern version of *Antigone*, Kierkegaard must first develop a distinction between ancient sorrow and modern pain. Sorrow arises from the character's ambiguous and vacillating relationship to "inherited guilt" and personal innocence. Sorrow thus necessitates a *fatum*, "the substantial categories of family, state, and race" while "our age," Kierkegaard claims, has lost this category, leaving the individual entirely to himself: "his guilt is consequently sin, his pain remorse." The Greek Antigone is the one *we* know, who subjugates her will to the "fateful necessity which visits the sins of the fathers upon the children," while the life of the modern Antigone "is not turned outward but inward, the scene is not external but internal; it is an invisible scene." Even if there is for Kierkegaard—as for Hegel, whose categories Kierkegaard echoes—no aesthetic interest in purely subjective suffering, even if it "nullifies the tragic," Kierkegaard will, after some hesitation, give Antigone "the daughter of sorrow a dowry of pain as a wedding gift. She is my creation," he announces and "it is as if I had rested with her in a night of love. . . ."

His knowledge of a secret so illicitly acquired puts Kierkegaard's pseudonymous Victor Eremita in an unlikely hermeneutical role which he must necessarily dramatize as a breach. In this context, Walter Rehm is right to argue, eloquently and persuasively, Kierkegaard's autobiographical interest in his Antigone.[19]

At first the young Antigone had had only "dim suspicions" of her father's crime of patricide and incest; but these suspicions were later confirmed with horrible certainty. There was thereafter no possibility for Antigone to reveal this secret; her father may not have known about it himself and to all appearance lived and died as a beloved and admired ruler. As Antigone grows into adulthood, the people honor and celebrate her father's memory whose secret, tormented guardian is Antigone. Unknown, shrouded in her secret, Kierkegaard's Antigone begins to exhibit the traits of Kristeva's melancholic sufferer. Absent from other people's meaning,

> . . . she does not belong to the world she lives in; even though she appears flourishing and sound, her real life is concealed. Although she is living, she is in another sense dead; quiet is her life and secretive, the world hears not even a sigh, for her sigh is hidden in the depths of her soul.

She has the same supreme metaphysical lucididty as Kristeva's sufferer: ". . . this introversion which lies in silence, gives her a supernatural bearing." Her silent and supernatural attributes make Antigone comparable not only to Kristeva's melancholic sufferer but also to Abraham, the incomparable knight of faith in *Fear and Trembling*. Like Abraham, Antigone neither desires anyone's knowledge nor can she hope to be understood. In the silent keeping of her secret, Kierkegaard's Antigone "is about to become wholly spiritual, something nature does not tolerate."

Kierkegaard's "fantastication" (as George Steiner called it) would significantly complicate the ensuing story if his night of love were to be taken into account when Kierkegaard's argument now plots Antigone's doom precisely in her betrothal to a young man. For it is her fiancé who as potential confidant presents himself as a threat to the secret she must keep lest she betray her father's honor. As Kierkegaard's essay draws to an end, he encounters "the dramatic interest— . . . Antigone is mortally in love." Now what was first taken to be only a metaphor, "the dowry of pain," Kierkegaard's "wedding gift," becomes the tragic flaw: "She cannot belong to a man without this dowry" and yet she cannot reveal her secret: could "she justify this to the dead?" And so "the secret conquers." Antigone dies, for only in death can she love without reservation and at the same time keep her secret.

Although Kierkegaard's story takes utmost poetic licence with Sophocles' play, Kierkegaard's reading of Antigone's death as paradoxical expression of secrecy seems plausible for Sophocles' *Antigone* as well. While alive, she is already dead "long ago" (559), and likewise: "our Antigone's life . . . is essentially over," Kierkegaard adds. "For me the doer, death is best," Antigone cries early on, and "Longer the time in which to please the dead / than that for those up here" (72, 75–76). When the chorus confidently predicts that no one would disobey Creon's edict because "No fool is fool as far as loving death" (220), they unwittingly name Antigone. To read, to *understand* the play and the character one must be in love with death, which is the story Kierkegaard tells—appropriately in an address to the fellowship of buried lives.

Antigone's death then is the emblem of the secrecy of suffering, a suffering one cannot know but in death and which presents itself in Sophocles' *Antigone* as the most impregnable hermeneutical obstacle. Antigone's role, one might say, is to enact the text's opacity, to darken it with her darkest thought. The tomb, "where the foot of man comes not" (773), is the darkest textual site, a tableau of her interiority, the locus of Antigone's secret which she embraces with amorous haste and impatience. Since everyone arrives too late at the site of such impenetrable secrecy, Antigone would become a character necessitating, as George Steiner shows in his book *Antigones*, numerous resurrections in subesquent poetic renditions—of which Kierkegaard's is but one.

PHILIPPE LACOUE-LABARTHE'S *ANTIGONE*

> The woman is perfected.
> Her dead
>
> Body wears the smile of accomplishment,
> The illusion of a Greek necessity . . .
>
> —Sylvia Plath, *Ariel*

In her book, *Mélancholie de l'art*, Sarah Kofman presents yet another, this time a veritably avant garde rendition, "an entirely different setting by that philosopher Lacoue-Labarthe. . . ."[20] Near the begining of her essay, Kofman points out that

> *La fonction pharmaceutique du théâtre* et *du théorique se réalise dans les deux cas au moyen de la* mimésis. . . . *la* transfiguration *en* spectacle *de tout ce qui provoque horreur et terreur dans la vie "réelle" et ce qui rend soutenable, supportable et même agréable ce qui ne peut d'ordinaire se regarder en face . . ."* (the redemptive function of theatre *and* of theory is realized in both cases through *mimesis. . . .* the *transfiguration* into *spectacle* of all that provokes horror and terror in "real" life and which renders bearable, supportable, even agreeable that which ordinarily could not be faced . . .).[21]

Theory, too, as her emphasis on the conjunctive *et* suggests, is based on the structure of specular representation. She writes with an irony reminiscent of Kierkegaard:

> *L'illusion fondamentale qu'apporte cette structure c'est que vous êtes un* sujet: *elle vous garde, vous protège de la folie et de la mort, vous permet de vous tenir debout—d'être bien d'aplomb—bien "assis," de dominer la scène ou se trouvent "représentées" souffrances et mort—et d'en jouir* (The fundamental illusion that makes possible this structure is that you are a *subject*, which keeps and protects you from madness and death, keeps you upright—in good equilibrium, well placed, in control and ready to enjoy the theatrical representations of suffering and death).[22]

How to perform *Antigone* so that this specular illusion of identity, separateness, exclusivity, and invulnerability is exposed? So that, one would assume, *Antigone* is not performed as philosophy, with its claims of separable insides and outsides? So that the theatrical perspective—which "convert[s] the other into a character and make[s] the world a stage for him," as Stanley Cavell has pointed out[23]—so that this structure of theatricality would be suspended? So that the unthinkable precisely could not be thought because it could not be represented? How to perform *Antigone* so that the performance would refute Creon's claims to make visible the soul, the mind, and the intent of any man? So that our seeing would precisely not show and not redeem Antigone's suffering—through our having seen it? So that we would *not* see it and thus *not* be distant from it? So that our not-seeing would itself be a suffering (of deprivation of knowledge, of blindness)?

Kofman's answer to these questions is offered in the example of *"un tout autre espace scénique"* by *"ce philosophe Lacoue-Labarthe"* who along with Michael Deutsch directed Hölderlin's *Sophocle's Antigone "au moyen d'une certaine césure"* (by way of a certain caesura).[24] The caesura, or "rupture," of this performance produced what Jacques Derrida in his essay on Artaud's theater of cruelty calls "a space that no speech could condense or comprehend . . ."[25]—not a catharsis *by means* of specular distance or understanding ("une *cathar-sis* par le spéculatif") but a catharsis *of* understanding itself ("*une* catharsis *du spéculatif même*"). The performance could therefore not take place in the theater with its defined assignment of separate categories such as actors and audience, fiction and reality, but at a place called *"l'Arsenal"* in Strasbourg, an abandoned military installation, condemned, ruined, with broken windows, *"un tout autre espace que celui de la scène classique, dans un lieu qui* déplace *singulierement le 'théâtre':* . . . *une zone marginale;* . . . *l'espace* de la césure, *qui brise celui de la 'représentation'"* . . . (an entirely different space than that of the classical scene, at a place which singularly calls into question theater itself: . . . a marginal zone; . . . the space of the caesura, which ruptures the space of representation).[26]

The "spectators" are at first not clearly distinguished from the chorus or from the actors and the audience follows them through this "nocturnal hell" past rooms wherein actors make ready for their entry, and where the *machinerie théâtrale* is visible—until one is seated close to the abyss into which Antigone is to disappear. The feet of the spectators in the first row dangle into the abyss. . . . Forced to give up their distance to the stage, Lacoue-Labarthe's spectators are to renounce the eye as the most speculative of the senses in favor of a more intimate form of knowledge.[27]

Though *spatially* the exact opposite, Lacoue-Labarthe's *mise en scène* is not so different from the original Greek theater. In her book, *In and Out of the Mind: Greek Images of the Tragic Self*, Ruth Padel explains,

> The spectators were far away from the performers, on that hill above the theater. At the center of their vision was a

small hut, into which they could not see. The physical action presented to their attention was violent but mostly unseen. They inferred it, as they inferred inner movement, from words spoken by figures whose entrances and exits into and out of the visible space patterned the play. . . . This genre, with its dialectics of seen and unseen, inside and outside, exit and entrance, was a simultaneously internal and external, intellectual and somatic expression of contemporary questions about the inward sources of harm, knowledge, power, and darkness.[28]

What is accomplished by the erasure of specular distance in Lacoue-Labarthe's mise en scene seems here accomplished by the extreme emphasis of specular distance. For, in neither space can the observer claim a perspective that would externalize, make objective the questions of (Antigone's) suffering. In both performances, these questions invade and involve the spectator. In neither performance, the sources of "harm, knowledge, power and darkness," as Padel calls them, can be unambiguously objectified. In neither performance are they clearly external allowing the subject purification or catharsis, objectification or distance from, and therefore representation of, these questions. They cannot be delegated, unburdened to an other (on a stage), they remain the other in the subject, just as the subject is the other on Lacoue-Labarthe's stage, or as the subject must "infer" internal motivations in external action, or else infer that these represent his interiority.

It therefore becomes questionable to speak of *understanding*, because understanding is an inference whose source is as uncertain as are the sources of harm, knowledge, power and darkness. They have exit and entrance in a twilight between the internal and external through which passage these worlds enter into mutual mirroring. It becomes then also questionable to speak of catharsis. While the distance of Greek theater might allow us the illusion (to which we can give our assent) that we are *not* in the presence of those who suffer, Lacoue-Labarthe's mise en scene explicitly erases this illusion and makes it impossible for the audience not to be in the presence of Antigone's suffering. Indeed, Lacoue-Labarthe's mise en scene might thus have restored a sense of the Nietzschean origin of tragedy in the Dionysian festival, where rather than being permitted to return via Aristotelian catharsis to calm civic order, the spectator must lose his good equilibrium (as Kofman would say), and surrender his control, and relinquish his separateness.[29]

ANTIGONE'S SUICIDE

> Corpses are virgin.
>
> —Mina Loy, "Photo after Pogrom"

If Antigone's suffering is present to us precisely because it is unrepresentable, we are in the presence of an unknown, in the presence of darkness and power, our feet dangling into the abyss. For the question is: How can the secrecy of suffering be kept as an intimate possession and how at the same time can it be shown without violating that intimacy? Antigone drives this question to its ultimate answer: her suicide. Here her pain expresses itself but only as a paradox of expression. Her death is the consummation of secrecy and revelation, of pain and language, of language and silence. Her suicide is her language of silence, a solitary unheard exclamation, a cry embodied in the most solitary, intimate, secretive act.

But if her death is the ultimate paradox of representation,[30] Polineices' corpse represents that paradox for the duration of the play. Thus, Polyneices' corpse must have always been an object of Antigone's suicidal obsession, a reminder of her secret, a prophecy of her death, a symbol of her desire. For like in her own death (wish), in Polyneices' corpse are suspended all familial, sexual, or political affiliations, all fathers' curses and all brothers' wars. The dead body is the site of the reconciliation of all difference, "the absolute calm of what has found its place," as Blanchot writes.[31] In its power to reconcile, Polyneices' body transcends war and politics, ethics and time and becomes therefore for Antigone the sublime, aesthetic symbol of her own desire. Blanchot's reflections on the cadaver as an image, his notion of the cadaver as perfectly self referential, as "the ideal expression of [a] . . . presence freed from existence, [a] . . . form without matter" these are the terms of Antigone's desire, which Polyneices embodies, which she will embody in her suicide, and which are always also embodied in the work that bears her name. Opposed to these eternities of death and art is Creon. By refusing burial to the body of Polyneices, by leaving the corpse in the light of the sun, Creon symbolically overextends himself, reaches into the timeless, draws the divine timeless into his secular time, the secrets of death into the light of reason. Hence, his blasphemous response when the guard points out the possibility of a divine first burial: "Unbearable, your saying that the gods / take any kindly forethought for this corpse" (282–83).

If one can say that Antigone is revealed in the act of burial, the play itself is structured by this paradox. The act of burial is necessary twice—the latter covering (of Polineices' corpse) revealing the first—since her first act of burial was itself concealed as a divine intervention: "Isn't this action possibly a god's?" proposes the chorus (279), thus offering Antigone a symbolic valorization but also concealment of consequences of her crime. On his first errand to Creon, the guard reports that the burial is "all accomplished, thirsty dust / strewn on the flesh, the ritual complete" (246–47). Although the sacred act seems accomplished with sufficient symbolic substance—"light dust upon him, enough to turn the curse" (255), as the guard explains—Antigone repeats the burial, which this time she seeks to render with the utmost publicity:

> So this same girl, seeing the body stripped,
> cried with great groanings, cried a dreadful curse
> upon the people who had done the deed.
> Soon in her hands she brought the thirsty dust,
> and holding high a pitcher of wrought bronze
> she poured the three libations for the dead.
> (426–31)

There is something willfully secular in this scene not only because it was not an unmarried girl's perogative to bury the dead,[32] but also because Antigone evidently deems the first burial and its divine attribution insufficient. Is the deed to be valorized not by its own symbolic power, not by having been performed once and sufficiently, but by Antigone's discovery, arrest, and punishment? Is she to rival the death of Polyneices? Obsessed with an unhinged greed for her very own bodily suffering and death, she tells Ismene: "Don't die along with me, / my death's enough" (556–57). Ismene's belated willingness to at least symbolically share in Antigone's punishment, or Haemon's belated solidarity appear woefully insufficient. Consequently Antigone's own burial will require no "light dust" but "a hollowed cave" "where the foot of man comes not" (774, 73). Nor is she, in fact, to die, as if death were too insubstantial: "she may manage not to die. / Or she may learn at last and even then / how much too much her labor for the dead" (778–80) says Creon ambiguously, and later on "let her choose death, or a buried life" (888). These pronouncements entail the possibility (or hope) of Antigone's failure to consummate her suffering in death. And yet it seems as if the proof of her suffering must lie in the total self-embodiment of it, in the art of it, so to speak. Thus, the tomb becomes symbolic of Antigone's radical interiority, her self-completion, her final retreat into herself, and the unrepresentability of her suffering. One would have to go into the tomb with her, as does Haemon, or one's feet would have to dangle into the pit wherein she disappears. Lacoue-Labarthe, if I understand Kofman's commentary correctly, assigns the site of the tomb for the representation of Antigone's interiority, which we or the actors can witness only by endangering our own fall.

The abyss becomes the scene of *Antigone's* internal pain which necessitates but at the same time makes impossible its translation, rewriting, interpretation, mise en scene from Sophocles, to Kierkegaard, to Lacoue-Labarthe. Lacoue-Labarthe's mise en scene, so Kofman seems to suggest, is itself the rupture of the illusion of representation. Mark Taylor, in his essay "Denegating God," assigns the crypt the same function in the un/revelation of the sacred. Like Antigone's suffering, the sacred is an incommensurable secret that "unsays all saying by leaving an empty space that renders all words hollow." Taylor's crypt resembles Antigone's cave (or tomb) in that both places, while negating or hollowing out speech, also keep that negativity or hollowness open before us. Like Antigone's cave, the crypt presents itself as "the no-place that haunts every place, the secret of the crypt leaves everything and everyone cryptic."[33]

In the tomb—physical fulfillment, and symbol of Antigone's "darkest thought"—*Antigone* has its beginning. From here it has its drive and will and legitimacy. *Antigone* is only, one might say, a transcription of the pit, a temporary bridge thrown across Antigone's darkest thought. On this bridge—Lacoue-Labarthe's mise en scene employs precisely this setting—Kofman wonders about the actors' "*qui jouent sur des passerelles, des échafaudages, des 'planches' sans garde-fous; qui montent et descendent, tour à tour, trois étages suspendus dans le vide*" (who perform on gangways, scaffoldings, planks without guardrails; who climb and descend, time after time, three stories suspended in the empty space).[34] Suspended above the empty space, which is the wound in Creon's city, the fabrications and machinations of representation become visible. One might fall into the abyss if one does not *act* well. From the (retro)perspective of the pit, above which we witness the coming and going of the actors, *Antigone* is but a fiction, the bridge over a hollowness. The messages carried by the actors, are all of Antigone's always having-been-dead. This death, suffered "long ago" in the past, was, now we know, in search of a plot, and of actors, in order to run its course.

Antigone's death is the final unrepresentable. Fittingly, she is not brought back onto the stage after her descent into her tomb. Unlike Jonah, Odysseus, Aeneas, or Dante, Antigone does not come back from her encounter with death. Her non-appearance redeems her from theatrical representation, redeems her from the specular curiosity of the spectators; it calls theater into question as a reliable medium for the expression of her suffering. Her invisibility is her final triumph, her purest recourse to the privacy and extremity of her suffering.

NOTES

1. Julia Kristeva, *Soleil Noir: Dépression et mélancholie* (Paris: Gallimard, 1987), 13 (my translation); *Black Sun: Depression and Melancholia*, trans. Leon S. Roudiez (New York: Columbia University Press, 1989), 3–4.

2. Sophocles, *Three Tragedies: Antigone*, trans. Elizabeth Wykoff (Chicago: University of Chicago Press, 1954. All quotations of *Antigone* are from this edition.

3. See Patrick Guyomard, *La jouissance du tragique: Antigone, Lacan et le désir de l'analyste* (Paris: Aubier, 1992): "Mais qu'est ce ici que cette morte? Est-ce un autre nom des dieux, des lois non écrites?" (52).

4. Maurice Blanchot, *The Gaze of Orpheus*, trans. Lydia Davis (Barrytown, N.Y.: Station Hill, 1981), 49.

5. Simon Richter, *Laocoon's Body and the Aesthetics of Pain* (Detroit: Wayne State University Press, 1992), 47.

6. See Jahan Ramazani, "Freud and Tragic Effect: The Pleasures of Dramatic Pain," *The Psychoanalytic Review* 78 (spring 1991), which is an excellent article on Freud's debt to tragic form. "Both patient and spectator can be led to a higher self-understanding, but only if self-reflection is delayed by formal devices of distraction until the self-reflected upon, now besieged by unconscious wishes, differs sufficiently from the former, repressed self" (80).

7. Georg Lukács, *Soul and Form* (1911), trans. Anna Bostock (Cambridge, MIT, 1974), 159. In the original: *Die Seele und ihre Formen* (Berlin: Luchterhand, 1971): "*Das Tragische is nur ein Augenblick: das ist der Sinn, den die Einheit der Zeit ausspricht und die technische Paradoxie, die darin enthalten ist, dass der Augenblick, der seinem Begriff gemäss ohne erlebbare Dauer ist, doch eine zeitliche Dauer haben soll, entspringt eben der Unangemessenheit jedes sprachlichen Ausdrucksmittels einem mystischen Erlebnis gegenüber*" (227).

8. Georg Lukács, *Theory of the Novel* (1916), trans. Anna Bostock (Cambridge: MIT Press, 1985), 45.

9. Blanchot, *The Gaze of Orpheus*, 39.

10. Martha Nussbaum: *The Fragility of Goodness: Luck and Ethics in Greek Tragedy and Philosophy* (Cambridge: Cambridge University Press, 1986), 66.

11. F. D. H. Kitto, *Form and Meaning in Drama* (London: Methuen, 1956), 149.

12. Kristeva, *Black Sun*, 137.

13. See Paul Ricoeur, *The Symbolism of Evil*, trans. Emerson Buchanan (Boston: Beacon Press, 1969): ". . . the Greek example is especially fitted to persuade us that the tragic vision of the world is tied to a spectacle and not to a speculation. . . . if the secret of tragic anthropology is theological, that theology of making blind [the tragic character's blind necessity of fulfilling his/her fate] is perhaps unavowable, unacceptable for *thought*" (212).

14. Although J. C. Kamerbeek does not substantiate this reading—"The form of the question . . . is certainly not calculated to offer Antigone the occasion of a negative reply," the very necessity of Kamerbeek's assertion does imply the possibility of reading the question in the way I suggest. See *The Plays of Sophocles: Commentaries*, vol. 3 (Leiden: E. J. Brill, 1978), 96.

15. See Lucien Goldman, "The Tragic Vision: The World," in *Moderns on Tragedy*, ed. Lionel Abel (New York; Fawcett Premier Book, 1967), 276 and note.

16. Georg Lukács, *Soul and Form*, 159. In the original: ". . . *das Vorbereitende ist nur für die Zuschauer da, ein Vorbereiten ihrer Seele für den Sprung der grossen Umwandlung. Denn achtlos überhört die Seele des tragischen Menschen alles Vorbereitende und blitzartig ändert sich alles, wird alles zum Wesen, da das Schicksalswort endlich erklang. Auch ist die Todesentschlossenheit der tragischen Menschen, ihre heitere Ruhe angesichts des Todes oder ihre lodernde Todesentzückung nur scheinbar heroisch, nur für die menschlich-psychologische Betrachtung; die sterbenden Helden der Tragödie—so ungefähr schrieb es ein junger Tragiker—sind schon lange tot, ehe sie starben*" (228).

17. Søren Kierkegaard, *Either /Or*, vol. 1, trans. Swenson and Swenson (Princeton: Princeton University Press, 1959), 137–262. I have omitted page references for the quotations since they are easily found in Kierkegaard's essay.

18. Søren Kierkegaard, *Fear and Trembling/ Repetition*, trans. Hong and Hong (Princeton: Princeton University Press, 1983), 77.

19. Walter Rehm, "Kierkegaard's 'Antigone,'" in *Begegnungen und Probleme: Studien zur deutschen Literaturgeschichte* (Bern: Francke Verlag, 1957) 274–316. Rehm excellently discusses Kierkegaard's Antigone in the context of German romanticism and also analyzes the essay's autobiographical connections.

20. See Philippe Lacoue-Labarthe, "The Caesura of the Speculative," in *Typography: Mimesis, Philosophy, Politics*, ed. Christopher Fynsk (Cambridge: Harvard University Press, 1989), 208–35.

21. Sarah Kofman, *Mélancholie de l'art* (Paris: Galilée, 1985), 76 (my translation).

22. Ibid., 76 (my translation).

23. Stanley Cavell, *Disowning Knowledge: In Six Plays of Shakespeare* (Cambridge: Cambridge University Press, 1987), 104.

24. Kofman, *Mélancholie de l'art,* 77. It seems that Cavell assigns a similar function to Shakespeare's *Lear* when he asks, "how are we to put ourselves in another's presence[?] . . . We must learn to reveal ourselves, to allow ourselves to be seen. When we do not, when we keep ourselves in the dark, the consequence is that we convert the other into a character and make the world a stage for him. There is fictional existence with a vengeance, and there is the theatricality which theater such a *King Lear* must overcome, is meant to overcome, shows the tragedy in failing to overcome. The conditions of theater literalize the conditions we exact for existence outside—hiddenness, silence, isolation—hence make that existence plain." See *Disowning Knowledge,* 104.

25. Jacques Derrida, "The Theater of Cruelty," in *Writing and Difference,* trans. Alan Bass (Chicago: University of Chicago Press, 1978), 237.

26. Kofman, *Mélancholie de l'art,* 78 (my translation).

27. See Sarah Kofman, *Nietzsche and Metaphor,* trans. Duncan Large (Stanford: Stanford University Press, 1993), 105.

28. Ruth Padell, *In and Out of the Mind: Greek Images of the Tragic Self* (Princeton: Princeton University Press, 1992), 77.

29. See Suzanne Gearhart, *The Interrupted Dialectic: Philosophy, Psychoanalysis, and Their Tragic Other* (Baltimore: Johns Hopkins University Press, 1992), 31.

30. See Richter, *Laocoon's Body and the Aesthetics of Pain,* 47.

31. Blanchot, *The Gaze of Orpheus,* 81.

32. Th. C. W. Oudemans and A. P. M. H. Lardinois, *Tragic Ambiguity* (Leiden; E. J. Brill, 1987), 167.

33. Mark C. Taylor, "Denegating God," *Critical Inquiry* 20 (summer 1994): 604–5.

34. Kofman, *Mélancholie de l'art,* 80.

6

LEAR
OR THE CAUSELESSNESS
OF SUFFERING

SUFFERING LOVE

> . . . cause is a concept that,
> in the last resort, is unanalysable—
> impossible to understand by reason . . .
>
> —Jacques Lacan,
> *Four Fundamental Concepts of Psychoanalysis*

> No cause, no cause.
>
> —William Shakespeare, *King Lear*

"Am I in France?" Lear asks, awakening from his madness; "In your
own kingdom, Sir" (4.7.75–76),[1] answers Kent. But it is a kingdom
without territory. Lear's "own kingdom" is what remains after he has
been stripped of all things illusory, crown and clothes. Kent's answer
may express his recognition of Lear's recovery of his own mental state
and his brief reign therein but it may hint, more mysteriously, at such a
kingdom as remains in spite of loss and defeat, a kingdom indefeatable

and immeasurable. The other kingdom, the one Lear had measured out and divided into (what turns out) two Machiavellian principalities strangely loses all substance in comparison to the immaterial kingdom into which Lear awakens at the end.

Where are we at the end of *King Lear*, and how did we get there? If the end of a tragedy is darkly predestined by a fatal necessity, the question of cause seems more enigmatic in *King Lear* than in any other of Shakespeare's tragedies.[2] What is the cause of Lear's suffering? Is it his obstinacy, his senility, his foolishness? Is it his loss of kingship? Or to ask differently: What is it that drives Lear mad? But is madness tragic? And if it is not, is filial ingratitude reason for madness? And if not, is ingratitude tragic? And if not, what is tragic in *King Lear* if not the love of Cordelia? "All her words are words of love," Stanley Cavell writes, "to love is all she knows how to do. That is her problem, and at the cause of the tragedy of King Lear."[3] But love as cause of tragic suffering seems as incomprehensible as suffering itself—and nothing is explained.

Although, as Cavell suggests, Cordelia's love is at the cause of Lear's tragedy, how can her love be cause for suffering? It makes no demands, needs no reward, and places upon Lear no conditions. Indeed, it says, ostentatiously

> Nothing, my lord.
> Nothing?
> Nothing.
> Nothing will come of nothing: speak again.
> (1.1.86–89)

And if it is precisely the undemanding, unconditional quality of her love that causes Lear's tragedy, we have only deferred the question about the cause of tragedy. We have substituted the question with love, but love is another question. For love's cause is "nothing." Were it not so, love would readily have entered into Lear's economic transactions in the opening scene.

> Tell me, my daughters,
> (Since now we will divest us both of rule,
> Interest of territory, cares of state)
> Which of you shall we say doth love us most?
> That we our largest bounty may extend
> Where nature doth with merit challenge.
> (1.1.47–52)

But will love be challenged? Goneril and Regan pretend, Cordelia refuses. Love will not be challenged. Love, as all three of Lear's daughters will emphatically prove, is not an object of commerce, measurable in terms of money and merit. Goneril's and Regan's rhetorical pretensions amount to the same "nothing" that Cordelia offers in response to Lear's challenge. For love, all three protest—albeit Goneril and Regan cynically—is nothing in comparison to political rule, territory, and state.

All three of Lear's daughters repay their father in extraordinary expressions of rebellion: Goneril will give "beyond what can be valued rich or rare" (1.1.56); Regan admits that she is "made of that self metal as my sister" (1.1.68), and Cordelia will give the paradox of "nothing," at once the most determinable and indeterminable of values.

If Lear is going to be reminded of Cordelia's love by his elder daughters' hate, he will be reminded not only in the antithetical sense in that they are *not* what she *is*,[4] but also in that their hate is as incomprehensible as her love, their presence as disastrous as her absence. Even if they are Cordelia's antithesis in all things, the diametrical precision of the antithesis renders them equally incomprehensible. In a functional (though not moral) sense, Goneril and Regan thus only repeat and perpetuate the incomprehensible. Like Cordelia's, their actions are inexplicable.

Instead of entering into Lear's economy of love, Cordelia answers:

> Unhappy that I am, I cannot heave
> My heart into my mouth: I love your Majesty
> According to my bond; no more nor less.
>   (1.1.90–92)

—no more nor less meaning that more or less is beside the question, irrelevant, impossible. Meanwhile, Lear assigns love a quantity in order to repress the bond, to repress nature, to replace family with state, nature with power, love with lines on a map. For Lear is the king who would conceive love spatially, geographically, monetarily, dividing shadowy forests and wide-skirted meads according to love: a love as a state in which one can rule and which one can abdicate, not a love to which one is subject. A love of which one is king. If such love as Lear would have is worth a kingdom, the kingdom Lear is willing to offer for love is the pawn for his fear of being subject to love, of being bonded, bondsman. His kingdom should buy him out of the bondage of love, but it sells him into it. The rest of the play, down to Lear's realization that man is "no more than this" (3.4.101) and up to his awakening that "this" is enough, is about his becoming a subject, a bondsman rather than a king.

Love must be suffered, it cannot be assigned or divided into equal parts, as if it were something. Love comes unbidden, beyond questions of "more" or "less," beyond what can be valued rich or rare. If it cannot be measured it cannot be avoided. The tragedy of *King Lear*, as Stanley Cavell observes, shows that the avoidance of love is impossible—as impossible, I would add, as the avoidance of suffering, which also comes unbidden, no more nor less, beyond what can be valued rich or rare. If Lear suffers love, he suffers love because it bears all resemblance to and shares all qualities with suffering, defying all speech, all comparison, all value and reason—as all his daughters foretell. All three of his daughters thus prophesy Lear's fate of suffering in terms of their incomparable love.

If incomparable, incomprehensible love is the subject of the tragedy of *King Lear*, Edmund adds very late in the play, in one of the most moving lines, the epitome of love's incomparability: "Yet Edmund was beloved" (5.3.238) which makes him no more nor less than Lear. While Edmund's insight comes only as he abandons his Macchiavellian logic: "Some good I mean to do, / Despite of mine own nature" (5.3.242–43) Lear, incorrigibly clinging to his system of causality, protests even at the end:

> I know you do not love me; for your sisters
> Have, as I do remember, done me wrong:
> You have some cause, they have not.
> (4.7.73–75)

The point is, of course, that just as Cordelia has no cause not to love, she has no cause to love, for that would draw love into the economy she wants so much to avoid. "No cause, no cause" (4.7.75) she therefore replies, which is the same as "no more nor less." Her reply is not only a fervent repudiation of his notion that she might in fact have cause to hate him, but also a fundamental negation of cause itself: "do not speak of cause" is what she is saying. In the same way she gives him "nothing" in order to preserve the giving of love itself.

While Cordelia's "nothing" dismantles the structure of Lear's economy of love, in his initial formula, "Nothing will come of nothing" (1.1.89), nothing is something. It is a part in a determinable structure of exchange. Lear, who wants to trade land for love, something for something, who wants to make love a commodity, will therefore not be ready to account for something out of nothing: Love for nothing. Loyalty for nothing. Cordelia for nothing. "He cannot bear love when he has no reason to be loved . . ." Stanley Cavell writes,[5] and therefore in order to learn love, Lear must, as he unwittingly prophecies, "be the pattern of all patience / I will say nothing" (3.2.37–38). Thus, Lear's redemption—if there is a hint of redemption at the end of the play—is nothing one can count out or plot on a map. To learn the lesson of love for "nothing" is to learn "the pattern of all patience," that suffering is for "nothing," but that in such suffering one may be subject to love. To learn this he will undergo, at the hands of Goneril and Regan, the reversal of his economic prescription: there he will receive nothing for love and nothing for loyalty.

In his book *Shakespeare*, Northrop Frye argues that the conception of nothing is comparable to "love, friendship, good faith, loyalty" because "[t]here is no 'why' about them: they just are. In putting on his love-test act, Lear is obsessed by the formula of something for something. I'll love you if you love me, and if you love me you'll get a great big slice of England."[6] But just as love has no why, neither, as Lear's daughters demonstrate, has hatred. "Here is no why," "'*Hier ist kein Warum*'" the SS guard is reported to have explained to Primo Levi upon entering Auschwitz.[7] Perhaps the common denominator between love and hatred is the gratuitous gift about which Mark Taylor says—incidentally in the same German phrase—that it is "always disinterested, the gift is *ohne warum*." Everything that Taylor subsequently lists under the qualities of agape, which is "giving that gives without demanding anything in return," is also a quality of the unconditional gift one receives in suffering: ". . . unmotivated, purposeless, indifferent. . . . eludes every economy. . . . can never be comprehended, is utterly gratuitous."[8] While eros, as Taylor explains, tries ceaselessly to fill the gaps opened by agape, Lear's economy tries ceaselessly to do the same.

But so does the aesthetic design or rational form of tragedy. Trying ceaselessly to fill the gaps opened by suffering tragedy also is an economy. It is this economy that Shakespeare's *Lear* withholds. By refusing to fill the gaps opened by suffering, the play makes 'visible'—if only by intimation as when Cordelia utters her "nothing" or when Lear cries "look there, look there"—something beyond the visions granted by tragic representation. The ultimate gratuitousness, Cordelia's death, is her embodiment of "nothing." Her dead body is love's final resistance to appropriation or representation. While ". . . the worst is not / So long as we can say 'This is the worst.'" (4.1.27–28), Cordelia's death is the worst, signifying the end of speaking. Like Antigone's, Cordelia's death is an allegory of the play's refusal to reveal the cause of suffering. The worst is beyond comprehension—but so is the best: Cordelia's love. By the withholding of cause, *Lear* demands the same rigor of renunciation that is required, according to François Lyotard, by avant garde art: a "letting go of all grasping intelligence and of its power, disarming it, recognizing that this occurrence . . . was not necessary and is scarcely foreseeable. . . ."9

Tell me how much you love me, he demands of his daughters, so that their words can fill the gap, the void, the nothing of love. By leaving it open the giving of love can happen. Analogously, in the gratuitousness of Cordelia's death the idea of love survives. If Cordelia had consented, she, too, would have substituted words for love. Being silent, saying "nothing," she gives love, makes love's present and makes love present—all of which is unbearably intimate. Lear is not used to love. He cannot bear to be in its presence without wedging a whole kingdom in between. Or perhaps because love's presence in Cordelia's silence points out the absence of love in Goneril's and Regan's words, he must banish love's presence. Lear's banishment of Cordelia is a banishment of the presence of love, a putting up of distance to avoid the unbearable intimacy Cordelia's "still-soliciting eye" (1.1.230) has invoked. From then on the Fool will be Cordelia: the blank of Lear's eye / I, his blind spot.

In Cordelia's word "nothing" Lear is seen: naked, blind, mad, a father, not a king. "You have begot me, bred me, loved me . . ." says Cordelia and returns these as duties as of a daughter to her father: "I return these duties . . ." (1.1.95–96) but for nothing, we might add, thus undoing Lear's economy once again. Having refused to wedge words between father and daughter, having refused the distances and displacements Lear wishes to establish, she has forced an encounter of unseemly immediacy: "I love your Majesty / According to my bond" (1.1.92). Momentarily she sees, not the king, but her father according to the bond between father and daughter: ". . . avoid my sight" (1.1.123) he cries and "Out of my sight!" (1.1.156).

The armor of words has been torn in Cordelia's refusal to speak. By not speaking she lets speak an intimacy, a familiarity, a love altogether impossible to render in purely civil or legal terms. She claims a love that comes about through nature, through the bond between father and daughter, not through kingdom but through kinship. Now Lear can be seen but he cannot look back. When he can she will be dead. He would prefer to see himself in the mirror of his elder daughters' response.

Goneril and Regan comply. Cordelia refuses. While her "nothing" names his lack, Goneril and Regan play mirror to Lear's demand. "For there was never yet fair woman but she made mouths in a glass" as the Fool says later on (3.2.35–36). Goneril and Regan respond to his narcissism by reflecting him. They reflect what he wants to see but they show him, with cruelty, that it is an imaginary projection, an illusion. While Goneril and Regan stroke Lear's ego, Cordelia is his blind spot, that which he cannot bear to see. Goneril and Regan love him according to his imaginary projections, Cordelia loves him according to his desire. She alone knows his lack and that no words can fill it. Or the same: she alone knows his desire and that no words can fulfill it. Her "nothing," "no more nor less," "no cause, no cause," are the expressions of this knowedge. It is in these words, naming his lack, that her "bond" is present. Banishing Cordelia is to banish his lack. When she dies he recognizes in her death the irreparability of his lack—recovers from it, momentarily to say, "look there, look there"—and dies, having seen "nothing"—but thereby having reestablished the bond between father and daughter. His death is the embodiment of that bond.

All characters in *Lear*, at one time or another, face the demands of love and cannot accommodate them. Unaccommodation is the plot of *Lear* even to the extent of its own structural and moral dissolution. The plot cannot accommodate the characters, the sequences, the consequences.[10] The many questions we must raise in response to Lear stand as unaccommodated as Lear on the heath.

Is Lear's stripping down to the unaccommodated man a model of understanding, of reading? Ought we to read Lear madly, nakedly, feelingly? Ought we to smell our way to the end of *King Lear* where "nothing" will be accomplished? Without preconceptions? Ready to forsake maps? Should we expect answers to the questions about the coherence of the play, Lear's motivation, the Fool's disappearance, Cordelia's death? Or is not the very presence of those questions, unanswerable as they remain, a way of inuiting Lear's lack and Cordelia's love? Lear's tragedy, I suggest, is not comprehensible in the way we understand *Lear* but in the way we do not. We need a hermeneutic of not understanding.

NOTES

1. William Shakespeare, *King Lear*, Arden Edition, ed. Kenneth Muir (London: Methuen, 1975).

2. Hence the continuing debate whether *Lear* has an ending at all. See Frank Kermode, *The Sense of an Ending: Studies in the Theory of Fiction* (London: Oxford University Press, 1966): "In *King Lear* everything tends toward a conclusion which does not occur . . ." (82). See also Stephen Booth, *King Lear, Macbeth, Indefinition, and Tragedy* (New Haven: Yale University Press, 1983): "Not ending is a primary characteristic of *King Lear*" (15).

3. Stanley Cavell, *Disowning Knowledge: In Six Plays of Shakespeare* (Cambridge: Cambridge University Press, 1987), 63.

4. "The antithesis with her sisters . . . brings her to mind whenever they are on the stage." See Harold C. Goddard, *"King Lear,"* in *William Shakespeare's King Lear*, ed. Harold Bloom (New York: Chelsea House, 1987), 27.

5. Cavell, *Disowning Knowledge*, 61.

6. Northrop Frye, *On Shakespeare*, ed. Robert Sandler (Markham, Ontario: Fitzhenry and Whiteside, 1986), 109–10.

7. Quoted in "The Obscenity of Understanding: An Evening with Claude Lanzmann," in *Trauma: Explorations in Memory*, ed. Cathy Caruth (Baltimore: Johns Hopkins University Press, 1995), 204.

8. Mark C. Taylor, "Denegating God," *Critical Inquiry* 20 (summer 1994):607.

9. Jean-François Lyotard, *The Inhuman: Reflections on Time* (1988), trans. Geoffrey Bennington and Rachel Bowlby (Stanford: Stanford University Press, 1991), 93.

10. This is excellently shown in Stephen Booth's first chapter of *King Lear, Macbeth, Indefinition*, 5–57.

SUFFERING
AND THE
REMEDY OF ART

MATTHEW ARNOLD: THE MODERN PAINFUL

MODERN PROBLEMS

> . . . the dialogue of the mind with itself
> has commenced; modern problems have presented
> themselves; we hear already the doubts,
> we witness the discouragement,
> of Hamlet and of Faust.
>
> —Matthew Arnold, "Preface to *Poems*" (1853)

> His gift knew what he was—
> a dark disordered city.
>
> —W. H. Auden, "Matthew Arnold"

The opening lines of W. H. Auden's poem "Matthew Arnold" attribute an insight to Arnold's poetry that Arnold lacked. It is perhaps also true—since Auden's lines are indeed so true—that Arnold himself had good Freudian reasons to keep his city in the dark:

> Doubt hid it from the father's fond chastizing sky;
> Where once the mother-farms had glowed protectively,
> Stood the haphazard alleys of the neighbor's pity.[1]

The city's dark disorder reappears not only in Arnold's poetry, which is altogether full of doubt and darkling thoughts, but also in Arnold's Preface to *Poems* (1853) where the same doubt awaits an "intellectual deliverance":

> The deliverance consists in man's comprehension of this present and past. It begins when our mind begins to enter into possession of the general ideas which are the law of this vast multitude of facts. It is perfect when we have acquired that harmonious acquiescence of mind which we feel in contemplating a grand spectacle that is intelligible to us; when we have lost that impatient irritation of mind which we feel in presence of an immense, moving, confused spectacle which, while it perpetually excites our curiosity, perpetually baffles our comprehension.[2]

Reading this passage from Arnold's essay "On the Modern Element in Literature," we may be reminded of Aristotle's "parallel in painting where the most beautiful colors laid on without order will not give one the same pleasure as a simple black and white sketch of a portrait."[3] Aristotle's painterly analogy is to illustrate the importance of plot as the organizing principle of tragedy. For when the immense moving specatacle moved in upon him, when the beautiful colors had spilled onto the page without order, Arnold would invoke an idealized notion of Aristotle's action, "an excellent action," to contain his own modern, irritated mind. The term, "excellent action," occurs in Arnold's Preface which opens with the confession that Arnold had omitted a certain poem in spite of its classical subject matter. It is a poem, Arnold writes, in which he had

> intended to delineate the feelings of one of the last of the Greek religious philosophers, one of the family of Orpheus and Musaeus, having survived his fellows, living on into a time when the habits of Greek thought and feeling had begun fast to change, character to dwindle, the influence of the Sophists to prevail. Into the feelings of a man so situated there entered much that we are accustumed to consider as exclusively modern.[4]

Rather abruptly we then hear Arnold repudiating "modern problems," "doubts," and "discouragement," all of which he darkly observes in the "painful, not tragic" suffering in *Hamlet* and *Faust*. Above all, we hear of the deplorable mark of the modern: the "dialogue of the mind with itself." Hamlet and Faust are the modern predecessors of Arnold's discarded *Empedocles on Etna*. Empedocles' modern problems (in Arnold's poem) are their bequest—even if such association leaves open the hopeful possibility that the rejected poem's very comparability to *Hamlet* and *Faust* might contain the promise of its future restoration. Indeed, restoration followed in 1868 "at the request of a man of genius, whom it had the honor and the good fortune to interest,—Mr. Robert Browning."[5] Empedocles' modern problems, it turns out, could be blamed on his "unpoetical age," the "damned times."[6]

Meanwhile, as Arnold's letters to Clough suggest, we may take as authentic—even to the point of implicating Arnold's own dark disordered city—that "suffering finds no vent in action" and "everything [is] to be endured, nothing to be done." "Odious" and "untragic," as Aristotle would have judged, this is the dreary opposite of the structure and soul of tragedy: "The worst situation is when the personage is with full knowledge on the point of doing a deed, and leaves it undone."[7]

> In such situations there is inevitably something morbid, in the description of them something monotonous. When they occur in actual life, they are painful, not tragic; the representation of them in poetry is painful also.[8]

Arnold's determination to become a "reformer in poetical matters,"[9] underscores his preference of the tragic over the painful. For it is nothing less than poetical matters that are charged with the advancement of an ideal aesthetic culture, a culture as art and of art as religion.[10] In such a culture the passive endurance of pain is an anti-cultural, unethical, pathological stance. The tragic, conversely, is associated with "excellent action" and "permanent passions." Eighty-three years after Arnold's Preface, three years before the war that would prove the impossibility of Arnold's excellent action either in life or in art, Yeats remembers Arnold in his introduction to the *Oxford Book of Modern Verse*. He affirms the same aesthetic principles as Arnold in his editorial decisions not to publish war poetry from the First World War: "I have rejected these poems for the same reason that made Arnold withdraw his *Empedocles on Etna* from circulation; passive suffering is not a theme for poetry. In all great tragedies, tragedy is a joy to the man who dies."[11]

In 1884, reviewing a production of *Hamlet* in the *Pall Mall Gazette*, Arnold still considers Hamlet "the plaything of cross motives and shifting impulses, swayed by a thousand subtle influences, physiological and pathological." Not surprisingly, "*Hamlet* thus comes at last not to be a drama followed with perfect comprehension and profoundest emotion, which is the ideal for tragedy, but a problem soliciting interpretation and solution."[12] If interpretation and solution are inferior to perfect comprehension and profoundest emotion, the fault is with the play which cannot resolve within its own rhetoric and form Hamlet's modern problems. Evidently, those are problems that will not be objectified in action and plot. For Hamlet's suffering is the epitome of the inexpressible, inward, mental suffering. He has "that within which passes show" and will not enter into rituals of mourning: "These but the trappings and the suits of woe"[13]—all of which necessitates a stern reprimand from Claudius:

> . . . to persevere
> In obstinate condolement is a course
> Of impious stubbornness, 'tis unmanly grief,
> It shows a will most incorrect to heaven,
> A heart unfortified, a mind impatient,
> An understanding simple and unschool'd. . . .[14]

What the king desires is a measure of, shall we say, aesthetic distance on the part of Hamlet, an aesthetic distance that would entail self-discipline, self-observation, distance from his sorrow: heaven itself would reward it, for to objectify one's mind is a sign of moral fortitude, courage, patience, and manliness, as well as of the rational faculties, understanding, and education. Arnold would not be pleased to be so closely allied to Hamlet's murderous uncle who here makes the same connections between self and society, aesthetics and religion as Arnold would in his book *Culture and Anarchy*.

The painful, then, is fundamentally at odds with "poetical enjoyment" because poetical enjoyment is pure, disinterested perception, knowledge held at a distance, and a distance sustained without desire. John Crowe Ransom unwittingly (or perhaps not) alludes to Hamlet's unaesthetic modes of behavior when he exemplifies the aesthetic distance in the ceremony of courtship by which a man's sexual appetites take "a circuitous road and become a romance," or the ritual of mourning, "the form of a pageant of grief," by which a man "is not obliged . . . to run and throw himself upon the body in an ecstasy of grief, nor go apart and brood upon the riddle of mortality. . . ."[15] If *Hamlet* then is the unabashed display of uncheck'd sexual appetite and excessive brooding upon the riddle of mortality, the play calls into question those classical values and forms which Arnold had hoped would "subsist permanently in the race," and which to him were "independent from time." Hamlet's modern problems rather imply a crisis of Arnold's "eternal objects of Poetry, among all nations and all times." Usurped and parodied, both in Denmark and in the play, Arnold's excellent action would compromise the state of Hamlet's modern mind. In its own painful state, the mind has neither country nor culture, neither stage nor state: the mind is objectless, morbid, monotonous, an exile in its own world and time. For pain is "not 'of' or 'for' anything," Elaine Scarry notes, "—it is itself alone."[16] Not surprisingly language becomes for Hamlet words, words, words.

The modern that stared out at Arnold in his *Empedocles on Etna*, although "accurate" (in which there is more than a faint admission of its cultural relevance),[17] was, he felt, morally deleterious: poetical representation demands "that it shall inspirit and rejoice the reader: that it shall convey a charm and and infuse delight. For the Muses, as Hesiod says, were born that they might be 'a forgetfullness of evils, and a truce from cares.'" Elsewhere Arnold asks: ". . . how can a man adequately interpret the activity of his age when he is not in sympathy with it?"[18] The question is central in his inaugural lecture as a professor of poetry in Oxford (1857) and outlines the homiletic compromises which can be seen as responsible for Arnold's abandonment of his "modern" poetry and the failure of particularly his later poetry to be any more than derivative. Answers to his question are given in the names and representative works of authors like Pindar, Aeschylus, Sophocles, or Aristophanes. These are compared to "the stages in literature which led downward . . ." but which, Arnold admits, "will be deeply interesting also."[19] The most illustrious example here is Lucretius, whose name and interpretative quality will represent "the characteristics stamped on . . . many of the representative works of modern times":

> With stern effort, with gloomy despair, he seems to rivet his eyes on the elementary reality, the naked framework of the world, because the world in its fullness and movement is too exciting a spectacle for his discomposed brain. He seems to feel the spectacle of it at once terrifying and alluring; and to deliver himself from it he has to keep perpetually repeating his formula of disenchantment and annihilation.[20]

The unintended autobiographical quality has been noted.[21] But because ". . . he who is morbid is no adequate interpreter of his age," Arnold turns to a representative of another age: Virgil. Here the criteria are less temperamental than formal. Virgil's gifts are epic, not dramatic. Strictly adhering to Aristotle's *Poetics*, Arnold favors action over Virgil's "melancholy," which is "a testimony to its incompleteness."[22]

Lucretius' gloomy despair and Virgil's melancholy represent Arnold's own "modern problems"; while they may have had their solution at a time "among august companions / In an older world, peopled by Gods, / In a mightier order" as we read in *Empedocles*, the historical and artistic limbo in which Arnold wanders is itself analogous to Empedocles' "continuous state of mental distress . . . unrelieved by incident, hope, or resistance." Lucretius' disenchanted philosophical gaze was not a position, after all, that could justify for Arnold his emotional unresponsiveness to a literary landscape that had, since Wordsworth, turned from "freshness" to "a wintry clime."[23] Empedocles, voicing Arnold's despairing conclusion to his poetic career, reads "[i]n all things my own deadness"; his woes are projected onto the "unallied unopening earth" in a thwarted romanticism that bespeaks Arnold's refusal to deploy a poetic argument or apology for the "heavenly wilderness" his Empedocles had discovered.[24]

BEYOND TRAGEDY

Auden seems to believe that Arnold's poetic gift

> . . . would have gladly lived in him and learned his ways,
> And grown observant like a beggar, and become
> Familiar with each square and boulevard and slum,
> And found in the disorder a whole world to praise.[25]

But if Arnold is either psychologically "homeless" (as Auden thinks) or historically exiled (as Arnold thought) from a better time that would redeem his "unpoetical" situation—a time whose fervent exponent the later Arnold would become—Empedocles' exile seems more permanent, perhaps fearfully prophetic of a general human condition that could not be remedied other than through suicide. For only Empedocles' leap into the fiery crater of Etna finally leaves open a speculative hope that one has moved beyond the "ceaseless opposition" (2.268) of subject and object, into a realm of unity and harmony, albeit non-verbal and unintelligible. But this would be the unacceptably modern or sublime sense of a tragic vision beyond the formal structures of tragedy. The final unintelligibility of Empedocles' "vision" reflects not Aristotle's action complete in itself, the ideal and ideology of form, but the vaster truth of more sublime closures beyond remedy or representation.[26]

Living in an age reputedly without tragedies, perhaps in a painful age, we have become, like Hamlet or Faust, doubtful about the curative faculties of a tragic aesthetic. Theodor Adorno advocates that "[i]n an age of incomprehensible terror and suffering," art must reflect the irrational, the negativity "of all that has been repressed by the established culture." If certain forms of the aesthetic might themselves be modes of repression, Adorno pleads for a ruthless demystification of beautiful illusions.[27] Similarly, Georg Lukács points out that it is in the opposition between dramatic action and the individual's solitude that the paradox of tragedy emerges. The dramatic, dialogic form of drama contradicts loneliness, which to Lukács is "the very essence of tragedy." "The language of the absolutely lonely man is lyrical, monological; in the dialogue the *incognito* of his soul becomes too pronounced. . . . loneliness has to become a problem unto itself, deepening and confusing the tragic problem and ultimately taking its place."[28] According to Stephen Booth, whose book *King Lear, Macbeth, Indefinition, and Tragedy* explodes the myth of tragedy as a unifying defining term: "*Tragedy* is the word by which the mind designates (and thus in part denies) its helplessness before a concrete, particular, and thus undeniable demonstration of the limits of human understanding." Tragedy, as an aesthetic genre, as a defining term, "denies the essence of what it labels: an experience of the fact of indefinition."[29] Summing up these notions of a fundamental difference between human suffering and the tragic, Karl Jaspers points out simply: "*Das Tragische ist geschieden von Unglück, Leiden, Untergang, von Krankheit und Tod, vom Bösen*" (the tragic is separate from misfortune, from suffering and defeat, from illness, death, and evil).[30] But how, then, can suffering be borne without the consolations of tragedy? How can we just suffer?

NOTES

1. "Matthew Arnold," in *The English Auden: Poems, Essays and Dramatic Writings,* ed. Edward Mendelson (London: Faber and Faber, 1977), 241.

2. Published as "On the Modern Element in Literature," *Macmillan's Magazine*, Feb. 1869; repr. in *The Complete Prose Works of Matthew Arnold: On the Classical Tradition*, vol. 1, ed. R. H. Super (Ann Arbor: University of Michigan Press, 1960), 20.

3. Aristotle, *Poetics* (ch. 6, 1450b), in *Rhetoric and Poetics of Aristotle*, trans. Ingram Bywater (New York: The Modern Library, 1954), 232.

4. Matthew Arnold, Preface to First Edition of *Poems* (1853), repr. in *On the Classical Tradition*, vol. 1,1.

5. Footnote to the edition of 1868.

6. *The Letters of Matthew Arnold to Arthur Hugh Clough*, ed. H. F. Lowry (London: Oxford University Press, 1932), 99, 111 (letters of Feb. 1849 and Sept. 23, 1849).

7. Aristotle, *Poetics*, 241 (1454a).

8. Arnold, Preface to First Edition of *Poems*, 3.

9. Letter of M. Arnold to his sister Jane, n.d., probably written in 1849, in *Victorian Poetry and Poetics*, ed. W. E. Houghton, G. R. Stange (Boston: Houghton Mifflin, 1968), 561.

10. See Vassilis Lambropolous, "Violence and the Liberal Imagination: The Representation of Hellenism in Matthew Arnold," in *The Violence of Representation: Literature and the History of Violence*, ed. Nancy Armstrong and Leonard Tennenhouse (London: Routledge and Kegan Paul, 1989), 171–93.

11. *The Oxford Book of Modern Verse*, ed. W. B. Yeats (Oxford: Oxford University Press, 1936), xxxiv.

12. *The Complete Prose Works of Matthew Arnold: Philistinism in England and America*, vol. 10, ed. R. H. Super (Ann Arbor: University of Michigan Press, 1974), 190–93.

13. William Shakespeare, *Hamlet*, Arden Edition, ed. Harold Jenkins (London: Methuen, 1982), 1.2.85–86.

14. Ibid., 1.2.92–97.

15. John Crowe Ransom, *The World's Body* (1938; repr. Baton Rouge: Louisiana State University Press, 1968), 33, 35.

16. Elaine Scarry, *The Body in Pain: The Making and Unmaking of the World* (New York: Oxford University Press, 1985), 162.

17. See A. Dwight Culler, "Matthew Arnold and the Zeitgeist," in *Matthew Arnold*, ed. Harold Bloom (New York: Chelsea House, 1987), 115–17.

18. Arnold, *On the Classical Tradition*, 33.

19. Ibid., 31.

20. Ibid., 33.

21. John P. Farrell, "Matthew Arnold's Tragic Vision" in *Matthew Arnold: A Collection of Critical Essays*, ed. David J. DeLaura (Englewood Cliffs, N.J.: Prentice Hall, 1973), 112.

22. Arnold, *On the Classical Tradition*, 35.

23. "Memorial Verses" in *The Poems of Matthew Arnold* (New York: Longman, 1979), 239.

24. "Empedocles on Etna," ibid. quotations are from section II, lines 321–22, 360, 291.

25. W. H. Auden, "Matthew Arnold."

26. See Murray Krieger's distinction between "tragedy" and "tragic vision" in *The Tragic Vision* (1960; repr. Baltimore: Johns Hopkins University Press, 1973), 2–5.

27. Theodor Adorno, *Aesthetic Theory*, trans. C. Lenhardt (London: Routledge, 1984), 27–28.

28. Georg Lukács, *The Theory of the Novel*, trans. Anna Bostock (Cambridge: MIT Press, 1985), 45.

29. Stephen Booth, *King Lear, Macbeth, Indefinition, and Tragedy* (New Haven: Yale University Press, 1983), 85.

30. Karl Jaspers, *Was ist Philosophie* (München: dtv, 1980), 385.

8

ROBINSON JEFFERS'
AESTHETIC OF PAIN

NATURE

> But Nature . . . is inexorable and immutable;
> she never transgresses the laws imposed upon her,
> or cares a whit whether her abstruse reasons and
> methods of operation are understandable to men.
>
> —Galileo, *Letter to the Grand Duchess Christina*

Like Arnold's speaker in "Stanzas from the Grande Chartreuse," Jeffers describes one of his characters as "lost between past and future just as the present world is."[1] And in his essay "Poetry: Gongorism and a Thousand Years," Jeffers echoes Arnold's similar prophetic stance, declaring with characteristic disenchantment:

> The present is a time of high civilization rapidly declining; it
> is not a propitious period for any of the arts; men's minds are
> a little discouraged, and are too much occupied with meeting
> each day's distractions or catastrophe.

Poetry, he goes on, must "break sharply away from the directions that are fashionable in contemporary poetic literature," ". . . there is no final reason why great poetry should not be written by someone, even today," although, Jeffers concedes, ". . . greatness is strange, unexpected and sometimes repellent. . . ."[2] Similarly, in his Foreword to *The*

115

Selected Poetry, Jeffers demands that poetry "concern itself with permanent things and the permanent aspects of life"; ". . . this excludes much of the circumstances of modern life, especially the cities." One of the strange and permanent things to be reclaimed in Jeffers' austere introduction is a certain "substance and sense, and physical and psychological reality." The "modern French poetry" or the "'most' modern of the English Poetry," Jeffers notes, is "in terror of prose," and "trying to save its soul . . . giving up its body," becoming "slight and fantastic, abstract, unreal, eccentric."[3] His subject, he recalls in one of his later poems, is the incomparably more solid and certain material world of mountains and ocean, rocks and water, beasts and trees. The human characters—perhaps in allusion to their decadent French and English relatives—play only the roles of "symbolic interpreters."[4]

Jeffers' characters do not submit too readily to their symbolic role. But while their resistance to Jeffers' materialist poetic may amount to tragedy, their suffering—given the immense temporal and spatial dimensions of Jeffers' universe—is almost invisibly implied, almost instantly subsumed or sublated in the eternal rhythms of a vast, sublimely purposeless natural process.

> The gods of Greece are dead, there is pathos in them but no poetry; the customs of Greece are dead, there is pathos in them but no poetry; Homer and the race he sired are alive, because light and darkness, mountains and sea, humanity and its passions, are permanent establishments.[5]

These "permanent establishments" will be claimed as the poetic potential of the Monterey coast: "[t]his coast crying out for tragedy like all beautiful places" (1:209).[6] Here Homer's spirit can be rediscovered in "the people living—amid magnificent unspoiled scenery—essentially as they did in the Idyls of the Sagas, or in Homer's Ithaca."[7] But Jeffers does not forget that Homer's race has since been subject to severe revaluation. Copernicus's and Darwin's discoveries, as one of Jeffers' characters explains,

> "pushed man
> Out of his insane self-importance and the world's
> navel, and taught him his place."[8]

If Arnold's "excellent action" sought to reassign man a central place in a moral universe, in Jeffers' work Arnold's "excellent action" is the "timeless excellence of things" (2:282): neo-classicism becomes philosophic materialism. While walking in the Oxfordshire fields during his stay in Great Britain in 1929, Jeffers recounts—in consciously anti-Victorian terms, it seems—that the landscape appeared in a "soft alien twilight / Worn and weak with too much humanity" (2:128):

> I remembered impatiently
> How the long bronze mountain of my own coast,
> Where color is no account and pathos ridiculous, the
>   sculpture is all. . . .
>
> (2:128)

The philosophic equivalent of this visual and philosophic difference makes Jeffers' world one that is not only post-Christian, but explicitly non-European, a world whose cultural and spiritual orientation is to "gray stars no Scottish nor Palestinian uplands but the godless hills of America / Like vacant-eyed bison lying toward the sea . . ." (2:352). Jeffers' movement from Europe to America, as Henry Wells observes, proceeds from the romantic tradition of pictorial representation to the sculpturesque style of a poetry that reclaims the world not as mother but as stepmother.[9]

> What I see is the
> enormous beauty of things, but what I attempt
> Is nothing to that. I am helpless toward that.
> It is only to form in stone the mold of some ideal
>   humanity that might be worthy to *be*
> Under that lightning. Animalcules that God (if he
>   were given to laughter) might omit to laugh at.
>
> (1:392)

Like the characters' tragedy, the artist's sculpture is a paradox, no more than a way of returning the pain of feeling to the "man-destroying beauty" of nature. ". . . [A]ll the arts lose virtue / Against the essential reality . . ." (1:110). Faced with this overwhelming fate, which we meet in Jeffers' work in the form of appropriately vast and sublime landscapes and geologic concepts of time, any human gesture, whether artistic or existential, is almost instantly obliterated:

> . . . I believe this hurt will be healed
> Some age of time after mankind has died,

Then the sun will say "What ailed me a moment?" and
      resume
The old soulless triumph. . . .

                                             (2:166)

But it is "a hurt" nevertheless—a hurt that articulates the paradox, calling forth, rendering visible the frail, brief existence of human kind.
"Without strain there is nothing," cries the hanged God, Jeffers' representation of a Schopenhauerian will to life: "Without pressure, without
conditions, without pain, / Is peace; that's nothing, not being . . . I have
chosen / Being, therefore wounds, bonds, limits and pain . . ." (2:482).
Human life need only submit to the amoral, irreducible principle of pain
according to which "No life / Ought to be thought important in the
weave of the world, whatever it may show of courage or endured pain;
/ It owns no other manner of shining . . . but to bear pain" (2:242).

THE SHINING

The presence of God "shines" indiscriminately in all phenomena: "each
atom has related atoms, and hungry emptiness around him to take / His
little shining cry and cry it back." But while God claims, "I am all, the
emptiness and all, the shining and the night" (2:481), Jeffers' characters
discover, tantalizingly, that they are yet "More shining than the other
animals." For if ". . . at the stricken moments" Jeffers' characters "can
shine terribly against the dark magnificence of things" (2:278), their terrible shining illuminates only the illusion of significance, of self, or of
meaning. Whether the word "shining," frequently used by Jeffers, signifies either lamp or mirror, light or reflection, epiphany or appearance,
ecstasy or illusion, these differences are all sublated in the totality of
nature.

The merely "seeming" signification of human life is played out in
Jeffers' poetic narratives in the texture of a vast semiotic landscape, signifying the eternal rhythms of ruin and restoration, vision and revision,
for "God [is] the exact poet, the sonorous / Antistrophe of desolation in
the strophe multitude." In its apocalyptic sum and total, "civilization
and the other evils" run their aesthetic course: they "remain / Beautiful
in the whole fabric, excesses that balance each other / Like the paired
wings of a flying bird" (2:310).

The flying bird appears in Jeffers' work repeatedly as the caged eagle or hawk, one of its wings broken, the divine natural balance temporarily out of joint. In a section of *Cawdor*, the caged eagle is eventually killed and the bird's death dream, prophetic and surreal, envisions a restoration of a sublime natural harmony. After pitifully eeking out its plot, toiling in the vain dialectic between civilization and other evils, the large-writ syntax of *Cawdor* suddenly contracts to intense lyrical caesura. When the caged eagle is shot,

> The great dark bird leaped at the roof of the cage
> In silence and struck the wood; it fell, then suddenly
> Looked small and soft, folded in its wings.
>
>   (*Cawdor* 99)

Eventually the lyrical small and soft, folded wings unfold as the eagle in its death-dream

>   . . . rose
> Possessing the air over its emptied prison,
> The eager powers at its shoulders waving shadowless
> Unwound the ever-widened spirals of flight
>
>   . . .

> Higher still, and saw the mountain dividing
> Canyon of its captivity (that was to Cawdor
> Almost his world) like an old crack in a wall,
> Violet-shadowed and gold-lighted; the little stain
> Spilt on the floor of the crack was the strong forest;
> The grain of sand was a Rock. A speck, an atomic
> Center of power clouded in its own smoke
> Ran and cried in the crack; it was Cawdor; the other
> Points of humanity had neither weight nor shining. . . .
>
>   (*Cawdor* 100)

Jeffers' philosophical perspective from "the height and desert space of unbreathable air" here stations itself beyond suffering, beyond darkness or shining, beyond difference. "Cold at heart [and] incapable of burning" (*Cawdor* 99), the dead eagle views nature from a temporal and spatial distance so vast that Cawdor's world appears as the scattered emblems of an enormous post-historical script, read through the eyes, as it were, of a god: the canyon is "an old crack in a wall," the forest a "little stain spilt on the floor," the rock is a "grain of sand," Cawdor is "a speck, an atomic / Center of power clouded in its own smoke." And yet, Cawdor's "shining" offers a small tortuous aperture in the dark magnificence of things, and briefly—for the duration of his suffering—converts the vast divine perspective to human dimension.

THE UNAVAILABILITY OF TRAGEDY

When Cawdor at the very end of the poem blinds himself, he unwittingly individualizes the unconscious blind will to life:

> All that lives [is] maimed and bleeding, caged or in blindness,
> Lopped at the ends with death and conception, and shrewd
> Cautery of pain on the stumps to stifle the blood. . . .
>
> (*Cawdor* 101–2)

Cawdor's inability to commit suicide and his ersatz mutilation suggest that Jeffers' human protagonists must find their suffering inescapable and their narratives interminable. While the eagle's death transcends suffering, Cawdor becomes the miniature exemplar of Jeffers' adaptation of Schopenhauer's blind will to life.

> . . . the archetype
> Body of life a beaked carnivorous desire
> Self-upheld on storm-broad wings: but the eyes
> Were spouts of blood; the eyes were gashed out; dark blood
> Ran from the ruinous eye-pits to the hook of the beak
> And rained on the waste spaces of empty heaven.
>
> (*Cawdor* 101)

What is denied to the human protagonist is a transcendence of suffering by accepting suffering as necessity, as epiphany, or as ecstasy of a principle of existence that exceeds human comprehension while demanding human participation. The last act of such acquiescence to merely material existence in a merely material universe would have been death, and death would have been the only embodiment of a truth beyond the illusions of human value and meaning. When this embodiment is refused by Cawdor, he becomes incurably human, civilized to the core. His refusal of death has its reasons in the dimensions of meaning and metaphysics, in the genre of tragedy itself, to which Cawdor through his self-blinding accidentally aspires. His allusion to Oedipus's similar self-mutilation seems at first confirmed by Fera, who is asked to play a part in this revised fragment of *Oedipus Rex* by becoming the Antigone who would "lead me by the hand" (*Cawdor* 109). But Cawdor himself deplores such allusions to tragic significance, or to moral responsibility, as "a pitiful self-indulgence"; he lacked "the strength to do nothing" (*Cawdor* 109). In his blindness he sees that the the beaked carnivorous desire of being inexplicably demands metaphysics, meaning, self-indulgent fictions. These are forms of God's self-torture, "a necessary / Ecstasy in the run of the cold substance . . ." (*Cawdor* 102). It is in such failed transcendence of suffering, and in such refusal of acquiescence to Jeffers' inhumanism, that his characters acquire their "shining."

As in *Cawdor*, the allegorical vehicle of transcendence is frequently the flying bird. Orestes in "The Tower Beyond Tragedy," for example, attempts "a fairer object" than to "waste inward / Upon humanity" (1:175). In order to fulfill his desire he will "fly like a freed hawk" and enter "the life of the brown forest / And the great life of the ancient peaks, the patience of stone . . ." (1:176–77). But such mystical sublation of individual suffering undermines representation itself: ". . . how can I express the excellence I have found . . ."? ". . . they have not made words for it" (1:177).

In "Give Your Heart to the Hawks," Lance's longing for punishment (2:372) resembles Cawdor's initial claims for justice: "'Justice. Justice. / Justice,'" Cawdor mutters, "but the third time of saying it the word / Was pithed of meaning and become useless" (*Cawdor* 68). Similar to Cawdor's murder of his son, Lance's crime of fratricide cannot be redeemed by any justice, either human or divine. The gods of Greece are dead and so are the customs of Greece; the hero is the statuesque "blind marble pillar stone" (2:368), the dispirited remnant of a post-Christian, post-classical age in which religious or moral jurisdiction is unavailable. "They had heroes for companions," Jeffers writes in "Soliloquy," "But you have invoked the slime in the skull, / The lymph in the vessels" (1:215). Thus, Lance should learn to abandon his aspiration to tragic status and embrace the sheer pain of existence, a cogito thrust at him by

> ". . . all
> The fire-maned stars like stallions in a black pasture,
>   each one with his stud of plunging
>   . . . and universe after
>   universe beyond them, all shining, all alive."

Hence Helen's question:

> "Do you think all *that* needs us? Or any evil we have done
> Makes any difference? We are part of it,
> And good is better than evil, but I say it like a prayer
> That if you killed him, the world is all shining."
>
> (2:374)

In an ultimate divine synthesis, nature's indifferent deconstruction of good and evil, other and self, annuls, Helen observes, "any difference." It is this dionysiac insight into the void, "the waste spaces of heaven," that throws into relief the moral and metaphysical groundlessness of Jeffers' characters. They are characters wrought by what Nietzsche would call "the truly tragic artist": "like a prodigal deity of individuation, he creates his characters—a far cry from mere imitation of nature—. . . then engulfs this entire world of phenomena, in order to reveal behind it a sublime esthetic joy in the heart of original Oneness."[10]

Lance in "Give Your Heart to the Hawks" is a case in point. His tragic role is presaged in the first part of the narrative in the allegory of the slow death of lobsters in boiling water; they ". . . Writhe at the sky, lives unable to scream" (2:317). Lance should bear his role in this way, "unhelped" (2:333) and "in lonely silence" (2:331), as he should have learned from the caged and dying hawk. But the nobility of a dying animal is denied to Lance who, being more than beast and less than a dionysian hero, cannot bear his fate in silence (2:388). Fayne, who develops into the spokeswoman of Jeffers' aesthetic, periodically invokes the "purifying" vistas of nature, urging Lance to a perspective from which he would judge his act as indifferent. "Where you and I / Have come to," she suggests near the end of "Give Your Heart to the Hawks," "is a dizzy and lonely place on a height; we have to peel off / Some humanness here or it will be hard to live" (2:404). But Fayne's vision of such sublime resolution of all worldly dialectic cannot assert itself against Lance's anachronistic guilt. This is the burden of a humanist tradition in Jeffers' narratives that will define the inhumanist position as unattainable through human action. Jeffers' "dizzy and lonely place"— attained by the death-dream of the caged eagle—is located on a height on which Jeffers' tragic hero will eventually be seen performing the death dance of the caged hawk, "Grotesque in action as the blackcock at dawn / Making his dance of love . . ." (2:373).

God's laughter (a possibility entertained in "An Artist") would have

lent suffering the value of a divine moral spectacle. But the sparsely pop-
ulated coastline where "men are few" (2:310) does not provide the social substitute for the absence of God, as is the case in Greek drama. The
desolation of Jeffers' California landscapes is therefore symbolically
functional, withholding the metaphysical referent that would enable individual suffering to be "reread in terms of a collective or communally
shared objectification."[11] Sent out into "the godless hills of America"
(2:352), Jeffers' characters signify nothing but their signifying.

If at the end of their narrative journey, Jeffers' characters see the
hanged God, the principle of being, in the incontestable reality of their
flesh, they earn their supreme vision only through their reluctant renunciation of all cultural and spiritual illusions. That includes as well the
narrative of their suffering. In light of this dionysian principle, their plot
is condemned to futility, the human cry silenced even if the human cry
paradoxically constitutes part of the self-consuming God. "Pain and
their endless cries," declares the self-torturing God, "How they cry to
me; but they are I" (2:481).

The teleology of Jeffers' long narrative poems, then, is the illusory
plot of human desire, dragged out over scores of pages towards a
hoped-for opening in an always closed, self-referential universe. As narrative types, Jeffers' characters must endure time in timelessness, they
must suffer their body as the body of a god. The incestuous self-referral
of their suffering both mirrors and completes the grander solipsism of
nature. Their desire to objectify their suffering in a bodiless idea, in justice, meaning, redemption, anything other than the sublimely material
nature of existence, inevitably drives them back to despirited matter
and being. Their desire for transcendence is thwarted by a principle
fiercely bent on foiling any escape from body to soul, from substance
and sense to the slight and fantastic, abstract, unreal, or eccentric that
Jeffers condemned in modern French and English poetry. Devoid of any
metaphysical or moral aperture other than its own phenomenal "shining," suffering appears in Jeffers' work as a radically reductive, fundamental, and in that respect, irreducibly natural phenomenon.

Jeffers' aesthetic aspires to be nothing but nature itself, refusing to
present itself as a transcendence of nature. "Here is the pain in myself
and all. Here is reality" (2:473), Gudrun concludes in "At the Birth of
an Age." Self-evident, unwilled and beyond doubt, suffering is as material as earth, and as resplendent as God, proof that man's origin and destiny is in nature. Human suffering finds itself therefore always already
implied and almost instantly obliterated in a larger universal suffering,

resolved without remainder in the self-sufficiency of time and space. Whether in the small radius of self or in the vast dimensions of nature, pain is a universal aesthetic principle, an inescapable circle of closure, where wounds are bonds and pain is limit: if "I have chosen / Being," declares the hanged God, "therefore wounds, bonds, limits and pain" (2:482)—therefore too, if Reave Thurso's pain "ever ended," he says, "I'd have to . . . burn my fingers with matches." Helen's response is in tune with the disinterest of aesthetic perfection: "I have not one grain of comfort / To answer with" (2:240). The tragedy of Jeffers' characters is their function in the ecstatic-aesthetic self-consummation of pain—pain as God. Their interiority is the exteriority of God. Incapable of projecting their pain unto an external order, they suffer themselves in a profoundly autonomous anonymity.

Although Jeffers presents a world unredeemed by transcendence, his reduction of culture to its primordial origins in pain implies a revisionary inauguration of epistemology and existential value. Suffering offers itself as irrefutable presence, material center from which to begin a reconstruction of human significance, even if such "significance" must appear doubtful or under erasure, since it cannot be defined other than in material terms. "I torture myself / To discover myself" (2:482) declares Jeffers' God, and the same epistemology is imposed on his characters. By providing us with innumerable myths and instances of suffering, Jeffers invents a modern tragic genre without the traditional Western self-delusions of magnitude, morality, and metaphysics. Beginning with pain, that inaugural and most primitive of human experiences, he articulates an epistemology of tragic value that might account for the very materiality and meaninglessness of suffering itself. Jeffers' refusal to perpetuate humanistic structures and their deferral of suffering thus compels the spectator or reader to admit his/her own vulnerability, drawing us into a more subjective, less mediated, intimacy with suffering itself.

Notes

1. *The Selected Letters of Robinson Jeffers*, ed. Ann N. Ridgeway (Baltimore: Johns Hopkins Press, 1968), 246.

Several critics have drawn attention to similarities between Jeffers and Arnold. In "Such Counsels He Gave to Us: Jeffers Revisited" *Parnassus: Poetry in Review*, 6 (fall/winter 1977): 185, Vernon Young refers to Jeffers' poetry as "the answer to 'Dover Beach.'" H. S. Commager notes echoes of Arnold in Jeffers. See *The American Mind* (New Haven: Yale University Press, 1950; repr.

1974), 131. See also Bill Hotchkiss, *Jeffers: The Sivaistic Vision* (Auburn, Calif.: Blue Oak Press, 1975) where Hotchkiss quotes Arnold's Preface and compares Jeffers to Arnold in terms of Arnold's advocacy for "an excellent action" (204).

2. Robinson Jeffers, "Poetry: Gongorism and a Thousand Years," *New York Times Book Review*, 18 Jan. 1948; repr. (Los Angeles: The Ward Ritchie Press, 1949), 4.

3. Robinson Jeffers, *The Selected Poetry of Robinson Jeffers* (New York: Random House, 1938), Foreword.

4. Robinson Jeffers, *The Beginning and the End and Other Poems* (New York: Random House, 1963), 50.

5. S. S. Alberts, *A Bibliography of the Works of Robinson Jeffers* (New York: Random House, 1933), 110–11.

6. *The Collected Poetry of Robinson Jeffers,* Volumes One (1920–1928) and Two (1928–1938), ed. Tim Hunt (Stanford: Stanford University Press, 1995). References are given in the text by volume and page.

7. Jeffers, *Selected Poetry,* Foreword.

8. Robinson Jeffers, *The Double Axe and Other Poems* (1948; rpt. New York: Liveright, 1977), 72.

9. Henry W. Wells, *The American Way of Poetry* (New York: Columbia University Press, 1943), 152–53. See also Robinson Jeffers, *Cawdor and Medea* (New York: New Directions, 1970), 29. References to *Cawdor* are indicated in the text.

10. See Alberts, *Bibliography,* 110.

11. Friedrich Nietzsche, *The Birth of Tragedy* and *The Genealogy of Morals,* trans. Francis Golffing (New York: Doubleday, 1956), 133.

12. Elaine Scarry, *The Body in Pain: The Making and Unmaking of the World* (New York: Oxford University Press, 1985), 288.

9

LYRIC SUFFERING IN W. H. AUDEN AND IRVING FELDMAN

AUDEN'S "MUSÉE DES BEAUX ARTS"

> His boy
> Icarus might have been here, in the picture,
> And almost was—his father had made the effort
> Once, and once more, and dropped his hands;
> he could not
> Master his grief that much.
>
> —Virgil, *The Aeneid*

In the sixth book of Virgil's *Aeneid*, Aeneas lands his fleet at Cumae's coastline where he seeks entrance into the underworld. At its gate are the elaborate carvings of Daedalus: scenes of his former life at the court of Minos in Crete and of his son Icarus who had plunged into the sea after their escape from Crete. But the scene of Icarus's fall into the sea had been left unfinished by Daedalus. Virgil implies the difficulties of Daedalus's artistic task when Aeneas and the Sybil stand mutely arrested before the fragment of that last scene: "The story held them; / They would have studied it longer . . ."—if no messenger had interrupted them. Since Virgil arranges for Aeneas's timely distraction, and since

127

Daedalus's repeated effort and failure to "Master his grief . . ." produced only a fragment, others less emotionally embroiled than Daedalus would have to complete his work and others less duty bound than Aeneas would henceforth have to study that scene.

Auden's celebrated "Musée des Beaux Arts" combines both responses, that of the Old Masters and that of the poet as belated visitor to scenes of suffering.

> About suffering they were never wrong,
> The Old Masters: how well they understood
> Its human position; how it takes place
> While someone else is eating or opening a window or just
>   walking dully along;
> How, when the aged are reverently, passionately waiting
> For the miraculous birth, there always must be
> Children who did not specially want it to happen, skating
> On a pond at the edge of the wood:
> They never forgot
> That even the dreadful martyrdom must run its course
> Anyhow in a corner, some untidy spot
> Where the dogs go on with their doggy life and the
>   torturer's horse
> Scratches its innocent behind on a tree.
>
> In Brueghel's *Icarus*, for instance: how everything turns
>   away
> Quite leisurely from the disaster; the ploughman may
> Have heard the splash, the forsaken cry,
> But for him it was not an important failure; the sun shone
> As it had to on the white legs disappearing into the green
> Water; and the expensive delicate ship that must have seen
> Something amazing, a boy falling out of the sky,
> Had somewhere to get to and sailed calmly on.[1]

Perhaps Auden was right. The Old Masters understood the human position of suffering. How it always takes place while someone is eating or opening a window or just walking dully along. How everything turns away quite leisurely. Auden's "Musée des Beaux Arts" is thus firstly not an ironic response to Virgil but the sad acknowledgment of the terrible anonymity of suffering. Then the poem also addresses the question of

Landscape with the Fall of Icarus by Pieter Brueghel the Elder
(Musées royaux des Beaux-Arts de Belgique)

spectatorship, of aesthetic distance, and of aesthetic representation. The human position of the sufferer elicits acknowledgment of the human position of the painter, poet, spectator, reader.

One such reader, Irving Feldman, found Auden's opening lines offensive, prompting the question: "Sir, respectfully, is it possible / ever to be *right* about 'suffering?'"[2] The question is audibly rhetorical: *right* is the wrong word. Feldman's argument for the authentic rather than the merely aesthetic is stridently sarcastic; his strategic cuttings and pastings of quotations mock Auden's didacticism and deference to the Old Masters:

> Schoolmaster Auden gave them full marks,
> "the Old Masters," for having understood
> "about suffering" its "human position."
> The view from Mt. Lectern was clear. They were,
>   he noted, "*never wrong.*"
>   One is pleased to see
> things put in place, grateful for instruction
> —though words like his might well inspire Job
> with ruddied fingernails once more to rasp
> excruciating music from festers and boils.
>   . . .
> I mean sir, our suffering is no
> Nativity, is never legendary
> Like Innocents slaughtered, Icarus plunging.
> We lack that consolation. *Our* suffering
>   is nameless (like us) and newly whelped
>   and dying just to claim us for itself.[3]

Does Auden's poem deserve this denunciation? Is the aesthetic distance of Auden's speaker indeed a moral distance as well? Is Auden turning towards the disaster or is he turning away? Or is Feldman's moral indignation already audible in the terrible calm of Auden's observations? The deferment of references—from poem to painting and from painting to legend and from poet to painter and from there to the spectator, and from there to the reader—complicate such questions about the moral accountability of art.

Three paintings by Brueghel are mentioned in Auden's poem, but only Brueghel's *Landscape with the Fall of Icarus* is named. The other two paintings are *The Census in Bethlehem* and *The Massacre of the Innocents*. If for nothing else, Auden's poem is remarkable for its effective condensation of three large canvases into the somewhat accidental economy of twenty-one lines. Faithful to Brueghel, Auden represents suffering as an almost indistinguishable part of ordinary life. Like the paintings, "Musée des Beaux Arts" refers to the abundance of the casual, unintended, accidental, marginal incidents that constitute quotidian and legendary life alike. In life—ours or theirs, quotidian or legendary—suffering always involves "someone else," it happens in "a corner, some untidy spot" while some "expensive delicate ship" has "somewhere to get to."

The list of the gratuitous that is assembled in Auden's poem to parody the pathos of suffering or the notions of tragic necessity, clashes, as does Brueghel's painting, with Ovid's original dramatization of Icarus's fall and drowning. Gazing "in absolute amazement" at the flight of Daedalus and his ill-fated son, Ovid's fisherman, shepherd, and ploughman cry out, "They must be gods!"[4] and the crime of hubris stands accused. Divine retribution must follow. The astonished gaze of Ovid's bucolic spectators[5] thus assigns to Icarus a tragic role in a divine spectacle. In Auden's poem, the ploughman's worldly indifference and the sun's equitable disinterest mute Icarus's forsaken cry; his pain is anonymous, unshared, unimportant, accidental. The world turning away in Auden's "Musée des Beaux Arts" dooms Icarus to fall into a world without gods, without trespass, and without tragedy. His legendary fall is summed up in Auden's perfectly minimal analogy to Brueghel's one and half legs. Icarus's fall is out of legendary, tragic contexts into the margins of a modern text.

As Michael Riffaterre notes, Auden's delegation of the task of valorization to the expensive delicate ship which "must have seen / Something amazing, a boy falling out of the sky" echoes Ovid's "absolute amazement" but displaces what were in Ovid's text *human* emotions onto an indifferent thing. The ship, in its incongruously costly and frail appearance, "leaving as it were the scene of the accident," parodies the unperturbed self-sufficiency of the beautiful. Leading straight away from any notions of moral involvement, the destination of the ship is "somewhere" which is everywhere, which bestows a thoroughly democratic value on aesthetic purpose: all events are equally valid of perception.[6] Meanwhile Icarus's "forsaken cry" goes unheard, and the boy's "white legs" disappear in a mere painterly or writerly hint. They seem (as has been widely noted) merely painted against their painted background.

The equanimity of Auden's observations, a succession of how's— "how well they understood"; "how it takes place"; "how . . . there always must be children"; and "how everything turns away"—now point either to the absence of any valorization of the events in the paintings or to a delicate emotional adjustment to the anonymity of suffering. The speaker notes with distance but therefore perhaps with terror, that everything—the children, the dogs and horses—is there not by purpose but by accident. Auden's phrase, "how every*thing* turns away," denotes everything's essential indifference, including the aesthetic indifference of the speaker/spectator, who may now begin to understand his own accidental human position. From that position he may acknowledge the anonymity of the sufferer. In painting that distance, in eliciting the acknowledgment, the Old Masters were never wrong.

It is perhaps useful to consult another of Auden's poems, "In Time of War," which predates "Musée des Beaux Arts" by a few months (both poems were written at the end of 1938) to ponder further the spectator's "human position." The following quotation is the seventeenth sonnet of the twenty-seven sonnet sequence, "In Time of War":

> They are and suffer; that is all they do:
> A bandage hides the place where each is living,
> His knowledge of the world restricted to
> The treatment that the instruments are giving.
>
> And lie apart like epochs from each other
> —Truth in their sense is how much they can bear;
> It is not talk like ours, but groans they smother—
> And are remote as plants; we stand elsewhere.
>
> For who when healthy can become a foot?
> Even a scratch we can't recall when cured,
> But are boisterous in a moment and believe
>
> In the common world of the uninjured, and cannot
> Imagine isolation. Only happiness is shared,
> and anger, and the idea of love.

The closing qualifications added to happiness and love—the "only" of happiness and the "idea" of love—echo dejectedly over the unaccountable purposelessness with which the poem opens: "They are and suffer; that is all they do." The truth—a Nietzschean dionysian truth—is measured by "how much they can bear," it is a truth wholly "in their sense," that is to say, its meaning is reduced to excruciating bodily sensation.

Love, in the face of such radical reduction of truth to suffering, is merely an insubstantial platonism. Happiness and anger, likewise, are mentioned only for what they cannot do. They cannot share suffering. Separateness is our human position and *that* is acknowledged here. We always stand elsewhere—elsewhere being, as in "Musée des Beaux Arts," "in the common world of the uninjured." If there were any sense of shared destiny in such a common world it would have to be articulated as in Stanley Cavell's observation: ". . . if I do nothing because there is nothing to do . . . [if] I am in awe before the fact that I cannot do and suffer what is another's to do and suffer, then I confirm the final fact of our separateness. And that is the unity of our condition."[7]

What the poem accomplishes is an acknowledgment of the failure of knowledge of another's suffering. Concealed by bandages, by its own corporeality, but concealed also by the "treatment that the instruments are giving," the sufferers are "remote as plants," their being is entirely reduced to their suffering. The poem's wry ironies and matter of fact tone admit the appalling distance between the spectator and the sufferer. In the common world of the uninjured we "cannot imagine / Isolation." To know would be to deny the acknowledgment, to understand would be to deny the isolation, it would be to imagine, to make an image of suffering.

FELDMAN'S "BYSTANDER AT THE MASSACRE"

In "The Bystander at the Massacre," a poem which like Auden's exemplifies its case with Brueghel's painting *The Slaughter of the Innocents*, Feldman addresses the moral question again:

> The bystander at the massacre of innocents
> might have seen his own innocence among the dying
> had not his distance from the spectacle of slaughter
> (not all that far off really) given him the space
> to entertain a doubt. . . . [8]

Here the spectator's doubt is not entertained with Auden's semblance of ease as in "Musée des Beaux Arts." Feldman transforms Auden's tranquility of tone into urgency: the spectator who stands before *The Slaughter of the Innocents*, or rather before a photographic reproduction of that painting "stabs his finger into the photo / as if to verify something incredible there. . . ." His doubt is about the morality of his distant gaze, perhaps more generally about the aesthetic distance itself, which is amplified by the reproduction of the painting into a photograph. Indeed, this spatial distance doubled through an unreliable reproduction is comparable to Auden's own aesthetic distance mediated through a similarly unreliable voice.

Though Feldman's spectator would wish to minimize that distance in his parenthetical soliloquy, his status merely as spectator rather than as suffering participant (*and* his denial of his distance) amount to the loss of his innocence. We hear—perhaps with terror because we hear it with so little surprise—the same loss of innocence in Auden's calm observations: how well they understood, how it takes place, how there always must be children and how everything turns away.

The genre of Feldman's poem, being a poem about a photograph and a photograph about a painting, draws a large circle of aesthetic distance, widening the moral chasm and separating the spectator from a reality never quite realized. Thus, allowance is made for that nostalgia for reality or for the painter's proprietary and precedent relationship to reality which Auden ironizes and which Feldman dramatizes. "At precisely this distance—standing by, looking on," Feldman writes, "[the spectator] can't get close enough ever to be certain / reality isn't some extraordinary matter. . . ."

> For his is the spectator's essential doubtfulness,
> this feeling that among the sum of appearances
> something important doesn't appear, and may never.

Envious of the reality concealed in the representation and lost in that perception, Feldman's viewer eventually (in the next poem of the sequence) seeks to recover his innocence when he reverts to pure pretense, whose place is appropriately in "Disney Village":

> . . . and look, we're kids again!
> simple and pure in heart, healed, grateful that we're us
> —because right now nothing ever really happened,
> and life never asked more of us than innocence—
> our new eyes behold not absence but color, our ears
> hear Mickey's sweet squeak, Donald's stormy funny grumble!
>
> Mickey and Donald want us to be happy. . . .

The satiric wit of Feldman's style here indicts sentimentality as bad faith and as a means of ignorant complicity in the causes of suffering.

In both Feldman's and Auden's poems the spectator of various scenes of suffering discovers that the Bloomean predecessor, the Old Masters who turn in Feldman's poem into the Schoolmaster, has always already been there and thereby concealed among appearances the nature of suffering. But while Auden would think of this as inevitable and our distance therefore as tragically unavoidable, Feldman hears at just this moment a moral imperative: "our names screaming—always / in our ears" and "our names / beseeching us from the sky. . . ." The names beseeching us would call us back from our exile from reality, or, as Charles Altieri has suggested, from our insubstantiality.[9]

But the essential doubt of Feldman's spectator, his morally dubious human position vis-à-vis the concealment of reality in suffering will not ultimately sustain itself against that imperative. What Feldman will show, and what Auden perhaps fails to show, is that the spectator's doubt cannot be morally maintained and finally robs the spectator of his moral and human substance.

Confronted with an inexhaustible sum of appearances, whose total accounting will always leave out the reality of suffering, the spectator comes to realize his complicity in suffering and in the moral questions its representation raises. Yet again, the same ethic is implicit in Auden's poem. The ship's ship-in-a-bottle qualities, the painterly qualifications of white legs and green water have led Michael Riffaterre to associate this scene in "Musée des Beaux Arts" with Williams' red wheelbarrow beside the white chickens. Such association results in a reading of Auden's poem as poem, of art as art. But precisely in its aesthetic autonomy, as Theodor Adorno has suggested, art mirrors the autonomy of suffering, even if art morally disfigures what it reflects: "what detracts from the gravity of art is the fact that aesthetic autonomy as the image of suffering remains fundamentally uninvolved in suffering, the source of its gravity." [10]

In Auden's as well as in Feldman's poems we are reminded of that fundamental uninvolvement, whereas in Williams' "Red Wheelbarrow" we are not. To be reminded of a fundamental uninvolvement cannot result in pure aesthetic pleasure. Auden's aesthetic distance in "Musée des Beaux Arts" indicts our own human position as morally dubious: separated from the source of the gravity of our aesthetic experience, we cannot entertain our distance, or the knowledge across that distance, with the kind of undesirousness which is the ideal and ideological nature of aesthetic perception.

These observations might suggest that not all occasions of aesthetic experience are equal, and that the gravity of a certain occasion might call into question, if not into crisis, the aesthetic experience itself. If Auden's poem calls the aesthetic experience into question, Feldman's calls it into crisis. Both poems suggest, but Feldman's more urgently so, that a purposeless perception, a state of undesirous knowledge might not in all cases be affordable. John Crowe Ransom unabashedly admits that the aesthetic experience has something to do with economic security and leisure: ". . . we propose to study our object, when we are more than usually undesirous and free and find the time to become curious about the object as, actually something 'objective' and independent."[11] Arguing from the political opposition to Ransom's view, feminist critics have drawn our attention to "the relative tranquility of the tone" of certain privileged aesthetic positions.[12]

The moral and aesthetic problems of such positions become explicit at several junctures in Feldman's "All of Us Here" sequence. At one point in "The Bystander at the Massacre," the spectator steps back from the aforementioned dramatization of his "essential doubtfulness." Then Feldman asks the aesthetic question, very much modelled on Ransom's formula, whether our forms of attention are a mere "curiosity? or a kind of revery?" At the end of his poem, that doubt turns, in an act of what one might call epistemological greed, to envy of those who suffer, an envy of their certainty, their substantive subjectivity:

> —. . . our evasion expands to enormous
> complicity, explodes in the spectator's rage
> and demented scream for more bigger quicker death,
> and we rush toward the time when, not lifting a finger
> —and yet we may fairly claim it our creation,—
> we spectators are gathered into the act
> and—for a second's intimate stupendous fraction—
> everything is beyond any doubt real.

While I. A. Richards speaks of "the essence of Tragedy" in similar terms as the momentary falling away of the fictions by which we live,[13] Feldman insists that such unmediated vision comes about only through self-deception. Though momentarily we may be gathered into the act, we do not lift a finger.

NOTES

1. W. H. Auden, *The English Auden: Poems, Essays and Dramatic Writings,* ed. Edward Mendelson (London: Faber and Faber, 1977), 237.

2. Irving Feldman, "Just Another Smack," in *Teach Me, Dear Sister* (New York: Penguin/Viking, 1983), 34.

3. Ibid., 34.

4. Ovid, *Metamorphoses*, trans. Rolfe Humphries (Bloomington: Indiana University Press, 1955), 188.

5. See Michael Riffaterre, "Textuality: W. H. Auden's 'Musée des Beaux Arts,'" in *Textual Analysis: Some Readers Reading*, ed. Mary Ann Caws (New York: MLA, 1986), 5.

6. Ibid., 8.

7. Stanley Cavell, *Disowning Knowledge: In Six Plays of Shakespeare* (Cambridge: Cambridge University Press, 1987), 110.

8. Irving Feldman, *All of Us Here and Other Poems* (New York: Viking, 1986), 14.

9. Charles Altieri, "Confession and Simulacra in Irving Feldman's Poetry," in *The Poetry of Irving Feldman: Nine Essays*, ed. Harold Schweizer (Lewisburg: Bucknell University Press, 1992), 82.

10. Theodor Adorno, *Aesthetic Theory*, trans. C. Lenhardt (London: Routledge and Kegan Paul, 1984), 57.

11. John Crowe Ransom, *The World's Body* (1938; repr. Baton Rouge: Louisiana State University Press, 1968), 44.

12. Patrocinio Schweickart, "Reading Ourselves: Toward a Feminist Theory of Reading," in *Contemporary Literary Criticism*, ed. Robert Con Davis and Ronald Schleifer (New York: Longman, 1989), 122.

13. I. A. Richards, *Principles of Literary Criticism* (New York: Harcourt Brace Jovanovich, 1930), 246.

10

PAUL CELAN: SUFFERING IN TRANSLATION

EDWARD HIRSCH'S "PAUL CELAN ..."

The circumstances of Paul Celan's emigration from his native Bukovina (in today's Romania) are well known and quickly told. He was born as Paul Antschel in November 1920 and raised in a German-speaking, Jewish home. In 1938, he studied at the medical school in Tours and returned to Bukovina after one year to study Romance languages. In June of 1942, his parents were deported by the Nazis and murdered in the fall of the same year. Paul Antschel escaped but was sent to labor camps where he hauled debris and rocks. In 1947, he left for Bucharest, from there he went on to Vienna (where his first volume of poems, *Der Sand aus den Urnen,* was published); after six months in Vienna he left for Paris where he became a lecturer in German at the École Normale Supérieure until his suicide in 1970.

"Paris, 1948," the notation following Edward Hirsch's poem, "Paul Celan: A Grave and Mysterious Sentence,"[1] marks the date of Celan's arrival in Paris. The title is repeated in the penultimate, eighth stanza:

> And now here is a grave and mysterious sentence
> Finally written down, carried out long ago:
> At last I have discovered that the darkness

139

> Is a solitary night train carrying my parents
> Across a field of dead stumps and wildflowers
> Before disappearing on the far horizon,
> Leaving nothing much in its earthly wake
>
> But a stranger standing at the window
> Suddenly trying to forget his childhood. . . .

The sentence that was carried out must now be written down, even if writing is a sentencing again. Thus, writing forms "An ominous string / Of railway cars scrawled with a dull pencil / Across the horizon at dawn." Haunted by such memory and necessity, the speaker stands at the window of his "small apartment":

> Soon the streets will be awash with little bright
> Patches of oblivion on their way to school,
> Dark briefcases of oblivion on their way to work.
>
> Soon my small apartment will be white and solemn
> Like a blank page held up to a blank wall,
> A message whispered into a vacant closet. But
> This is a message which no one else remembers
> Because it is stark and German, like the silence,
> Like the white fire of daybreak that is burning
> Inside my throat. If only I could stamp it out!

Hirsch's poem movingly chronicles Celan's poetic destiny at the crucial point of his arrival in Paris, where the question of language—what language after the Holocaust? How to write after what happened?—must have stood out in exemplary clarity. Though Celan had already published his first volume in German, his residence in a French-speaking city must have recast the question whether German would remain Celan's poetic vehicle. Was it the appropriate language, capable of remembering or would it become the language of forgetting, would the stark German render the white fire of silence, would it bring speechlessness to speech? These are questions implicit in Hirsch's presentation of Celan's poetic calling as a blank page held up to a blank wall, as the speechlessness of the survivor held up to the silence of the dead. His poetic message—which Celan at a moment of more hopeful intentions likened to a "*Flaschenpost*," a message in a bottle[2]—is here at this point of silence before speech only whispered into an empty closet. Rarely has a poetic vocation stood in such hesitant and exemplary way before its linguistic destiny.

For Hirsch, to position Celan at a window, haunted by images of smokestacks and railway cars, rehearsing lines of "Death Fugue"—the "sickly, yellow film of sperm and milk" covering the buildings—envious or contemptuous of the bright patches of oblivion and the dark briefcases of forgetfulness outside, is to position Celan in a mental and linguistic no-man's-land. Though the outside-inside metaphors are inverted when Celan tells Yves Bonnefoy (as Olschner reports), "'*Vous êtes chez vous, dans votre langue, vos références, parmi les livres, les oeuvres que vous aimez. Moi, je suis dehors . . .*'" (You are at home in your own language, in your references, among your books, the works you love. I am outside; [my translation])[3] the same sense of linguistic exile is there. While the writing of German poetry by a Romanian Jew in a French-speaking city replicates in some sense the political dislocations of his own past life in his native Bukovina, German is at the same time the only continuity in these geographic, historic, and linguistic transformations.

CELAN'S GERMAN

> All of Celan's poetry is translated *into* German.
>
> —George Steiner, *After Babel*

> Where there is understanding,
> there is no translation but speech.
>
> —Hans-Georg Gadamer, *Truth and Method*

In his essay on Paul Celan's translations, Leonard Olschner quotes one of Celan's early poems,[4] *"Nähe der Gräber,"* written in the winter of 1942–43, where Celan asks his mother

> *Und duldest du, Mutter, wie einst, ach, daheim,*
> *den leisen, den deutschen, den schmerzlichen Reim?* [5]

> And, Mother, will you suffer, as once at home, the quiet, the German, the painful rhyme? (my translation)

"So much / ash to be blessed," Celan writes in his poem "Chymisch," but, Derrida asks, "How may one bless these ashes in German?"[6] How hospitable is the German language to a poet whose parents had been murdered by the Germans in the same winter?[7] In her introduction to *Last Poems*, Katherine Washburn quotes the biographer of Celan's early years, Israel Chalfen, as remembering Celan's own response to the problem of writing in German: "'Only in one's mother tongue can one express one's own truth. In a foreign language the poet lies.'"[8] Yet, Celan's residence in France imports the distance and estrangement of one whose mother might deny the request of *"Nähe der Gräber"* and whose mother tongue, like his native country, has been irreparably transformed by the Nazi and the subsequent Soviet occupations. Nevertheless, in his Bremen Address (1958) Celan writes:

> Only one thing remained reachable, close and secure amid all losses: language. Yes, language. In spite of everything, it remained secure against loss. But it had to go through its own lack of answers, through terrifying silence, through the thousand darknesses of murderous speech. It went through. It gave me no words for what was happening, but went through it. Went through and could resurface, "enriched" by it all.
>
> In this language I tried, during those years and the years after, to write poems: in order to speak, to orient myself, to find out where I was, where I was going, to chart my reality.[9]

Celan would likely share Maurice Blanchot's hope "in the materiality of language," where "the reality of the earth continues to exist," affirming "the presence of things before the *world* exists, their perseverance after the world has disappeared, the stubbornness of what remains when everything vanishes. . . ."[10] But the passage of language on its journey through a thousand darknesses of murderous speech proves difficult. Celan's poetry frequently renders the survival of language in allegories of the etymology of translation, *übersetzen*, to ferry across. When langauge arrives on the other side of darkness, on the whiteness of the blank page, it resurfaces enriched with blood, silence, murder, and history.[11] In the wounded, disfigured syntax of Celan's poetry, language is a "messenger of readable blood-clots . . ."

> *Lesbare Blutklumpen-Botin,*
> *herübergestorben, trotz allem,*
> *von wissenden Stacheldrahtschwingen*
> *über die unverrückbare*
> *Tausendmauer getragen.*[12]

Readable blood-clot-messenger, died hither, in spite of all,
borne across the immovable thousandwall by barbed wire
waves. (my translation)

"Glad for passage," Celan imagines in another poem a group of
refugees in a ferry, at their side is *"mitgewanderte[] Sprache"* (camp-
following language). But the ferry leaves a wake *"buchstabenähnlich"*
(letter-like),[13] suggesting the violent linguistic dislocations that would
consign Celan's post-structural *Schrift* to become the exemplary twentieth-
century allegory of the Jewish diaspora. Celan's poetry, as he puts it in
one poem, is written by the *"mit-/schreibende / Ferse,"* the "co-/writing
/ heel"[14]

> past the poison—
> palatinates, past the cathedrals
> . . .
>
> by the tinily flaring, the
> free punctuation marks of
> the sequestered writ that
> has dis-
> persed
> into the
> countless, un-
> utterable,
> to be uttered
> names. [15]

"German poetry is going in a very different direction from French
poetry," Celan replied to a questionnaire from a bookstore in Paris.
"No matter how alive its traditions, with most sinister events in its
memory, most questionable developments around it, it can no longer
speak the language which many willing ears seem to expect. Its language
has become more sober, more factual. It distrusts 'beauty.'"[16] No pre-
Holocaust images or metaphors, no traditional aesthetic, can render
what happened; art deserves Celan's contemptuous comment: "Nothing
but art and mechanics, nothing but cardboard and springs. . . . It is all
very fine to talk about art."[17] "If art is to survive the Holocaust—"
Shoshana Felman writes, "to survive death as a master—it will have to
break, in art, this mastery, which insidiously pervades the whole of culture and the whole of the esthetic project."[18]

As Celan's language goes through what happened, his German

must resemble the stones and debris he hauled in the labor camp, and the ashes and bones of the dead. "So don't talk to me about flowers," Hirsch writes,

> . . . those blind
> Faces of the dead thrust up out of the ground
> In bright purples and blues, oranges and reds.
> And don't talk to me about the gold leaves
> Which the trees are shedding like an extra skin:
> They are handkerchiefs pressed over the mouths
> Of the dead to keep them quiet. . . .

But how to remove the gold leaves of language? How to write in language without a history of language? How to write speechless poetry? How to write as a Jew in exile? How to write in German? How can one reappropriate a language in which one was silenced and exiled? Perhaps by forcing the same language to undergo the same exile and silence—to bear suffering and death in its own morphology and syntax—or, as Emmanuel Levinas writes, by "interrupting itself ceaselessly so as to let its other voice enter into these interruptions. . . ."[19] Or, as Celan explains in the "Meridian," to undo the poetic, to lead the poetic tropes *ad absurdum* so that gold leaves become "MERKBLÄTTER-SCHMERZ," "leaflets-pain,"[20] flowers become truth:

> A RUMBLING truth
> itelf has appeared
> among humankind
> in the very thick of their
> flurrying metaphors.[21]

"It is a 'greyer' language," Celan writes in his reply to the bookstore's questionnaire, "a language which wants to locate even its 'musicality' in such a way that it has nothing in common with the 'euphony' which more or less blithely continued to sound alongside the greatest horrors."[22] Celan's German thus becomes the language that resists the *Metapherngestöber*, the thick metaphoric forgetfulness of language. Rather it is a language that brings to speech the absence of those who have been murdered so that the Jew, the exile, the murdered would be meant, remembered, addressed by the same German in which they were forgotten, obliterated, erased.[23] Celan's poetry, Felman notes, strives "to subvert, to dislocate and to displace the very essence of esthetics as a *project of artistic mastery* by transforming poetry—as breakage of the word and as drifting testimony—into an inherent and unprecedented, testimonial *project of address*."[24] But will such address, mutilated and broken as it is, throw itself across the silence of the dead?

In his essay on Celan, Derrida points out that Jewish writing bears the mark of circumcision, it is the language of "ciphered wounds," or of "cut words," which makes Jewish writing universal, addressed to all: all poets, as Derrida declares after Marina Tsvetayeva, are Jewish: "the wound is . . . universal, a differential mark in language. . . ."[25] If such a language echoes in its very writing its ruptures, in its very speaking its speechlessness, in its words its silences—it must speak against itself.

ATEMWENDE

His poetry, Celan explains in the "Meridian," is the language of *Atemwende*, of the turning of breath. *Atemwende* is a duplicitous word, epitomizing in its metaphoricity the fundamental respiratory gesture of Celan's poetry: both breath and death, spirit and matter, word and silence. *Atemwende* is exemplified in the absurdity of an outrageous gesture of suicidal *Gegenschrift*, counter-writ,[26] or "*Gegenwort*," a "counter word," or "word against the grain" delivered by Büchner's Lucile from *Danton's Death*, quoted in the "Meridian." Lucile is Celan's impersonation of the counter-poetic. Though her undoing of language is her own undoing, though her defiant shout, "Long live the King" amounts to a self-betrayal (which is also the revelation of her self to her self), a sentence that is her death sentence, and although her "Long live the King" is immediately 'understood' by the revolutinary citizens who arrest her in the name of the Republic, such speaking, though suicidal, nevertheless amounts to a poetic liberation. Lucile's cry intimates that only by such extreme claims to language-as-resistance, only by means of its suicidal absurdity, can she name herself and plot her liberation from historic determination. That Lucile's liberation comes at the cost of a misunderstanding (the citizens believing her to be a monarchist) or that such liberation could only be achieved by murder, prompts Lacoue-Labarthe to speak of poetic language as catastrophe. Such catastrophe—begun with the turn of breath, continued in Celan's call for the transformation of mechanical art into sublime avant garde poetry, illustrated by Lucile's counter word, and culminating in a self-sentencing and suicidal "*Heimkehr*" (homecoming)—[27] now finds its most concentrated, *verdichtet*, existence, in Celan's language of choice: German.

Because it is a language of choice, Celan may speak it as counter-German in which German takes revenge on German, subverting, dissembling, and reassembling itself in a lawless linguistic freedom to which history itself has given licence. The most suggestive terms for this self-liberation of self and language are offered in George Steiner's brilliant remark:

> All of Celan's . . . poetry is translated *into* German. In the process the receptor-language becomes unhoused, broken, idiosyncratic almost to the point of non-communication. It becomes a "meta-German" cleansed of historical-political dirt and thus, alone, usable by a profoundly Jewish voice after the holocaust.[28]

By Steiner's definition of "good translations," an "alienness and felt 'at-homeness' remains unresolved, but expressive." A good translation finally is "elucidative strangeness."[29] These terms echo Celan's poetics of the "Meridian," where poetry is defined in terms of a dialogic movement to another, and finally in the arrival in "*etwas Unheimliches.*"[30] The translation, 'something uncanny' for "*etwas Unheimliches,*" is perhaps less descriptive of Celan's poetic ambition than Steiner's "elucidative strangeness" or the unresolved "alienness and felt 'at-homeness.'"

If Celan's language of translation is an exemplary instance of a language of suffering, a language not at home in its own writing, it is also the language where understanding is in question. Celan's work is remarkable for the way it puts understanding into question by presenting itself as a dialogic language, frequently exemplified in literalized references to the German word '*übersetzen,*' to ferry across, as for example in one of Celan's poems from *Atemwende* where the poem allegorizes Celan's linguistic destiny as a translation of *Wundgelesenes,* "wound-readings," "woundwords," or "reading-wounds":

> . . .
> *Die in der senk-*
> *rechten, schmalen*
> *Tagschlucht nach oben*
> *stakende Fähre:*
>
> *sie setzt*
> *Wundgelesenes über.*[31]

The upward punting ferry, in the vertical, narrow abyss of day, it carries across the reading of wounds. (my translation)

"The example of translation," as Gadamer notes, "makes us aware that language as the medium of understanding must be consciously created by an explicit mediation."[32] Perhaps Jewish writing in the wake of the Holocaust must necessarily express itself as explicit mediation, a recovery of language itself. It cannot be language as blissful oblivion that makes its quotidian use functional "alongside the greatest horrors." It must be a language under reconstruction, putting itself back together by borrowing its material from a tradition in ruins. Celan's halting, fragmentary, fissured style reflects this language-as-bricolage, as trial-language or meta-language, a language in which one is *dehors* (as Celan told Bonnefoy), outside, speaking it always as a foreign language. In "Conversation in the Mountains" Celan writes: ". . . for the Jew, you know, what does he have that he really owns that's neither borrowed nor lent and never returned . . . ?"[33]

When the poet mentally revisits the graves of the murdered in "The Straitening," he encounters the question of words and names. Can death be named in language? Can words serve as passage for the memory of the dead? Or does language interpose itself as an obstacle to such desire?

> The place where they lay, it has
> a name—it has
> none. They did not lie there. Something
> lay between them. They
> did not see through it.
> Did not see, no,
> spoke of
> words. . . .

In the next stanza we hear that "it is I, I, / I lay between you . . ." and the speaker becomes a means of passage for speech. "Your breathing / obeyed. . . ."[34] Animated by the breath of the dead, Celan's poetry recovers the words that lay between them. In a much later poem, we read: "The death / you still owe me, I / carry it / out"[35]—and we understand how difficult and suicidal the recovery of words has been. "He elected to write in German," Jed Rasula notes, "while being Rumanian and living in France, because his affinities with the victims of the Holocaust declared themselves most explicitly in the smaller linguistic gestures with which he *executed* the language from within."[36] The word "executed" is fitting and appropriately ambiguous: it not only implies the suicidal strain in Celan's language, but also indicates the paradoxically affirmative gesture inherent in language—even in the German language. The

German "*austragen*," "to carry out," connotes the sense of a period of gestation or labor so that we end up with the more tortuous paradox of a bringing of death to birth in language. But the speaking of death is the speaking of the unspeakable, requiring an *Atemwende*, a counter-speaking, or a speaking that encounters its own speechlessness. In his structural analysis of Celan's poetic fissures caused by the other's radical alterity, Krzysztof Ziarek speaks of "a 'translation' into words of what says itself only as the unsaid."[37] Or to say this yet in another way: writing in German is both rebirth and reburial of the dead, it is a return to the scene of the murder, it is an uncovering and recovering of a wound. To carry out, *austragen*, is thus one of the versions of Celan's translations, condensing Celan's ambiguous poetics of recovery and suicide.[38] We read in "The Straitening":

> . . .
> Years, years, a finger
> feels down and up, feels
> around:
> seams, palpable, here
> it is split wide open, here
> it grew together again—who
> covered it up?

There are perhaps two answers to that question. The first is implicit in Celan's neologisms, which are predominantly *Wortzusammensetzungen*, likened by Nina Cassian to "the union of organic cells."[39] The second answer is in that because *Wortzusammensetzungen* are only metaphoric coverings, always implying a gaping wound at the core, they remain metaphoric passages whose allegorical dramatizations are played out in Celan's address to a dialogic "you."

> *Zu*
> *Entziffernde du.*
>
> *Mit dir,*
> *auf der Stimmbänderbrücke, im*
> *Grossen Dazwischen,*
> *nachtüber.*[40]

> You, to be decifered. With you, on the bridge of the vocal cords, in the large inbetween, nightly. (my translation)

While this dialogic address is the chief poetic allegory of the "Meridian," there, as in Celan's poetry, the address remains unconsummated, unfinishable "in the large inbetween." The path from you to you is an impossible "*Heimkehr*" to a no-land, a u-topia. The poetic process is an "*unbefahrbares Schweigen*," an impassable silence.[41] The ferry to translate the speaker is the poem that does not exist, as Celan concludes in the "Meridian." Writing, as we read in the opening and closing lines of "The Straitening," is (always) a writing asunder—"(. . . / Grass. / Grass, / written asunder)"[42]—widening the wound at the core. In her Introduction to Celan's *Collected Prose*, Rosmarie Waldrop writes: "He can only hope that out of his insistence will come a new language which can fill the gap and include the other side."[43]

Thus, Celan's poetry seems finally less a "*project of address*," as Felman conceives of it, than a project of language. The other side is not (only) a historical "you," the addressee not (only) a reader but the implicit "you" by which language *as such* is possible—the you "meant" by language. Celan's new language, therefore, is not a new, revisionist political or historical project but rather a Benjaminian dream of pure language wherein German would be freed from its historical burdens so that it could speak again in self-forgetfulness—

> TO STAND in the shadow
> of the woundprints in the air
>
> To stand-for-no-one-and-nothing
> Unrecognized
> for you
> alone[ ][44]

. . . so that speaking itself, speaking for-no-one-and-nothing, Benjamin's *reine Sprache*, could be rescued to guarantee an inexhaustible reserve—after the world has disappeared . . . so that the speechless, the unspoken, could be spoken and affirmed again. Yet, throughout, Celan's language remains an unfinishable passage towards such a pure language, leaving the poem open like a wounded consciousness, a desire, or a freedom, unattained: "*du / kommst nicht / zu / dir*" (you do not come to yourself), which is reiterated as a rhetorical question in the "Meridian": "*Sind diese Wege nur Um-Wege, Umwege von dir zu dir?*" (are these [poetic] routes only detours, detours from you to you?). Even if the implied answer is yes, the voice itself becomes audible in this impossible address:

"Aber es sind ja zugleich auch . . . Wege, auf denen die Sprache stimm-haft wird . . ." (But these are at the same time the paths on which language becomes voice). The poetic expression of this miracle of poetic presence is in one of Celan's late poems from *Lichtzwang*:

> DURING THE DARK BLOWS I found out:
>
> you live towards me, nonetheless,
> in the standpipe,
> in the
> standpipe.[45]

As the little counter-word "nonetheless" (*dennoch*) asserts itself against an insurmountable, interminable linguistic detour, as the voice gropes towards some incomprehensible truth in language, Celan's poems all tragically deny a homecoming. His poems are always, as he points out in the "Meridian," "lonely and en route," uttered between a perpetual-parting and a never-arriving:

> I CAN STILL SEE YOU: an echo
> that can be groped towards with antenna
> words, on the ridge of
> parting.
>
> Your face quietly shies
> when suddenly
> there is lamplike brightness
> inside me, just at the point
> where most painfully one says, never.[46]

Yet again, in spite of a passage of translation that has become interminable, the dejected "never" is the beginning of speech. Where one most painfully says "never," the first affirmation has already been made.

Even if Celan's poetry amounts to a "*Genicht*,"[47] a neologism joining *Gedicht* and *nicht*, "poem" and "not" into one compound, a word that reiterates the silence of alterity, the *unbefahrbares Schweigen*—then nothing and silence are the conditions of speaking. For *Genicht* is not only the nihilistic, suicidal assent to Nothing but also the betrayal of the assent—for if it *speaks* of Nothing, how could the poem not speak against it? Thus, the act of speaking itself is the hope and substance of Celan's poetry, the materiality of his language, the presence of voice, *Atemwende*. Lucile, as Celan explains, has the ear to hear such speaking, such breath, because she does not listen to the talk of art:

Aber es gibt, wenn von Kunst die Rede ist, auch immer wieder jemand, der zugegen ist und . . . nicht richtig hinhört. Genauer: jemand, der hört und lauscht und schaut . . . und dann nicht weiss, wovon die Rede war. Der aber den Sprechenden hört, der ihn "sprechen sieht," der Sprache wahrgenommen hat und Gestalt, und zugleich auch . . . Atem, das heisst Richtung und Schicksal.

But when there is talk of art, there is often somebody who does not really listen. More precisely: somebody who hears, listens, and looks . . . and then does not know what it was about. But who hears the speaker, "sees him speaking," who perceives language as a physical shape and also, . . . breath, that is, direction and destiny. [48]

TRANSLATING CELAN

The translator's job, Celan's as well as Celan's translators', is thus to hear language itself, and in language the breath which is the gesture of a fundamental affirmation of speaking as such: the turn from breathlessness to breath, Celan's *Atemwende*. A listening to speaking itself requires as Celan (allusively?) notes *Konzentration* (concentration) and *Aufmerksamkeit* (attention).[49] In such listening there is no *Rede von Kunst*, no gratuitous hermeneutics but a deeper, perhaps thoroughly aesthetic perception without understanding. Krzysztof Ziarek articulates this in Heideggerian or Gadamerian terms: "It is a hermeneutics that, rather than simply reading and interpreting, attempts to deliver a message, to let it say itself, without covering or explaining away what remains baffling and other in it."[50] Good translations then—if Celan's poetics amounts to a theory of translation—ought not to understand as much as to hear the speaker, see him speak, perceive language as breath, direction, and destiny. If these requirements result in the lean whisper, the near breathlessness of Celan's poetry, it is the very near-silence of his poetry that bespeaks all the more the great labor implicit in such speaking—and listening.

And how do these requirements to translate the breath apply to the translator of Celan's poetry? How can these requirements apply at all if (as John Felstiner notes) "Celan's barest utterances can make so strong a call on us that in translating, one is tempted to interpret them"?[51] How to translate fate, how not to translate fact, if translation is always interpretation?[52] Michael Hamburger suggests that the translator's "attention is something other than what is normally meant by 'understanding'. I am by no means sure," he admits, "that I have 'understood' even those of his poems . . . which I have been able to translate over the years. . . ."[53] Indeed, the translator ought not to understand, so that Celan's own answerlessness would be carried over into other languages. But if it is the German language that is answerless, if his speechlessness is explicitly in the shame and failure of that very language,[54] how can another language appropriate such a linguistic, historic, and moral predicament?

The problems that I am alluding to are anticipated in the misprinting of the first edition of *Der Sand aus den Urnen*, published in Vienna in 1948, where the printers had 'understood' and 'corrected' what they deemed Celan's spelling mistakes: *unirdisch* (non-terraneous) becomes *unterirdisch* (sub-terraneous), *rauchendes Wasser* (smoking water) becomes *rauschendes Wasser* (streaming water) and so forth.[55] Since the well intended corrections obliterate Celan's neologisms and misunderstand his counterspeaking just as the Parisian Citizens in *Danton's Death* misunderstand Lucile's counterspeaking, Celan withdrew the volume. I find this sentencing of his first volume prophetic of the sentencing that Celan's poetry became. The death of that first volume resembles Lucile's suicidal speech as it foretells Celan's suicide.

Do English translations accelerate such destiny when they analytically reason apart Celan's synthetic neologisms, when *Durchbruchscheibe* becomes "pane for breaching," *Seinstrog* becomes "trough of being," *Beilschwärme* becomes "Hatchet-swarms," *Dunkelschläge* becomes "dark blows"? Perhaps *"das Unheimliche und Fremde"* (the uncanny and foreign),[56] the elucidative strangeness in Celan's neologisms ought to have remained in the legitimacy—however subversive—which the new words assume in their paradoxical appearance of solid verbal unity and outrageous, lawless freedom.[57] The uncanny strangeness, however, is made public, made explicit, drawn attention to, in the labor of the English reconstructions. Strangeness visible, understood, is perhaps no longer strange,[58] and Celan's translations are perhaps no longer translations when they occur in translation.

NOTES

1. Edward Hirsch, *Wild Gratitude* (New York: Knopf, 1992), 50–52.
2. Paul Celan, Ansprache anlässlich der Entgegennahme des Literaturpreises

der freien Hansestadt Bremen, in Paul Celan, *Gesammelte Werke*, 5 vols. (Frankfurt: Suhrkamp, 1983), 3:186.

3. Quoted by Leonard Olschner, "Anamnesis: Paul Celan's Translations of Poetry," *Studies in Twentieth Century Literature (STCL)* 12 (summer 1988): 170.

4. Ibid., 170.

5. Celan, *Gesammelte Werke*, 3:20.

6. Jacques Derrida, "Shibboleth" (for Paul Celan), in *Midrash and Literature*, ed. G. H. Hartman and S. Budick (New Haven: Yale University Press, 1986), 346.

7. See *Poems of Paul Celan*, trans. Michael Hamburger (New York: Persea Books, 1995), 21.

8. Paul Celan, *Last Poems*, trans. Katherine Washburn and Margret Guillemin (San Francisco: North Point Press, 1986), viii.

9. "Speech on the Occasion of Receiving the Literature Prize of the Free Hanseatic City of Bremen," in Paul Celan, *Collected Prose*, trans. Rosmarie Waldrop (Riverdale on Hudson, N.Y.: Sheep Meadow Press, 1986), 34. The original text reads as follows: "*Erreichbar, nah und unverloren blieb inmitten der Verluste dies eine: die Sprache.*

Sie, die Sprache, blieb unverloren, ja, trotz allem. Aber sie musste nun hindurchgehen durch ihre eigenen Antwortlosigkeiten, hindurchgehen durch furcht bares Verstummen, hindurchgehen durch die tausend Finsternisse todbringender Rede. Sie ging hindurch und gab keine Worte her für das, was geschah; aber sie ging durch dieses Geschehen. Ging hindurch und durfte wieder zutage treten, 'angereichert' von all dem.

In dieser Sprache habe ich, in jenen Jahren und in den Jahren nachher, Gedichte zu schreiben versucht: um zu sprechen, um mich zu orientieren, um zu erkunden, wo ich mich befand und wohin es mit mir wollte, um mir Wirklichkeit zu entwerfen" (*Gesammelte Werke*, 3:185–86).

10. Maurice Blanchot, *The Gaze of Orpheus and Other Literary Essays*, trans. Lydia Davis (Barrytown, N.Y.: Station Hill, 1981), 46–47.

11. See Christopher Fynsk, "The Realities at Stake in a Poem" in *Word traces: Readings of Paul Celan*, ed. Ars Fioretos (Baltimore: Johns Hopkins University Press, 1994), 164.

12. Celan, "Schieferäugige," in *Gesammelte Werke*, 2:98.

13. Celan, "Osterqualm," in *Gesammelte Werke*, 2:85.

14. *Poems of Paul Celan*, 232, 233.

15. Ibid., 265.

16. Celan, "[Reply to a Questionnaire from the Flinker Bookstore, Paris, 1958]" in *Collected Prose*, 15.

17. Celan, "Der Meridian" (Rede anlässlich der Verleihung des Georg-Büchner-Preises, Darmstadt, am 22. October, 1960) in *Gesammelte Werke*, 3:188. The translation is from Philippe Lacoue-Labarthe, "Catastrophe: A Reading of Celan's 'The Meridian,'" *Oxford Literary Review* 15 (1993):9.

18. Shoshana Felman, "Education and Crisis, or the Vicissitudes of Teaching," in *Trauma: Explorations in Memory,* ed. Cathy Caruth (Baltimore: Johns Hopkins University Press, 1995), 39.

19. Emmanuel Levinas, "Being and the Other: On Paul Celan," *Chicago Review* 29 (1978):17.

20. Celan, "Leaflets-Pain," in *Last Poems*, 98.

21. *Poems of Paul Celan*, 271.

22. Celan, *Collected Prose*, 15–16.

23. See Johann Babtist Metz, "Suffering unto God," trans. J. Matthew Ashley, *Critical Inquiry* 20 (summer 1994). Metz's comments on biblical traditions of perceiving the world might well apply to Celan: "This anamnestic reason resists forgetfulness. For anamnestic reason, being attentive to God means hearing the silence of those who have disappeared. It does not relegate everything that has vanished to existential insignificance. Knowing remains a root form of missing, without which not only faith but even the human him- or herself would disappear" (615).

24. Felman, "Education and Crisis," 43.

25. Derrida, "Shibboleth," 340, 341.

26. Ibid., 341.

27. Celan, "Der Meridian," 201.

28. George Steiner, *After Babel: Aspects of Language and Translation* (Oxford: Oxford University Press, 1975), 389.

29. Ibid., 393.

30. Celan, "Der Meridian," 192.

31. Celan, "Dein vom Wachen," in *Gesammelte Werke*, 2:24.

32. Hans-Georg Gadamer, *Truth and Method* (1960), trans. Joel Weinsheimer and Donald G. Marshall (New York: Crossroad, 1989), 384.

33. Celan, "Conversation in the Mountains" in *Last Poems*, 207.

34. *Poems of Paul Celan*, 141–43.

35. Celan, *Last Poems*, 15.

36. Jed Rasula, "Paul Celan," *STCI* 8 (fall 1983):115.

37. Krzysztof Ziarek, *Inflected Language: Toward a Hermeneutics of Nearness* (Albany: State University of New York Press, 1994), 198.

38. See Felman, "Education and Crisis": "Celan's poetic writing therefore struggles with the German to anihilate his own anihilation in it, to reappropriate the language that has marked his own exclusion . . ." (33).

39. Nina Cassian "'We Will Be Back and Up to Drown at Home': Notes on Paul Celan," *Parnassus* 14 (1994):128.

40. Celan, "Schieferäugige," in *Gesammelte Werke*, 2:98.

41. Celan, "Niedrigwasser," in *Gesammelte Werke*, 1:193.

42. *Poems of Paul Celan*, 153.

43. Celan, *Collected Prose*, viii.

44. Celan, "To Stand," in *Poems of Paul Celan*, 233; note my departure from Hamburger's translation of the second line.

45. Celan, *Last Poems*, 44.

46. *Poems of Paul Celan*, 307.

47. Celan, "Weggebeitzt," ibid., 238.

48. Celan, "Der Meridian," 188. "The Meridian," in *Collected Prose*, 39.

49. Ibid., 198.

50. Ziarek, *Inflected Language*, 10.

51. John Felstiner, "Paul Celan in Translation: 'Du sei wie du,'" *STCL* 8 (fall 1983): 93.

52. Gadamer's hermeneutics, as Gerald Bruns explains, implies precisely that "What we recognize is reality as other, not as the same: reality as that which is more Fate than Fact." See Gerald Bruns, "On the Tragedy of Hermeneutical Experience," in *Hermeneutics Ancient and Modern* (New Haven: Yale University Press, 1992), 186.

53. *Poems of Paul Celan*, 20.

54. See Theodor Adorno, *Aesthetic Theory*, trans. C. Lenhardt (London: Routledge and Kegan Paul, 1984), 111.

55. Celan, *Gesammelte Werke*, 3:19,39.

56. Celan, "Der Meridian," 193.

57. While many of Celan's neologisms are entirely original, James K. Lyon has pointed out that many of them are simply excavations of scarce terms or words no longer in use. See "Poetry and the Extremities of Language: From Concretism to Paul Celan," *STCL* 8 (fall 1983): 40–68.

58. Celan's decision eventually to withdraw the "Todesfuge" from further anthologizing reflects the fact that the readers had succeeded and the poem had become too familiar and had, counter to its intentions, familiarized the reader with the horror of the Holocaust. A similar fate has befallen Picasso's *Guernica*.

11

THE FAILURE
OF THE
REMEDY OF ART

SYLVIA PLATH'S *ARIEL*

> . . . never has art had so little cathartic potential.
> —Julia Kristeva, *Black Sun*

"What we have here," writes Irving Howe about Sylvia Plath's poem, "Daddy," "is a revenge fantasy, feeding upon filial love-hatred, and thereby mostly of clinical interest."[1] Hugh Kenner, who would have agreed with Howe's judgment, remarked that one could read Plath's earlier, formal poems as "the work of a very intelligent girl in her mid twenties" and as a "set of habits that . . . had kept her producing and alive."[2]

The very intelligent girl in her mid-twenties serves as the embodiment of an aesthetic in which, as Eliot would have advised, the man who suffers and the mind which creates are to be separate. A strictly formalist aesthetic did not—and this kept her alive—allow for any mixing of poetry and pathology. But even Eliot, albeit the later Eliot, made allowances for the untidy overlap of suffering and the aesthetic. In *The Use of Poetry and the Use of Criticism*, he permits that "ill health, debility or anemia may (if other circumstances are favorable)

157

produce an efflux of poetry. . . ."[3] But if illness can produce poetry, can poetry produce health, can it keep alive? How much illness can it contain?

In the case of Sylvia Plath we are predisposed to answer these questions negatively. Knowing her violent end, we cannot but approach her work retrospectively, finding it full of intention, warnings, prophecies. One such prophetic intention, foreshadowing the extremity and violence of suicide is prefigured, I suggest, in Plath's envious identifications of Jewish suffering in the Holocaust. In the context of the questions above, then, we can ask, should these identifications have been preemptive or preparatory? Did they help or hinder Plath's suicidal desires? Should the moral and aesthetic excess of her Jewish identifications have served as a metaphoric substitution for her personal holocaust?

If we turn to Jacqueline Rose's *The Haunting of Sylvia Plath*, we find in it a fine tuned reading of Plath's poems both in its aesthetic, psychoanalytic, and political dimensions. On the last page there is a quotation by Marguerite Duras' *La douleur* which traverses, Rose maintains, a "psychic terrain" similar to "Daddy."[4] I will return to Duras below. Rose's major argument in the last chapter of her book is to analyze the psychic terrain of Plath's poetry and thereby to respond to formalist readings such as Howe's or Kenner's. Much of their and of others' critique focuses on Plath's appropriations of Jewish identity, particularly in the poem in question, and it will therefore provide a good example of what is at stake on that psychic terrain. The most contested lines are these:

> I thought every German was you.
> And the language obscene
>
> An engine, an engine
> Chuffing me off like a Jew.
> A Jew to Dachau, Auschwitz, Belsen.
> I began to talk like a Jew.
> I think I may well be a Jew. (50)

Rose's defense of Plath's problematic appropriation of Jewish suffering is to highlight the paradox or impossibility of identity itself.

Plath's identity, Rose argues, is her non-identity—a paradox epitomized by Jewishness, but also by the German language in which Plath both finds and loses her father.[5] Then the paradox of identity is traced back to the master paradox of the paternal law, summed up by David

Rosenfeld (whom Rose quotes) as an instance of the "'logical-pragmatic paradox' facing the children of survivors: 'to be like me you must go away and not be like me; to be like your father, you must not be like your father.'"[6] Jacques Derrida in turn, also quoted in the same context, explains the essentially self-negating, self-contradictory, essence of Jewishness: "'The Jew is also the other, myself and the other; I am Jewish in saying: the Jew is the other who has no essence, who has nothing of his own or whose essence is not to have one.'"[7] François Lyotard places these paradoxical forms of identification into the existential dimensions of the Holocaust: "'if death is there [at Auschwitz], you are not there; if you are there, death is not there.'" All these forms of impossible identification, Rose claims, are anticipated in Freud's structural paradox between the superego and the ego: "'You *ought to be* like this (like your father)'" and "'You *may not be* like this (like your father).'"[8]

The conclusion drawn from these multiple structural analogies of identification is that the paternal law is analogical in "its cruelty, and its force" to the structural relations between Jewish victim and Nazi torturer. Thus, the very title of the poem "Daddy" and the unstable, interchangeable roles of father and Nazi, daughter and victim, in all their permutations, suggest to Rose the "intolerable psychic conditions" under which any process of identification must run its course. But this amounts to an exceedingly tragic rendering of the structure of identity. If "Daddy" is about the intolerable psychic conditions under which identity labors—comparable to Jewish victim and Nazi torturer—does not Rose's reading confirm the clinical interest that Irving Howe found in Plath's poem? Or is "Daddy" more than the record of a pathology?

Rose's answers to these questions seem to be given by assigning the poem an internal distance from its own concerns, not unlike Eliot's aesthetic distance between the mind which creates and the man who suffers: "Daddy" is "about its own conditions of linguistic and phantasmic production."[9] The poem's propensity to simile—"I began to talk like a Jew. / I think I may well be a Jew. / I may be a bit of a Jew"—testify to "a partial, hesitant, and speculative identification between herself [Plath] and the Jew."[10]

Yet, in view of the very extremity of Plath's claims of identification, can there remain an external point of residual identity from which one may remain aesthetically partial, hesitant, speculative? Can one partially, hesitantly, speculatively, appropriate the Holocaust to create an *univers concentrationnaire* as linguistic and phantasmic production?[11] Plath's near punning of "jaw" with Jew in "The tongue stuck in my jaw" intimates an ambivalent answer to such for Plath not entirely rhetorical questions—just as in the breathless repetition of "Ich, ich, ich, ich" (49), the excessive protesting implies both a self-forgetfulness and a self-consciousness, a simultaneous confession and denial of her identificatory desires.

If these ambiguities and confusions amount themselves to some poetic trauma it might imply that one cannot appropriate another's suffering as image, as speculative possibility, as partial truth, without suffering the loss of aesthetic reflection and speculation. In "Daddy," then, the aesthetic would subject itself to excess perhaps precisely so as to indict its own speculative distances and hesitations. The poems' propensity to simile may indict poetry itself: its similes cannot forge comparability of the incomparable. This could be an admission of the betrayals of the trauma poetry attempts to name. "Daddy" is a poem, then, whose reflections, hesitations, and speculations doubt less Plath's assumption of Jewish identity than the poem's ability to absorb such identity. Haunted though it may be by hooks and cries, Plath's poetic necessarily misspeaks the suffering which is its subject and which therefore remains its obsession.

If for Plath everything attains truth only through suffering, suffering remains the coveted, envied certainty beyond aesthetic distances and beyond the impossible approaches and approximations of language. Poetry is merely a Nietzschean "illusion of a Greek necessity" (84) or a temporally inverted dream of the fated future where the dreamer attempts to attain some control over that dark, feathery thing that inhabits her. Or perhaps Plath's invocations of the Holocaust should have served as the aesthetic substitution preventing her eventual imitation of the Holocaust in her own domestic gas oven. But the incommensurability of the Holocaust, the impossibility of its transformation into simile or metaphor, dooms its employment as poetic therapy.

Like Duras' work, Plath's poetry eschews the "festive" implications of the aesthetic.

> . . . never has art had so little cathartic potential. Undoubtedly and for that very reason it falls more within the province of sorcery and bewitchment than within that of grace and forgiveness traditionally associated with artistic genius. A complicity with illness emanates from Duras' texts. . . .[12]

Kristeva asks, "How can one speak the truth of pain, if not by holding in check the rhetorical celebration, warping it, making it grate, strain, and limp."[13] After Auschwitz and Hiroshima, she writes, "the difficulty in naming no longer opens onto 'music in literature' (Mallarmé and Joyce were believers and aesthetes) but onto illogicality and silence."[14]

Antonin Artaud demanded that language cede its place to mise en scene, and that gesture replace words. Cesare Pavese's last entry in his diaries reads: "Not words. A gesture. I shall not write again."[15] But poetry must remain in language and must wait to be rendered more truly in the gesture and the act, not in writing but in the body. The desire for such embodiment of her suffering seems audible in Plath's poetry. Her language tonally tears and ruptures, but also, conversely, words give way to a predominance of pre-verbal rhythm and repetition, and vowels lengthen and become echoes of a primordial music of pain:

> You do not do, you do not do
> Any more, black shoe
> In which I have lived like a foot
> For thirty years, poor and white,
> Barely daring to breathe or Achoo. (49)

There might be, as the psychic conditions worsen, some poems keeping track of the progress of an inexorable existential fate, sometimes symbolized by a metal or silver track devoured by an engine. In "Getting There" the speaker inquires, "How far is it? / How far is it now?" (36). But the poems, one feels, hardly delay and begin to keep record of a desire that will exceed, eventually, their figurative substitutions: "The train is dragging itself, it is screaming—/ An animal / Insane for the destination . . . (37). Richard Blessing comments,

> Perhaps in poetry intensity and velocity are one, emotion the exact equal of motion. At any rate, when Plath closes "Elm" by raising the murdering force of the "isolate slow faults" to the third power or when she urges the applicant to "marry it, marry it, marry it," she has managed to close on a note of pure frenzy. One has the sense that the rest is not so much silence as energy too intense for articulation.[16]

In "Years" Plath declares:

> What I love is
> The piston in motion—
> My soul dies before it.
> And the hooves of the horses,
> Their merciless churn. (72)

Some poems' narrative impatience is as fated as the calm prophetic certainty of others:

> I smile, a buddha, all
> Wants, desire
> Falling from me like rings
> Hugging their lights.
>
> The claw
> Of the magnolia,
> Drunk on its own scents,
> Asks nothing of life. (78)

In a radio interview on BBC, Plath offhandedly confirms the desire of her poetry to transcend its words for a truth less doubtful than the passion of her excessive identifications. Her analogy for the relevance of personal experience is in "the larger things, the bigger things, such as Hiroshima, Dachau, and so on,"[17] against which any individual experience would appear insignificant, at least by measure of the kind of apocalyptic epistemology she seemed to have sought for a proof of the truth or value of her experiences. But if poetry cannot measure up to such ambition, nor perhaps can suicide. Plath's addition, "and so on," indicts even Hiroshima and Dachau as lacking in force and relevance, and one must suspect her death might have been insufficient as well. The apocalyptic imagery of Plath's poetry and eventually her death suggest that she was in search of "things" large and big enough so that their ontology would be sublimely self-evident, like that of Hiroshima or of Dachau, outside of which one would no longer search for relevance or reference. Hiroshima and Auschwitz are the ultimate reference. Plath's suicide might reveal itself thus as a tragically incomplete substitution for that sublime surplus of signification which, for Plath, only Hiroshima or Dachau could attain.

Plath's poetry thus becomes emblematic of the modern work which cannot be completed within its own formal parameters, always awaiting its closure in a catastrophe the aesthetic cannot deliver.

ROBERT LOWELL'S *DAY BY DAY*

> So many secondary troubles,
> the body's curative diversions.
>
> —Robert Lowell, *Day by Day*

One could hardly conceive of a more pronounced difference in style and intensity than between Plath's *Ariel* and Robert Lowell's last volume of poems. Published one year before his death in 1977,[18] *Day by Day* measures out life in coffee spoons, aligning one tired episode with another. Judged by the once innovative, "muscular" style of the poems that made him famous, or by the political protest and confessional candor that made him the avant-garde of a new poetic generation, *Day by Day* is Lowell's mostly melancholy inventory of last breakdowns and record of his circus animals' desertion:

> I was surer, wasn't I, once . . .
> and had flashes when I first found
> a humor for myself in images,
> farfetched misalliance
> that made evasion a revelation? (121)

The former farfetched misalliances and evasions that could turn into revelations only because misalliances and evasions are sometimes themselves revelatory now seem to yield to the more urgent question, "Is getting well ever an art, / or art a way to get well?" (124). But the interchangability of art and cure assigns art only some therapeutic function, no aesthetic refuge from "this final year" (58), no transcendence of the aging body. Books are merely "the body's curative diversions" (17), their remedy is temporary, their form episodic not tragic: "Those blessed structures, plot and rhyme," Lowell asks belatedly in the book, "why are they of no help to me now . . ." (127).

Day by Day is appropriately structured by the passing of time, beginning with recollections of literary ancestry and ending with ruminations and reminiscences of the autobiographical past (excepting the three translations which conclude the book). The poet's inability to connect and unify the various episodes into plot and rhyme deepens his questions about the redemptive powers of poetry. The most fundamental structural and thematic question arises therefore when Lowell asks

>   Can one bear it; in nature
>   from seed to chaff no tragedy? (57)

The question seems not so much in respect to the allegorical "struck oak" mentioned in the poem as to the unredeemed "natural" structure, as it were, of Lowell's work, a work, which, as autobiographies go, follows life from seed to chaff but will not amount to tragedy. Tragedy's aesthetic and spiritual dimensions remain elusive. Like Plath's, these poems must find their completion and confirmation elsewhere.[19]

Elsewhere is mostly the autobiographical past. Several of the poems of *Day by Day* seek to settle a score with Lowell's parents. But each attempt only repeats betrayals and accusations already levelled twenty years earlier. Although efforts to even the score are made when Lowell writes in "To Mother": "It has taken me the time since you died / to discover you are as human as I am . . . / if I am" (79) or when he allows his father to respond, "it's your life, and dated like mine" (81), one cannot fail to note the addition of the petulant qualifications.

In other poems Lowell revisits old themes and old images, and we are back in familiar hospital settings:

>   The immovable chairs have swallowed up the patients,
>   and speak with the eloquence of emptiness.
>   By each the same morning paper lies unread:
>   *January 10, 1976.*
>   I cannot sit or stand two minutes.
>   . . .
>   Less than ever I expect to be alive
>   six months from now—
>   *1976,*
>   a date I dare not affix to my grave.
>   The Queen of Heaven, I miss her,
>   we were divorced. . . . (114)

"Doomsday Book" opens with the line "Let nothing be done twice—" (54) but it reminds us of the earlier "Skunk Hour" ("The country houses that rolled / like railways are now / more stationary than anthills— / their service gone. Will they / fall . . ." (55)).

Much is recalled rather than imagined, repeated rather than remade, and the advice at the end of *Day by Day*, in a poem entitled "Epilogue," should have been offered in a prologue. "Epilogue" is the most explicit but ironically belated announcement of a new poetic intention: "I want to make something imagined, not recalled" (127). This, being almost the final statement of the book, seems retrospectively only to confirm its failure but at the same time it announces a departure from the retrospective, autobiographical teleology of the book to a more romantic, transcendent realm:

> I hear the noise of my own voice:
> *The painter's vision is not a lens,*
> *it trembles to caress the light.*
> But sometimes everything I write
> with the threadbare art of my eye
> seems a snapshot,
> lurid, rapid, garish, grouped,
> heightened from life,
> yet paralyzed by fact.
> All's misalliance.
> Yet why not say what happened?
> Pray for the grace of accuracy
> Vermeer gave to the sun's illumination
> stealing like the tide across a map
> to his girl solid with yearning.
> We are poor passing facts,
> warned by that to give
> each figure in the photograph
> his living name. (127)

As hope to history, or as art to time, grace, painting, and naming are opposed to fact, to photography, and to writing. The question is: How can fact turn into grace, photography into painting, writing into naming? How can we poor passing facts receive a name? While the painter's vision acknowledges the light—perhaps Socrates' light as metaphor of the transcendent Good—the lens cannot caress the light, cannot acknowledge it, and "All's misalliance."

These late, veritably spiritual notions do not entirely spring from the unreflective "noise" of Lowell's own voice, although that line ought to have suggested the poet's unselfconscious "yearning" towards his new romantic vision. Auden's "The Composer" may have served as model, assigning similar redemptive powers to "imaginary song" as Lowell assigns the painter. In Auden's poem,

All the others translate: the painter sketches
A visible world to love or reject;
Rummaging into his living, the poet fetches
The images out that hurt and connect,

From Life to Art by painstaking adaption,
Relying on us to cover the rift . . .

You alone, alone, O imaginary song,
Are unable to say an existence is wrong,
And pour out your forgiveness like a wine.[20]

In light of Auden's Stevensian invocation of imaginary song, the transcendent aesthetic dimensions of Lowell's intention may become clearer. For a poet who had made his career with snapshots of family members and "'the injuries of time,'" which are, as Susan Sontag notes, "the camera's special aptitude,"[21] Lowell's poetic of forgiveness now hopes to restore grace to truth, light to fact, name to word. Forgiveness should add that indefinable notion of accuracy, for which Lowell's example becomes the Dutch realist, Vermeer, particularly, as Helen Deese has noted, his *Woman in Blue Reading a Letter*.[22]

But can such sudden spiritual powers assigned to a poetic naming redeem the "poor passing facts" of mere life in time, of life that might not amount to tragedy? Since we are told in the opening poem, "Ulysses and Circe," that "things changed to the names he gave them, / then lost their names," can the poet's pen-turned-brush give back to the figure in the photograph "his living name?" The overtly rhetorical question, "Why not say what happened?" yearns towards "yes." It is both defensive and hopeful, the latter implying the slightest possibility that grace might perchance add miracle to mimesis.

"Notice" anticipates the warning of "Epilogue." The scene, as in several poems of this volume, is a hospital ward, and the poem opens with an encounter between science and art, medicine and poetry, with each, it seems, having reached the limits of their explanatory powers:

The resident doctor said,
"We are not deep in ideas, imagination or enthusiasm—
how can we help you?"
I asked,
"These days of only poems and depression—
what can I do with them?
Will they help me to notice
what I cannot bear to look at?" (118)

The same question that is asked in terms of painting and photography in "Epilogue" is here asked in terms of "noticing" and "looking." If the answer is tentatively positive, *yes, poetry will help me to notice what I cannot bear to look at,* we must ask: in what sense is noticing deeper, more imaginative, more enthusiastic than looking? In what sense is it a help the doctors cannot give? The latter question suggests that its non-conceptual, non-empirical nature allows *noticing* to become aesthetic perception, where *looking* remains based on concept and prejudice, paralyzed by fact, a lens, not an eye.

The poem ends with the speaker's arrival

> . . . home—I can walk it blindfold.
> But we must notice—
> we are designed for the moment. (118)

I am not sure how much contradictory force the "but" has. Seeking to reassert a poetics of a-temporal, spiritual intimation of the moment—hence the narrator's blindness—the last two lines feebly affirm aesthetic perception as redemption: We are designed for the moment (of death) so as to ensure a design of beauty; we do not see but we may notice.

In the next poem, "Shifting Colors," the unbearable moment can once more be imagined, not through the lens but through the painter's redemptive vision. The verse painting of "Shifting Colors" is throughout of creatures "more instinctive" than "poor measured, neurotic man" (119). The poet's eye is here likewise to be more instinctive; it is to perceive without the imposition of poor measures and meaning, it is to see with the grace of accuracy:

> I see
> horse and meadow, duck and pond,
> universal consolatory
> description without significance,
> transcribed verbatim by my eye. (119–20)

We hardly need the subsequent, interpretive lines

> This is not the directness that catches
> everything on the run and then expires—

or the mention of Mallarmé "who had the good fortune / to find a style that made writing impossible" (119–20) to realize that such writing yearns for its own obliteration.

But the title of Lowell's last book implies also the interminability of writing—a writing that only prolongs the illness that called for it: "in this tempting leisure, / good thoughts drive out bad; / causes for my misadventure . . . come jumbling out . . ." (121). Or: "Alas, I can only tell my own story" and the friend must take on the role of analyst "to keep up conversation" (121). While such writing, telling, and listening may delay the end, evasions now are no longer revelations, but evasions. And consequently, as in a Freudian script, the narrator lapses back into repetitions of the past, to keep avoiding what cannot be looked at.

The question

> Is getting well ever an art,
> or art a way to get well?

must be reciprocal. For neither life nor art can be prescribed to the other as remedy. The autobiographical dimension of *Day by Day* is its erasure of difference between life and art. Art cannot transcend the life of the body, its dimensions are the same as those of the finite mind. If Lowell nevertheless advocates such remedial measures as the painter's eye to tease a spirituality out of life, the effort remains intermittent and feebly desired like an echo whose diminishing strength forebodes a death.

NOTES

1. Irving Howe, "The Plath Celebration: A Partial Dissent," in *Sylvia Plath*, ed. Harold Bloom (New York: Chelsea House, 1987), 11.

2. Hugh Kenner, "Sincerity Kills," in Bloom, 75–76.

3. *Selected Prose of T. S. Eliot*, ed. Frank Kermode (London: Faber and Faber, 1975), 89.

4. Jacqueline Rose, *The Haunting of Sylvia Plath* (Cambridge: Harvard University Press, 1992), 238.

5. Ibid., 227.

6. Ibid., 230.

7. Ibid., 217.

8. Ibid., 230.

9. Ibid., 230.

10. Ibid., 228.

11. Quoted in Lawrence L. Langer, *The Holocaust and the Literary Imagination* (New Haven: Yale University Press, 1975), 52.

12. Julia Kristeva, *Black Sun: Depression and Melancholia*, trans. Leon S. Roudiez (New York: Columbia University Press, 1989), 228.

13. Ibid., 225.

14. Ibid., 222.

15. Cesare Pavese, *Il mestiere di vivere* (Torino: Guilio Einaudi, 1952).

16. Richard Allen Blessing, "The Shape of the Psyche: Vision and Technique in the Late Poems of Sylvia Plath," in *Sylvia Plath: New Views on the Poetry*, ed. Gary Lane (Baltimore: Johns Hopkins University Press, 1979), 60.

17. "Sylvia Plath," in *The Poet Speaks,* ed. Peter Orr (London: Routledge, 1966).

18. Robert Lowell, *Day by Day* (New York: Farrar, Straus and Giroux, 1977); page references in the text refer to this edition.

19. I cannot therefore agree with Helen Vendler who defends the aesthetic value of the book. Although we are not to look "for the hard-driving compression of the late sonnets; not for the transforming and idealizing power of lyric . . ." she nevertheless discovers in the poems Lowell's listening "to the inner life of the poem, deciding with mysterious certainty when it was finished, when it had found its equilibrium." These seem to me contradictory claims testifying to Vendler's own attempt to redeem the poems from their failing aesthetic. See "Last Days and Last Poems," in *Robert Lowell*, ed. Bloom, 104 and 112.

20. *The English Auden,* ed. Edward Mendelson (London: Faber and Faber, 1977), 239.

21. Susan Sontag, *On Photography* (New York: Farrar, Straus and Giroux, 1977), 69.

22. See Helen Deese, "Lowell and the Visual Arts," in *Robert Lowell: Essays on the Poetry*, ed. Steven Gould Axelrod and Helen Deese (Cambridge: Cambridge University Press, 1986), 180–216.

12

THE MATTER
AND SPIRIT
OF DEATH

SHARON OLDS' *THE FATHER*

> A large part of the popularity and persuasiveness of
> psychology comes from its being a sublimated
> spiritualism: a secular, ostensibly scientific way
> of affirming the primacy of 'spirit' over matter.
>
> —Susan Sontag, *Illness as Metaphor*

> When we understood it might be cancer,
> I lay down beside you in the night . . .
>
> —Sharon Olds, *The Dead and the Living*

Sharon Olds' poetic sequence *The Father*[1] records her father's death
from cancer. Each breath, cough, spit of mucus, and stool is accounted
for. The book is obsessed with waiting, with breathing, with bodily
functions of the most intimate and ultimate kind, as if the poet wanted
to wrest a secret from the slow process of dying, being present to her father's dying so as not to miss the split second when the secret might leap
out of the body. The book lingers, at times with an astonishing patience
and insistence, particularly over the exact moment of his death, which is
the title of one poem. Olds releases her father slowly and with costly

tenderness, letting go only after he has begged for it in the manner of
Jacob (23). The book is a work in slow motion, an anticipatory and retrospective grieving, a pity and fear, all in ritual passage reminiscent of
the monastic schedule, with the poems bearing such titles as "The Waiting," "The Pulling," "The Lumens," "His Stillness," "The Want," "The
Lifting," and so forth.

Above all, the book is about matter. Olds seems to learn with relief
that that is all it is: "I have always longed to believe in what I am seeing"
(32). The father's death, where it might have most strongly called this
longing into question, most strongly reconfirms it. Indeed, it seems as if
the suffering and death of the father was a last occasion to prove that
truth must be in the particular, in the body, not in the soul, in history,
not beyond it.

> When I come to his hospital doorway in the morning
> and see, around the curtain, the motionless
> bulge of his feet, under the sheet,
> I stop breathing. I walk in,
> the starved shape of his body rises
> and falls, and I breathe again,
>   I sit and breathe with him. . . . (22)

The line ending on "his body rises . . ." may offer a momentary illusion
or allusion to the body rising from the dead, but it is the law of matter
that seeks its destiny, breath not spirit, matter not metaphor. Father and
daughter lie not in heaven but "somewhere on the outskirts / of the gar-
den of Eden . . ." (22).

> I wish I could say I saw a long
> shapely leg pull free from the chrysalis, a
> wet wing, a creature unfold and
> fly out through the window, but he died down
> into his body. . . . (57)

The spiritual does become—perhaps necessarily if matter wants to be
truth—the narrative's dialectical opponent; it has to be called forth to be
called off. How else could one say that the body is enough, other than
that the poet, having known her father "soulless" all her childhood (39),
would have descended and looked for his soul if he could have been
helped (62)? But since these possibilities are denied, even salvation will
be absorbed by matter. Will matter shine with its own salvation? Will
salvation matter?

The book begins and ends with matter, frames its argument with matter and with all of its declensions and conjugations, as noun and verb, material and moral truth. The opening reference to Genesis where the father is "night-/watchman of matter, sitting facing / the water—the earth without form, and void, / darkness upon the face of it, as if / waiting for his daughter" (3–4)—makes a grand, perhaps intentionally too grand, announcement of a romantic creative rivalry between God and daughter, spirit and matter. The daughter is not always creator of her own world and language (23) and, being subject to the father-God's breath, she is also subject to the father's uncreative powers: "I was an Eve / he took and pressed back into clay . . ." (71). That the daughter survives is only due to the stronger power of death. Death is the daughter's liberator.

In retrospect one realizes that even the very first line of the book—"No matter how early I would get up . . ." announces, allusively, the matter of this book. But while this is a book about matter its purpose is thoroughly redemptive: it is to redeem the clay into which he had pressed her. The body of her dying father is the site of redemption. The last page closes with the father's voice from the dead, "I am matter, / your father . . ." framing, thematizing this book in between whose covers there is the body of the father, still or restless, first sitting, then lying, then sinking down, in pain and in sleep, all minutely observed. There is a veritable poetics, a creative theory, in the father's relentless decline deeper into body and ash and earth and the daughter's rising, not higher, but also deeper into her conviction that soul is nothing, matter all, and yet that death can do what life undid. The bitter memories of what life undid, or what the father did, accelerate their appearance in the second part of the book. The book therefore, one senses, is a last chance of healing and helping what could never be healed or helped in life.

Each poem is a measurement of minute increments of time, of inexorable, irreparable progress, granting only the smallest reprieves and returns to previous scenes and settings. There is only one seeming remission when the father "is better, he is dying a little more slowly" (11); otherwise the narrative of this sequence is obedient to the strict authority of time and disease and death. Many of the poems begin by marking time, "How early . . ." "The last morning . . ." "Every hour . . ." "Now . . ." ". . . and there are three weeks left." "I waited . . . ," and so forth. In the middle of the book, the book of waiting contracts to briefer increments of time. The diary of dying which had been a living with time, becomes now a living on the verge of timelessness. The question of whether one can continue where death ends looms somewhere in that intense narrow margin of time/lessness marked by the imminence of death. Then, after ten or so pages of return and repetition of death and reflection on the moment of death itself, time expands by leaps "Beyond Harm," "One Year" into the future where even memory is torn down ("The Motel") and the father's death not only recedes, but also rises up again in myth and dream.

The certainty of death is the book's telos from which it derives its assurance of arrival and survival as well as its style. The breath of the author is dependent first on the breath then on the death of the father, the matter of his breath and death is finally reflected by a style marked by lucid, factual clarity. Caring for the father is equally therapeutic for the daughter. Mutuality is one of the book's themes and is frequently encountered in the father's breathing, where the daughter discovers her dependency, the source of her own breathing and writing. Nor is there a question about authorship or reference or autobiography. The unproblematic analogy between life and art suggests instead that the death need not be, cannot be, transformed through art, and that art, likewise, seeks no transformative powers beyond being simply the power of witness and attendance, a *being-there* as factual as a back rub, although as much a labor of love. It is only in the latter part of the book, in what one might call the "memory-poems," where the desire for the indifference of matter leaves the remainder of an "unearned desire" (63) and the incompletions of love (65, 68).

The narrative contingency and continuance depends on seeing the father safely through to the fire (43), a resistance to the pull of death (66) and a liberation from death (52). But eventually the achievement of the book, when the telos of the father's death has been consummated, is to continue continuance itself. The book therefore eventually asks the question: what writing can survive a death? How does one write after the most consummating narrative event? How does one write after one has written to the end? Perhaps that is why the sequence lingers at that latter point, returning to and rewriting and repeating the death until it releases the writer into freedom: "I suddenly thought, with amazement, he will always / love me now, and I laughed—he was dead, dead!" (52)

Many of the issues I have mentioned here in summary are addressed in a poem entitled "I Wanted to Be There When My Father Died" (71). The title seems more idealistic than the qualification that follows immediately: ". . . because I wanted to see him die—." Indeed, *The Father* is a book almost exclusively of seeing. "I have always longed to believe in what I was seeing" (32). It is a curious admission since it implies other beliefs, which are, presumably, tested out at the site of the father's dying and found wanting. It is here in "I Wanted to Be There . . ." that we learn one of the secret motivations of the poet's presence at her father's deathbed, a motivation that explains partially the distance implied in "seeing":

> because I wanted to see him die—
> and not just to know him, down to
> the ground, the dirt of his unmaking, and not
> just to give him a last chance
> to give me something, or take his loathing
> back. (71)

The dimensions of the daughter's relationship with the father and her childhood are present in other poems as well where we learn that if the daughter now has "nothing for him, no net, / no heaven to catch him," it is because he taught his daughter "only / the earth, night, sleep, the male / body in its beauty and fearsomeness" (24). But besides fear she returns to him also pity. "The Look" gives one of the most moving examples. The last lines of the poem read:

> . . . I could touch him from deep in my heart,
> he shifted in the bed, he tilted, his eyes
> bugged out and darkened, the mucus rose,
> I held the cup to his lips and he slid out
> the mass and sat back, a flush came into
> his skin, and he lifted his head shyly but
> without reluctance and looked at me
> directly, for just a moment, with a dark
> face and dark shining confiding eyes. (17)

In the balance of pity and fear, these remain cherished moments, encounters of which there is not much likeness, to my knowledge, in modern American poetry. *The Father* is a book in search of a catharsis and clarification of fear and pity, that they may be offered in right measure and balance. If Sharon Olds' book wants to be such an offering, the catharsis that the narrative ought to work out for its author remains one of the book's major labors, born in poem after poem, throughout the long summer of the father's dying. "All summer he had gagged, as if trying / to cough his whole esophagus out." We read on in "I Wanted to Be There . . ." :

surely his pain and depression had appeased me,
and yet I wanted to see him die
not just to see no soul come
free of his body, no mucal genie of
spirit jump
forth from his mouth,
proving the body on earth is all we have got,
I wanted to watch my father die
because I hated him. Oh, I loved him,
my hands cherished him. . . . (71)

The Father is an articulation, a verbal extension of the "Oh," held pre-cariously between the two forces of love and hatred, fear and pity. But eventually even the hands that cherished him will delegate their task to "other hands" into which it might be better to "commend this spirit," for not all issues between love and hatred have been, can be, resolved in poetry.

The hands that cherished him cherished the body, meaning the par-ticular, the historical, Aristotle's "that which was." It is no body if it can be generalized, just as one cannot generalize caring, washing, nursing, helping, witnessing. Hence, the particularity of the descriptions and ac-counts of mucus, spit, and stool. Even the language of the poems follows the law of material truth: it avoids poeticizing this particular death, lest it might turn into Aristotle's poetic universals and thereby into a belying of individual suffering and dying. Thus, each poem, redescending into the labor of moments and situations, also refuses to let suffering, death, and caring become transformed into art.

What we admire in this volume is firstly not the art of writing but the art of nursing. What we admire must be first the exemplary moral determination and love of the daughter to nurse her father—she who "had stopped / longing for him to address [her] from his heart" (14). Her father, we learn progressively, at times would not speak for a week, had never asked his daughter for anything, had never really looked at her, had regularly passed out on the couch in alcoholic stupor, and had only when he sickened turned to his wife and daughter. In spite of this grim record of her youth, there is not an instant of hesitation as the book begins—significantly "early"—in the daughter's moral determination. To the father she must have appeared like a Cordelia, proving in the nu-merous instances of closeness and intimacy a loyalty and affection rare and difficult.

He gargled, I got the cup ready,
I didn't vary the stroke, he spat, I
praised him, I let the full pleasure
of caressing my father come awake in my body,
and then I could touch him from deep in my heart. . . . (17)

Such attention, merging as it does pain with pleasure and matter with spirit, reconnects the world in its deepest fundamentality. Perhaps not surprisingly, it is in this poem that we find one of the epiphanies of the book, when the father momentarily responds with his "dark shining confiding eyes." If the world needs an ethical foundation, its beginnings would be in such small, intimate, and brief mergings of pleasure and pain. "This is the world where sex lives, the world / of the nerves, the world without church, / . . . outside the world of the moral" (9), as Olds points out in "Death and Morality." The book is the record of the strategies of the will, of the small, small acts of attention, measured by the paced continuance of the sequence, by which this merging of pleasure and pain could be possible and consciously attended to. The originality of Olds' book is in the particularity of the death and deed, in which service she left behind, as Kierkegaard would say, both the category of ethics and of aesthetics. *The Father* tells of the incomprehensible category beyond. Olds' denial of spiritual revelation, her insistance on the body demands that the church find itself in hospitals rather than "far away, in a field," where one can hear "the distant hymns of a tent-meeting . . ."(9).

TESS GALLAGHER'S *MOON CROSSING BRIDGE*

Is grief contain'd
in the the very deeps of pleasure?
—John Keats, *Endymion*

The inflections of joy. The inflections of
suffering. And strangely
sometimes the mixing
of the two.
—Tess Gallagher, *Amplitude*

In a good number of Tess Gallagher's poems of grief and sorrow, and of frail, desperate substitution of words for love, of absence for the beloved's presence—"how did we live so well before / with nothing missing?"—we attend the narrative of a somnabulist whose excessive syntax is what Julia Kristeva would call an "archaic 'semiotic' . . . constituted by preverbal self-sensualities."[2] Or it is, one might say, a night-groping for conjunctions, correspondences, continuities, each line throwing a line to the next, in a sinuousness of logic, that makes almost all of Gallagher's poems always also disposed to pleasure.

> All bird and no recall, she
> thinks, and lives in his birdness, no burden
> but strange lightness so she wants to be up at dawn,
> the mountains fogged with snow, a world
> that sleeps as if it were
> all the world and, being so, able to be seen
> at its beginning, freshly
> given as sleep is, bleak fertility of sleep when
> she thinks far into his last resting
> wherein she drifted, drifts, slow and white,
> deeply asking, deep with its dark below.[3] (6)

How easily one could have made that last line end with a rhythm of a somber triad of iambs: "déeply ásk/ ing, déep / with dárk / belów." The "its," which makes such self-mystification impossible, paradoxically assigns the deep "its" dark where the *assigning* removes and distances, and one is slightly safer.

Yet Gallagher's language, always seeking its sources in music, becomes inevitably a celebration of its own soundings, a listening to its own enchantments: "I gleam. I mourn"; or: a "listening hand / bending one of the notes as pain-in-transit bends / language to purposes outside meaning" (98). Some lines announce programmatically the difficulties of Gallagher's *poesis* of absence, of making something out of something missing.

> . . . who's assigned this complicitous extension,
> these word-caressings? this night-river
> full of dead star-tremors, amazed floatings, this
> chaotic laboratory of broken approaches? (60)

The book is not only "to confirm what is forever beyond speech" (49), it is yet to be perplexingly like "a poem missing even the language / it is unwritten in" (54)—where "even" might have to mean "especially." For the un-written is the language of the dead, whose language is missed, whose speech can not be recovered. As the "unwritten pages" (60) of the dead "lift an ongoing dusk in me," the ambiguous "lifting" bespeaks the mental state of the mourner whose dusk is neither lifting to yield the remaining light of day nor the darkness of night. Mourning is writing-in-twilight, it speaks neither the language of the dead nor that of the living; its syntax mirrors amazed floatings and complicitous extensions. "[W]ords are candles I blow out / the moment I set them down" (62).

Nevertheless, the book, which announced an affirmative "yes" as its very opening gesture, writes, or wants to write, a recovery in metaphors of light. The first of the six parts begins with "dark," "sleep," "night," "dawn," then proceeds to "last light," then "Muslin half light," "arctic light." Suddenly all shines in a "brightest now" and we are only on page twelve and there are almost ninety pages left. The love poems at the end of the book make this impatience for recovery more explicit.

What to do with so much light in a book of darkness, so much pleasure in a book of mourning? In the opening poem of the second part, "He was suffering from too much light . . ." (19), then the light metaphors proceed somewhat more economically and more ambiguously from "deep blue morning" to a "breaking off at both ends into daylight" to "morning and the light uncoupled" and eventually in the last section "Light begins" and "He wants me all in light. . . ."

If one can take this diminishing of darkness as a telos of Gallagher's poetic narrative, the title poem should be of exemplary importance, promising as it does in its title, a frail bridge of light:

> If I stand a long time by the river
> when the moon is high
> don't mistake my attention
> for the merely aesthetic, though
> that saves in daylight.
> Only what we once called worship
> has feet light enough to carry
> the living on that span of brightness.
> And who's to say I didn't cross
> just because I used the bridge in its witnessing,
> to let the water stay the water
> and the incongruities of the moon to chart
> that joining I was certain of. (59)

One of the few things, perhaps the only thing, that is certain in this difficult poem, is the metaphor of crossing. It is conceivable that the book is supposed to accomplish such a crossing. Evidently the crossing is supposed to happen at night when "the moon is high," and the speaker addresses an unknown other, afraid that the "long time" of her attention might be misunderstood as "the merely aesthetic" which in turn only "saves in daylight" not at night, since the aesthetic is based on distance, disinterest, and sight (at least metaphorical), some of which, however, is available to the speaker: "the moon is high." What saves at night, if not the aesthetic, must be "what we once called worship," which has perhaps, despite its anachronism, capablities of mystical transport across "a span of brightness."

Perhaps the book, if it is inscribed with the title of this poem, is supposed to be a span of brightness, or a bridge of light—but then there are difficulties. Why the sudden rhetorical posturing: "who's to say I didn't cross / just because I used the bridge in its witnessing. . . ." Who would deny it? Who would say "she didn't cross" if one cannot exactly make it out in all this incongruous moonlight? Is the book to be used as a witnessing for a crossing, or "joining" as we read in the last line? But then, how is one to read the conjunction "*to* let the water . . . ?" Does it mean "in order to," or "so that" the water would "stay the water"? What water? Why "stay"? "Stay" in what sense? And why the shift from present tense to past tense?

The implicit disquiet of such questions, of such wondering and inquiry in these sinuous turnings of lines and phrases, in this and in other poems as well, intimates the difficulties of moon-crossing, of crossing on a span of light, of joining what one "was certain of." It cannot be done in daylight. The crossing is undertaken with "feet light enough," that is to say, not with anything that would ruffle the water so that it can "stay the water," and with a moon inconstant enough to do no more than "chart" or map the journey across this legendary river of death, a moon that is also reputedly unreliable, building a bridge of light that might fall and fail to bring about "that joining"—all these assignments and conditions are acknowledged. But the joining does not take place. "Wake" is the physical encounter with the impossibility of joining with the dead. There Gallagher asks rhetorically, "Did I want to prove how surely / I'd been left behind?" (5)

In "Moon Crossing Bridge," the question, "Who's to say I didn't cross"—not requiring a question mark (because already answered?)—is likely directed to the speaker herself. For where are the necessities for such defenses other than in the speaker's own doubt that the crossing would not accomplish the joining, that there would perhaps be no crossing at all. The past tense in the last line confirms the doubt—". . . that joining I was certain of"—for we now know that the joining has been disconfirmed. The poem entertained it on a "span of brightness." The poem has been (only) a "witnessing" of desire and impossibility.

How else could the bridge lead to "lives of solitude," as the note on the Togetsu Bridge indicates at the end of the book? Is the joining only accomplished in solitude, in a spiritual meeting, having to do with worship? But the answer to this question is also negative since "what we once called worship" makes that possibility truly an anachronism. Joining does not take place this side of life, the river keeps flowing undisturbed under the bridge, the moon is no Acheron. As the epigraphs preceeding part 5 of *Moon Crossing Bridge* warn, even to attempt such a crossing requires one's death. Only in death can "Horses pass over it, donkeys pass over it, cats and dogs, tigers and elephants pass over it, men and women, the poor and the rich. . . . They all pass over it." But the desire of joining the other side is like the monk's desire for a solid stone bridge.

This poem then, perhaps against the intentions of its author, disconfirms its certainty as much as "the master" disconfirms the monk's desire to cross over to death with certainty and without danger. The poem is the poet's master. Like the stone bridge of the Togetsu Bridge legend (which turns out to be "a rotten piece of board, a plank"), the poem will not hold up, will not transport the speaker to the other side. Its task is to collapse to leave the wish unfulfilled.

If "Moon Crossing Bridge" has a death wish, its wish is the dialectical other of death. The river is the river of death across which beckons the wished-for joining with the beloved. The poem promises passage but the crossing is impossible. The certainty of the joining, now considered in a dejected retrospective, is only the certainty of the lyric imagination: that span of light which would carry one across, surely and safely as a stone bridge. In reality, and when the time comes, one needs a rotten plank.

The light of day, towards which the whole book yearns and awakens, is the "merely aesthetic . . . that saves in daylight." The real yet untenable consolations, those not offered by the aesthetic would be, would have been, in "what we once called worship."

"Two of Anything" (20–21), begins with a "small tug" and "two barges" crossing. But the speaker's request for permission from the dying mate to accompany him, is refused: "'Someone, you know, / has to stay here and take care of things.'" The "you know" has most intimate significance since only the one who knows can properly "stay here."

The desire for death, for a suicidal crossing and joining is already rehearsed "serene / and afloat on the strange broad canopy" (5) of a world abandoned in the third poem of this long sequence, as the speaker is left alone with "the powerful raft of his body" (49). The wish for death is repeated in glimpses throughout *Moon Crossing Bridge,* at the end of "Corpse Cradle," at the end of "Reading the Waterfall," or in "Black Pudding." But the book is also inscribed with the pleasure of the deferments of dying of which the last part offers delightful erotic enchantments:

> let's shine awhile
> without touching. Sensuality is,
> after all, a river that is always waiting.
> Let's wait another way. Not for
> anything, but because waiting
> isn't part of nature. I don't want
> to take a step toward death
> in anyone's company, not even
> for love's sake. (87)

But even the title poem ambiguously, less ecstatically, begs the river to wait, to "let the water *stay* the water"; for there too the river plays the role of time which is to be crossed for a joining. Is then the structure of the love poems in the final section of the book the same as the structure of the poems of grief? Can we learn from the love poems how it is to wait in "the abandoned world" (5), to wait against nature, to "stand a long time by the river / when the moon is high"?

Assuming that the answer to these questions is affirmative, this similarity between death poems and love poems presents itself in the desire for a consummation of an interminable waiting. But unlike love, mourning has no dialogic other, and if the mourner finds a beloved in the last section, he is but another metaphor of crossing, a span of brightness. The desire for dying—in both of its senses, the occasionally literal and more often figurative—pervades *Moon Crossing Bridge,* especially in the ambivalence of pleasure and pain, sex and death. The "Yes" of the first poem may well be taken as an affirmation of such conjunctions: "Do you want me to mourn? / Do you want me to wear black?" (3). Subsequently the speaker enacts her grief in the role of lover: "I climbed up beside you into our high bed" (5) and the dead one appears to her as otherworldly lover: "So the weight of his leg / falls again like a huge tender wing / across my hipbone" (9).

In spite of its last section of love poems, the most faithful lover remains solitude itself.

> There is that getting worse at saying
> that comes from being understood
> in nuance, because the great illiteracy
> of rain keeps writing over my days
> as if to confirm the possibility
> of touching everything so it glistens
> with its bliss bent aside by some soft
> undirected surpassing. (67)

While the act of writing here becomes a substitute object for the missing object of mourning, the very necessity of substitution may explain Gallagher's symbiotic syntax and imagery, her almost private language. The only dialogic object remains writing itself. It "confirm[s] the possibility of touching everything." The abundance of sensuous phenomena—the illiterate rain, the moonlight, the glistening and gleaming, the sleep—are all figures representative of Gallagher's style, which is throughout a language "keenly obscured" (68), a weeping weather of words, incessant, dark and light as moonlight, unconscious or pre-conscious as dream and sleep. Even hermeneutical inquiries might be misapplied, as when "Corpse Cradle" opens with the prohibiting gesture:

> Nothing hurts her like the extravagance
> of questions, because to ask is
> to come near, to be humbled at the clotted nucleus.
> One persistent cry bruises her cheekbones and she lets
> it, lets the open chapel of her childhood brighten over
> her with tree-light. Gray-white future
> of alder, hypnosis of cedar as when
> too much scent-of-nectar combs
> her breathing. Rain on rain
> like an upsurge in his sudden need to graze her
> memory. . . . (6)

As a language of the unconscious, semiotic rather than semantic, "memory prepares a quick untidy room / with unpredicatble visiting hours" (10) for the absent one's "sudden need." Or, as a pendant to

these sudden painful grazings, her grief is felt in flashes of earliest childhood scenes which her mate's death has unpredictably uncovered:

> How I climbed
> like a damp child waking from nightmare to find
> the parents intimate and still awake.
> And with natural animal gladness, rubbed my face
> into the scald of their cheeks, tasting salt
> of the unsayable—but, like a rescuer who comes
>   too late, too
> fervently marked with duty, was unable to fathom
>
> what their danger and passage had been for. . . . (10)

If the experience of death becomes a repetition, or uncovering of a primal injury, then *Moon Crossing Bridge* is a return to the danger and
passage the child had sensed in the parent's intimacy. Again, death and
sexuality are closely linked as primal and culminative experiences. To
return to these experiences, to cross over to them, is the burden of
Moon Crossing Bridge. If to write about death is to write "what is forever beyond speech" (49) Gallagher must write—in one of the most
moving descriptive insights—

> . . . the way a child hums to the stick
> it is using to scratch houses into the dirt, still
> it is a silky membrane and shining
> even to the closed eye. (49)

Notes

1. Sharon Olds, *The Father* (New York: Knopf, 1992). All page references in the text under part I are to this edition.

2. Julia Kristeva, *Black Sun: Depression and Melancholia*, trans. Leon S.
Roudiez (New York: Columbia University Press, 1989), 205.

3. Tess Gallagher, *Moon Crossing Bridge* (St. Paul, Minn.: Graywolf
Press, 1992). All subsequent page references under part II are to this edition.

13

SUFFERING AND
SAINTHOOD

ANNIE DILLARD'S *HOLY THE FIRM*

> . . . illness is not a metaphor, and . . .
> the most truthful way of regarding illness—
> and the healthiest way of being ill—is one most
> purified of, most resistant to, metaphoric thinking.
>
> —Susan Sontag, *Illness as Metaphor*

In his essay "Suffering unto God," Johann Baptist Metz responds to what he sees as a contemporary tendency to reduce the suffering of Christ to a theological or aesthetic concept. Frequently "in the language of the suffering God," he argues, suffering is eternalized, universalized, sublated in a Hegelian "self-movement of absolute spirit," or secretly aestheticized. But suffering, he concludes, "which makes us cry out or finally fall wretchedly silent, knows no majesty."[1] I want to pursue the implication of these observations in a reading of Annie Dillard's book, *Holy the Firm*,[2] where these tendencies, I believe, are particularly visible.

In the second part of this symbolically tri-partitioned book, spanning three days from November 18 to 20, an airplane crashes and "Julie Norwich seven years old burnt off her face" (36). The fiery crash splits the world into two opposing dimensions: world and God, irredeemable matter and indifferent God, time and eternity. Can this division be healed? Can the burnt face of Julie be the site of this healing? *Holy the Firm* answers these questions too unequivocally. Burning and fire are the chief metaphors of the book; they become the metaphoric terms for an eternalization of Julie's suffering, a sublation of individual suffering in cosmic, religio-aesthetic concept.

In part one, we encounter the metaphor of burning in a celebrated passage about a moth which flies into a candle and becomes its wick. The description is a masterpiece of close observation:

> All that was left was the glowing horn shell of her abdomen and thorax—a fraying, partially collapsed gold tube jammed upright in the candle's round pool.
> And then this moth-essence, this spectacular skeleton, began to act as a wick. She kept burning. The wax rose in the moth's body from her soaking abdomen to her thorax to the jagged hole where her head should be, and widened into flame, a saffron-yellow flame that robed her to the ground like any immolating monk. (17)

But the writer too is aflame, so is the artist, so are the seraphs, nuns, and thinkers: "A nun lives in the fires of the spirit, a thinker lives in the bright wick of the mind . . ." (22). Even the cat's tail catches fire. . . . Such are the temptations and pitfalls of allegory and metaphor. Dillard's book becomes an extended metaphysical conceit yoking together heterogeneous ideas such as cats and nuns, artists and burn patients, with "a little violence here and there in the language, at the corner where eternity clips time" (24). Eternity and time, God and Julie Norwich, converge by a violence visible in Julie's wounds as much, Dillard hopes, as in the comparable wounds of writing. For artists, she claims, are "pyrotechnic fools" (50). This metaphor, in turn, seems in a flash of self-revelation, so to speak, to point to the dangers of Dillard's promethean quest for the god in Julie Norwich's burns. While the burning of the moth in the flame of a candle may strike one as romantically appropriate for the consuming desire of artist or saint, how reducible to metaphor, how employable as conceit, is the burning of the face of a child in an airplane accident? How comparable is Julie Norwich's suffering to the suffering of the artist, to the desire of the nun, to the death of a moth, to the tail of a cat?

These questions are answered by the tri-part structure of the book itself which can be said to frame, to preface and to postface, to anticipate and to resolve, the burning of Julie Norwich in the allegories of the moth, the nun, and the artist. When the second part of *Holy the Firm* begins with the sentence "Into this world falls a plane" (35), we are to understand that this falling is the "freak chance" that splits "the skin of illusion" (48). It calls into question the world established in the first part of the book, which is "the world at my feet, the world through the window . . . an illuminated manuscript whose leaves the wind takes, one by one," and which draws the writer into a luminous self-referential textuality: "and I am dazzled in days and lost" (24). The ominous prophetic burning of the moth, of the writer, of the nun, indeed the notion of illumination itself here resound as figures of a transcendental desire wholly innocent, wholly shutting out the real. All fires burn in this first section of *Holy the Firm* to illuminate but a fictional world, one not yet real, still "bound to itself and exultant" (30), happy and hopeless like a spiritual aesthetic, or an aesthetic spirituality into which no plane has yet fallen. As yet a vision beyond "the colorful thought" of the pastoral first part is impossible: "the colors wrap everything out" (29). It is November 18. On November 19,

> Little Julie [is] mute in some room at St. Joe's now, drugs dissolving into the sheets. Little Julie with her eyes naked and spherical, baffled. Can you scream without lips? Yes. But do children in long pain scream?
>   It is November 19 and no wind, and no hope of heaven, and no wish for heaven, since the meanest of people show more mercy than hounding and terrorist gods. (36)

The questions are redundant. Their superfluousness is underscored by the fact that on November 20, on the third day in this trilogy, Dillard will reclaim the world as illuminated manuscript: "There are no events but thoughts . . ." (62). But how can Julie Norwich's suffering be thinkable? Can the facial burns of Julie Norwich become an allegory of something other than the destruction of her face? Does her burning illuminate anything other than her disfigurement? Is suffering not irredeemable matter, event beyond the scope of thought and writing?

Such acknowledgment of the unthinkable is briefly pondered when Dillard laconically remarks, "I heard it go. The cat looked up" (35). But the indifferent gaze of the animal, who is the appropriate respondent to the indifference of events such as airplanes falling out of the sky, is rationalized when Dillard adds, "There was no reason . . ."—for even to negate reason is to reclaim some authorial omniscience.

From the moment of the airplane's crash, Julie Norwich's burn serves as metaphor for the author's own creative / spiritual desire. A few pages after the description of the accident, Dillard not only identifies with the girl—"we looked a bit alike"—she also identifies with the deeper, invisible unreason of her suffering: "We *looked* a bit alike. Her face is slaughtered now, and I don't remember mine" (41). Julie's face is here both metaphor and mirror, the *ars poetica* of *Holy the Firm*.

In what precedes and follows (since the book frames Julie's suffering) the artist, writer, thinker, seraph and angel, nun, (even the cat) all burn prophetically and redemptively for Julie Norwich. All become a Julie Norwich of sorts, whose name moreover suggests that her burning is also a medieval spiritual allegory, or a scene in heaven: as Julie screams without lips, the seraphs cry: holy, holy, holy. As the intensity of the seraphs' love ignites them, Julie gets her face burnt off. As her drugs dissolve into the sheets, the seraphs' love dissolves them. In the second part of the book, fire is thus possibly, Dillard muses, a sublime self-enclosed "power play of fire" in which we are "victims, falling always into or smashed by a planet slung by its sun" (48). But such amplification of Julie's accident in cosmic imagery and its allegorical replay in scenes of angelic worship only belittles the enormity of Julie's, indeed of any, suffering. Dillard's language in this book is a playing with fire in which the author becomes herself "bound by the mineral-made ropes of [her] senses" (48), victim and captive of her style and redemptive imagination.

In the third part, the author encounters Christ in a vision of his baptism. As "He lifts from the water" (67), Christ's movement seems to cancel Julie's falling to earth and Dillard sees, in the manner of John Donne, the whole world contracted into one small drop of water and "all has fused" (67). The fusion has been wrought by the redemptive artist who, "in flawed imitation of Christ" (72), spans all contradictions and opposites "from here to eternity" (72).

Dillard's world has returned in this third part of *Holy the Firm* to a universal pastoral, a vision of the world as illuminated manuscript page, illuminated by the artist who sets the world aflame and whose life goes up in the work like a moth in a candle, who burns sacrificially like the seraphs to "lighten the kingdom of God" (72). We glimpse Julie Norwich once again, this time as an aesthetic image of divine sublation, mutely contained in the consummation of all difference. Three pages from the end she is summoned once more:

There is Julie Norwich. Julie Norwich is salted with fire. She is preserved like a salted fillet from all evil, baptized at birth into time and now into eternity, into the bladelike arms of God. For who will love her now, without a face, when women with faces abound, and people are so? (73)

All the accouterments of the aesthetic as a denial of the world are here: Julie is preserved, plucked out of time and the social world of women and worldly love into the artifice of eternity ("you got there early, the easy way"). Never—excepting Dillard's sudden reversals in the last paragraph of the book—shall she take her bodily form from any natural thing.

Meanwhile, the last pages of *Holy the Firm* seem not wholly unequivocal about aesthetic denial and repression and displacement. Although the next paragraph begins with a statement at best ambiguous: "You might as well be a nun" (74), and Julie returns briefly as the patient in the burn ward waiting to be handed the mirror, these penultimate paragraphs now examine the physical and the spiritual in their mutual exclusion and confrontation. The struggle is palpable. Yet Julie's pain and crying is transformed into the joy and praising of the seraphs, and the pain is erased in spiritual ecstasy: "Held, held fast by love in the world like the moth in wax, your life a wick, your head on fire with prayer, held utterly, outside and in, you sleep alone, if you call that alone, you cry God" (76). But these metaphors of pain, these rhapsodic sublimations of suffering eventually yield to a more worldly form of redemptive imagination. The last paragraph of *Holy the Firm* closes by resorting to the sudden and wholly unexpected availability of a worldly remedy: "Julie Norwich, I know. Surgeons will fix your face" (76) and one is jolted once again—this time uncertain what might constitute the more grievous hubris: to spiritualize Julie's suffering, or to presume one "knows" surgeons will fix her face.

This last remedy must be, among all the others, another metaphor by which Julie's suffering can be thought rather than event, evasion rather than truth. But such displacement is only possible, it seems, by the author's last, Christlike, act of taking upon herself the suffering of Julie: "I'll be the nun for you. I am now"—a sacrificial act that had been foretold in Dillard's transferences and projections, particularly the one where the artist spans "all the long gap with the length of his love, in flawed imitation of Christ on the cross stretched both ways unbroken and thorned" (72). The flaw here is that Dillard, having appropriated Julie's suffering as artistic/spiritual metaphor, cannot resist doing the same with Christ's suffering. Thus, the book is not only consumed by the metaphors of fires but also by the allegory of Christ's all embracing sacrifice which conjoins all opposites and bridges all paradox.

Likewise, conjoining ends with beginnings, *Holy the Firm* arches back to its opening scene where Dillard, the nun, thinker, writer, burning visionary lives "alone" on northern Puget sound, in Washington (13). In this nunlike, secluded, aloneness Julie's cries of pain, cries of spiritual ecstasy, and cries of marital love are prefigured already in the first paragraphs where the author awakens allusively embracing in her own cry the cry of the burn patient, of the nun, of the wife: "someone is kissing me—already. I wake, I cry 'Oh,' from the pillow." (11–12). In its circular, triunal structure the book and its author lastly present themselves as the aesthetic totality within which the unthinkable realities of joy and suffering are—too neatly—resolved.

The forsakenness of the cry of Jesus, Johann Baptist Metz insists, elicits no echo of desire: God is "more and other than the answer to our questions."[3] It is not coincidental that God's radical otherness is most lucidly perceived by those in pain: Christ and Job, but also the Julie Norwich who lives as I write this. For it is in the cries of the sufferer that the more and other of God is audible. To hear God in less than the cry of the sufferer (the cry which is also the language of prayer), or to make God the same as desire, is to reduce the hope for a more radically other consolation than the one we can provide ourselves.

NOTES

1. Johann Baptist Metz, "Suffering unto God," trans. J. Matthew Ashley *Critical Inquiry* 20 (summer 1994):619.

2. Annie Dillard, *Holy the Firm* (New York: Harper and Row, 1977). All page references in the text are to this edition.

3. Metz, "Suffering unto God," 621.

14

THE REMEDY
OF WRITING

RAYMOND CARVER'S "BLACKBIRD PIE"

> . . . pain is the most powerful aid to mnemonics.
>
> —Nietzsche, *On the Genealogy of Morals*

When Michael Schumacher asked Raymond Carver what he encouraged his students to read, Carver answered "letters"—Flaubert's, for example. "Every writer should read those letters. And Chekhov's letters and the life of Chekhov. I'll recommend a great book of letters between Lawrence Durell and Henry Miller."[1] The one book, besides his own, Carver gave me was a collections of letters by Richard Aldington and Lawrence Durell, entitled *Literary Lifelines*. Evidently life and letters enjoy a particularly close correspondence. Letters promise versimilitude, perhaps truth. They do not usually cultivate illusionary methods or draw attention to their own genre or fictional nature. Letters represent those virtues which Carver praised in good stories; neither "circuitous or overblown," letters "work invisibly";[2] they have the same qualities that Ann Vliet attributes to Carver's stories: "it is impossible to extract what is being told from the telling of it."[3]

But just such assumptions about the reliability of letters are in question in that most unusual of Raymond Carver's stories, "Blackbird Pie."[4] There the precise remembering of a lost letter, even possibly the writing of "more letters" ought to ensure the continuance of a past whose lack of continuity dictates continuity. Yet despite his good memory and alleged success in factual tests, the narrator of the story cannot accomplish the task of remembering. Finally, the task is, however ambivalently, delegated to his wife: ". . . history will now have to do without me—unless my wife writes more letters. . . ." Curiously, those future letters like the unread letter in the story, will eventually—so the narrator hopes—be read by "someone [who] can look back on this time [and] interpret it according to the record, its scraps and tirades, its silences and innuendos." If the fragmentary and incomplete nature of this "record" cries out for interpretation, Carver does his best to complicate that task.

Unlike any of his other stories, and in uncharacteristic metafictional manner, "Blackbird Pie" foregrounds problems of writing and narrative. If the chief aim of narrative, as Peter Brooks has claimed, is "the recovery of the past,"[5] the letter presents an allegorical instance of the puzzling uncertainties attending any such reconstructive attempt. As in Poe's "Purloined Letter," the letter itself in "Blackbird Pie" is absent and available only through Carver's parody of the narrator's perfect memory: "I have a good memory. I can recall every word of what I read. My memory is such that I used to win prizes in school because of my ability to remember names and dates, inventions, battles, treaties, alliances, and the like. I always scored highest on factual tests. . . ."

If narratives customarily do not get the business of recovery done to the letter, so to speak, this narrator hopes to prove that assumption wrong. But predictably the story that results from his recall of the mysterious letter is hardly any more reliable than the authorship or content of the letter itself. In the suddenly uncertain world of words created in "Blackbird Pie," where letter means both epistle and typographical character and where "history" is also 'his story,' it is hard to imagine that Carver is not poking fun at those who would claim him for the dirty realist camp.

Armed to the teeth with historical facts, the narrator's memory reveals only that "speaking from hindsight . . . tends to confirm the obvious." "Blackbird Pie" thus develops into a critique, replete with irony and a good deal of humor,[6] of the realist narrative genre and of memory, its oldest muse. The story finally amounts to a major retraction of what has been critically assumed to be Carver's realism.

In the course of the story the narrator abdicates his alleged "good memory" of facts in favor of fictions. He will recall the letter in its partialities and claims, but only so as to revoke it; he will change it—"recreate" is his euphemism—to delay its final verdict. Life might yet be assigned a meaning other than "the obvious." Indeed, "Blackbird Pie" attains an *other* end in an unusual narrative feat: a lyrical postlude with horses wandering in the fog.

The horses make an unprecedented appearance in Carver's stories; their origin appears to be less in Carver's own poems than in the poetry of his wife, Tess Gallagher. Always surreal if benign accomplices of the mental process, horses in Gallagher's poetry announce a "sumptuousness of presence . . . the weight of living so clear a mandate / it includes everything. . . ."[7] Mysterious and revelatory presence, in other words, cannot be attained through a pedantic insistence on "every word." If pursued to the letter, such greedy desire for the fulfillment of life reveals only its "decline," a process which Carver attributes to history. The end of "Blackbird Pie" must therefore be "outside history," a realm of miraculous lyrical recovery "—like horses and fog."

In "Blackbird Pie" Carver presents remarkable insight into the subliminal aspects of narrative and the desire that is its motor. If narratives are to recover the past, the narrator in "Blackbird Pie" with his obsessions about history, autobiography, and memory ought to present a model narrative. But his memory does not stand outside the history it seeks to recover. Memory itself becomes a concealer, covering rather than uncovering the pains of the past.

In spite of his hunger for facts and love of the literal, the narrator's own looking back proceeds by way of particular strategies of evasion and denial. Carver renders these strategies with psychoanalytic instinct and symbolic acumen in a conspicuously absent letter which allegedly the narrator "didn't keep," or protests to have "lost," "or else misplaced," all of which, he claims, happened "accidentally" and entirely "uncharacteristically." The Freudian implications are spelled out boldly enough, suggesting that the narrator's story will itself resound with silences and innuendos. The wife's letter, shoved underneath the door of the protagonist's study, introduces all of the elements of a sudden conversion on Carver's part to a postmodern narrative: "a greater explicitness in the abandonment of mimetic claims, a more overt staging of narrative's arbitrariness and lack of authority, a more open playfulness about fictionality."[8] The letter is unaccountably present, then absent; its authorship is questionable; its claims to truth are denied. Like the minister in Poe's "Purloined Letter," Carver's narrator comes under the spell of the letter, or, as Lacan has called it, under the "twilighting" conditions of narrative. The dubious qualities of the letter become the mise-en-abîme of the narrator's own crisis in telling his story. If his is the story of a last attempted recovery of the past, it is claimed with evasions and qualifications so numerous that they indict the unreliability of the narrator himself rather than that of the author of the letter:

> I would go so far as to say that every word of this entire letter, so called (though I haven't read it through in its entirety, and won't, since I can't find it now), is utterly false. I don't mean false in the sense of "untrue," necessarily. There is some truth, perhaps to the charges. I don't want to quibble. I don't want to appear small in this matter; things are bad enough already in this department. No. What I want to say, all I want to say, is that while the sentiments expressed in the letter may by my wife's, may even hold *some* truth—be legitimate, so to speak—the force of the accusations leveled against me is diminished, if not entirely undermined, even discredited, because she *did not* in fact write the letter. Or, if she *did* write it, then discredited by the fact that she didn't write it in her own handwriting! Such evasion is what makes men hunger for facts.

Even if facts remain elusive, the narrator's suspicions may well be justified. If he doesn't fool us with his memory, his wife writes like Raymond Carver and Carver may well be wryly reading himself. Thus, words themselves become the object of their meaning, most notably when the narrator literally draws "the merest <u>line</u> under a word. . . ." To claim that the story is exemplary of the "more garrulous, less plotted"[9] quality of Carver's seven new stories in *Where I'm Calling From* is therefore to put it mildly.

In "Blackbird Pie" letters, or words, are refused their former reference to life; they no longer yield self-effacingly to that prescriptive authority accorded to "autobiography, the poor man's history," as the protagonist puts it. Here that authority, personified by the wife about to leave her husband, is called into doubt: we learn early on that "the handwriting *was not her handwriting.*" The letter can therefore be purloined, the authority of its narrative prescription can be altered:

> Instead of beginning to read the letter through, from start to finish . . . I took pages at random and held them under the table lamp, picking out a line here and a line there. This allowed me to juxtapose the charges made against me until the entire indictment (for that's what it was) took on quite

another character—one more acceptable, since it had lost
its chronology, and, with it, a little of its punch.

The theory of fiction that Carver is offering here assumes a deeper significance than in any of his other stories. That the letter cannot be produced allows it to be re-produced, and that things cannot be put down
to the letter allows them to be made up, all of which serves to "re-create
the letter." But in spite of the narrator's assurance, "I mean what I say,"
to say and to mean are here not the same. Although he supposedly recalls every word of what he reads, he digresses into fiction even as he digresses into history, reading a past notably more vast and distant than intended in the letter: ". . . names and dates, inventions, battles, treaties,
alliances."

These supposedly factual proofs of his good memory are delivered
with the same kind of "territorial view" that characterizes the vista beyond the couple's house. The narrator's explanation of "territorial view"
as "having to do with a vista appreciated only at a distance," turns out
to be the precise definition of his own fearful narrative point of view in
regard to his own personal history. History in "Blackbird Pie" is a displaced territorial view of suffering, of the pain the narrator has inflicted
and endured. The distance and vastness of the historic facts he quotes intimate the contrary structure of the narrator's memory where the forces
of repression must battle against the forces of an overwhelming personal
responsibility. These forces, in the guise of wars and truces, compulsively
"stick in [his] head;" they come painfully unbidden to his unforgiving
memory like nursery rhymes: "Thermopylae, Shiloh, or the Maxim gun.
Easy. Tannenberg? Simple as blackbird pie. The famous four and twenty
that were set before the king."

While past histories in this story are recalled as relentlessly and fas-
tidiously as in Carver's other stories, all with date and place "down to
the last comma [and] the last uncharitable exclamation point," their significance amounts grotesquely to "the equivalent . . . of a fully loaded
jumbo jet crashing every three minutes from breakfast to sundown."
Perhaps we should read the analogy as a stumble, a slip, bespeaking the
narrator's desire for a final apocalyptic event in which history—his story
as well—would be forced to resolve and reveal itself in all its horrific debris of detail. But Carver, the master of speechlessness, at the same time
reduces to utter absurdity any attempt to find an "equivalent" to the irreducible intimacy of personal history and individual suffering. The

image of a jumbo jet crashing every three minutes all day long underscores in its very absurdity and amplification that suffering has no verbal equivalent, and that it is incomparable to the historic facts and figures the narrator rattles off.

Thus, his story of suffering, even in its telling, remains untold. The place of its composition or rather of its de-composition—"my room"— dooms the narrator to the same kind of isolation that, as William Stull observes,[10] characterizes the existential realism of Carver's earlier work. At the opening of the story, the reference to "my room" indicates a severance of the relationship and a mutual privacy which turns into unsharable solitude. Solitude and separation, as we learn from the narrator, has always been the nature of the couple's relationship: "My wife had no friends here in the country, and no one came to visit. Frankly, I was glad for the solitude. But she was a woman who was used to having friends. . . ."

When the protagonist notes that "It didn't take long to see that my wife wasn't in the house," he is only pointing out a fact established long before her actual leaving in the symbolic layout of the house itself: "(The house is small—two bedrooms, one of which we refer to as my room or, on occasion, as my study.)" The writing which presumably goes on in the house serves paradoxically only to intensify the incommunicable separateness of husband and wife. Both husband and wife write, he writes stories, she letters, but neither of them can read what the other has written. If "things have gone from bad to worse," as he remembers her to have written, it is because they have to write—because the opportunity when "we could have talked . . ." must be written about. And writing always bears the marks of a history accessible only in that most elusive of tenses, the past subjunctive.

This retrospective tense denoting a past possibility and a present impossibility underlies most of Carver's stories, stories of suffering that always have inscribed within themselves a need for talking. As that habitually fails, the need for further writing and re-writing is exacerbated to keep alive the desire for talking—even if each instant of writing also repeats the impossibility of talking: "*I want to talk about us,*" writes the wife, "I want to talk about *now*. The time has come, you see, to admit that *the impossible* has happened."

It is fair to say then that not only talking, but also writing itself is in crisis in stories of suffering. "Blackbird Pie" opens with the narrator's pointing in puzzlement to writing: he stumbles over "purport," a word over which, as Carver shrewdly anticipates, the reader would have stumbled as well. Purport is an unusual word in the context of Carver's laconic style, a word that draws attention to itself as it draws attention to the promises, claims, and appearances that come with letters or words. "Purport" temporarily rends Carver's style. It arrests the relentless "decline" of his plot. It works as a catalyst, inciting the writer to look twice, to re-write, to revise, and to "re-create," so as to deny and to delay. Thus, the story about to depart onto the typical Carverian downward slide "from bad to worse" and from there "to the end of the line," halts at the very beginning. The narrator's resolve to cut and paste the letter's indictment against him appears, in this sense, as a self-conscious effort to revise the ultimate consequences of a personal history of suffering.

But the *self*-conscious narrative finally tells an *un*-conscious tale. The desire to recall the letter in order to revoke it, so that its verdict of an end could be delayed, finally reveals the intimate mental site where that desire originates:

> ... withdrawing farther into ... a small enough thing, but ... talcum powder sprayed over the bathroom, including walls and baseboards ... a shell ... not to mention the insane asylum ... until finally a balanced view ... the grave.

"At this point"—the point of the revelation of a previously repressed and displaced small inward lyricism—the narrator "heard the front door close." The shuffled pages are "dropped," and (in italics): "to let the record show: *every light in the house was burning*." The volatile narrative circumstances of Carver's story, fraught as they are at this point with the weight of too much significance—cannot sustain itself and levels to a lyrical tableau. The records and facts so carefully shored against the ruins of the burning house suddenly appear irrelevant:

> Suddenly,—I don't know how to say this other than how it was—a horse stepped out of the fog, and then, an instant later, as I watched, dumbfounded, another horse. These horses were grazing in our front yard. I saw my wife alongside one of the horses. . . . She was standing beside this big horse, patting its flank. She was dressed in her best clothes and had on heels and was wearing a hat.

Although, in appropriate realist fashion, Carver gives the horses good reason to seek the abundant pastures of this couple's "shaggy" lawn, their appearance marks an unusual lyric pause, both in the story's plot as well as in Carver's style.

Such lyric pauses—tableaux of the desire for a remedy for his story—are anticipated in other stories: most serenely in the drawn space of the cathedral in the story of that title, or in the cathedral-like "high, pale cast of light in the windows" of the bakery in "A Small, Good Thing." There, according to William Stull, Carver transcends the existential realism of the earlier stories and attains a "vision of forgiveness and community rooted in religious faith."[11] Here the Judeo-Christian allusions of "Cathedral" and "A Small, Good Thing" are more likely Romantic and pagan. The same philosophical development that Stull traces in Carver's work is visible in the development of "Blackbird Pie" in the characters' movements from inside to outside, from history to lyric vision, or from writing to a symbolic or pictorial form of understanding. In Carver's own commentary "On *Where I'm Calling From*," he traces the origin of "Cathedral" to a "time-out," a similarly inexplicable non-historical caesura as we witness in "Blackbird Pie," a time filled with "some poems and book reviews . . . And then one morning something happened. After a good night's sleep, I went to my desk and wrote the story 'Cathedral.' I knew it was a different kind of story for me, no question. Somehow I had found another direction I wanted to move toward. . . ."[12]

The altered mental and narrative circumstances initiated with the writing of "Cathedral" seem thus not only repeated but emphasized in the lyrical tableau of "Blackbird Pie." Its more literal origins are attributed to a poem entitled "Late Night with Fog and Horses." Written during what Carver described as an "astounding experience" in 1983, a time of unprecedented poetic activity, the poem suggests that "something had ended, / something else rushing in to take its place."[13] However, the poem itself does not live up to that promise. It ends by reverting to Carver's obsessions about "disastrous phone calls, and maledictions," whereas in "Blackbird Pie" the narrator resolves to remain "outside history," left to contemplate the insufficiency of historic, linear, or factual narratives to account for, and to redeem, the inward life. The "question of the handwriting" finally conjures up one more time the unforgiving literality of "the things I can't forget . . . ," but his compulsive memory yields finally, and one might suppose unexpectedly, to more "subtle things . . . like horses or fog."

The metaphoric totality of the lyrical image, closing as it does an otherwise interminable spiral of autobiographical 'his stories,' appears as the redemptive unplotting of the "history" which the protagonist unwittingly took when he took a wife. If "to take a wife is to take a history," "Blackbird Pie" in its final tableau unwrites that history and expels the former muse: ". . . I'm outside history now—like horses and fog. Or you could say that my history has left me. Or that I'm having to do *without history*. . . . I'm saying good-bye to history. Good-bye my darling."

The story that follows "Blackbird Pie" in Carver's last collection would confirm such a redemptive narrative transformation. "Errand" takes us, significantly, to Europe and an earlier time, far from the settings and times of the former autobiographical allusions and references.[14] If "Blackbird Pie" can thus be read as an act of narrative remedy, its cause appears to lie only externally in the unexpected economic and creative opportunities which Carver experienced in 1983 when he received the Harold and Mildred Strauss Award. Carver's poem, "Late Night with Fog and Horses," seems likewise no more than a draft of the story. The more likely precursor, in terms of the import of the lyrical moment "out of history," appears in such poems as for example "Listening" in *Where Water Comes Together with Other Water*:

> It was night like all the others. Empty
> of everything save memory. He thought
> he'd got to the other side of things.

Even if the poems ends:

> Once more he found himself in the presence
> of mystery. Rain. Laughter. History.
> Art. The hegemony of death.
> He stood there listening.

What the speaker of "Listening" is listening for is the revelation that seems temporarily granted in "Blackbird Pie" where the speaker transcends 'his story' "to the other side of things."

Horses, as I have suggested, figure prominently in several of Tess Gallagher's poems, precisely in those poems which Carver urged her to delete from her *Amplitude: New and Selected Poems*, the book nearing

completion when Carver was in his own poetic phase and when the
"New Stories" existed in draft.[15] In one of Gallagher's poems, the
horses' appearance intimates, like the image of the horses in "Blackbird
Pie," a "sumptuousness of presence," and in another poem their appearance suggests a dream world of "cloud shadows / drowsy as a mind that
can't shout, can't / beseech . . ."—which would lend itself as a fitting epi-
graph to Carver's last scene in "Blackbird Pie." Similar to the narrator of
"Blackbird Pie" who is "outside history," Gallagher writes in "Death of
the Horses by Fire":

> Only when the horses began to burn
> in the funnel of light hurrying in one place
> on the prairie did we begin to suspect
> our houses, to doubt at our meals
> and pleasures. We gathered on the ridge
> above the horses, above the blue smoke
> of the grasses, and they whirled in the close
> circle of the death that came to them, rippling in
> like a deep moon to its water. With
> the hills in all directions
> they stood in the last of their skies
> and called to each other to save them.[16]

The title of Carver's *Where I'm Calling From* seems like an echo to these
closing lines. As in Gallagher's poems, horses in Carver's story appear
from without history. They seem supernaturally equipped, giving off "a
surge of power" but also inspiring fear.

The fact that Carver preferred Gallagher's more straightforward,
narrative poems to her surreal, lyrical ones, and yet that the surreal nevertheless became a catalyst for the kind of "metamorphosis" Carver
wished to undergo,[17] suggests that her influence worked on deeper than
conscious levels. The narrator's sudden liberation from a history which
provided distant images of war and violence for the narrator's compulsive displacements of his own painful history, leads in "Blackbird Pie" to
a sudden understanding—indebted to Gallagher's influence—of the subliminal patterns of his narrative imagination. If Carver reads himself in
"Blackbird Pie," then the closing paragraph might amount to a cathartic
experience, a summing up and repudiation of a fictional pattern.

Whether the late time of its composition, its penultimate place-
ment in Carver's last book of stories and the story's compositional origin
intimate that this is a new direction much abbreviated by Carver's early

death, is an open question. But what seems clear is that "Blackbird Pie" marks a further swerve initiated by "Cathedral" and "A Small Good Thing," away from what Aristotle would call history toward poetry, from what has been towards what might be.

NOTES

1. *Conversations with Raymond Carver*, ed. Marshall Bruce Gentry and William L. Stull (Jackson and London: University Press of Mississippi, 1990), 221.

2. Ibid., 126.

3. Ann Vliet, review of *Where I'm Calling From*, *Dallas Morning News*, June 19, 1988.

4. All quotations of "Blackbird Pie" are from *Where I'm Calling From: New And Selected Stories* (New York: Atlantic Monthly Press, 1988).

5. Peter Brooks, *Reading for the Plot* (Cambridge: Harvard University Press, 1984), 311.

6. See Cynthia Gail Thompson-Rumple, "'It's Grave, Life is, Tempered with Humor': Counterpoint Humor in Selected Stories of Raymond Carver," Thesis (East Carolina University, 1991), 84–92.

7. Tess Gallagher, *Amplitude: New and Selected Poems* (St. Paul, Minn.: Graywolf Press, 1987), 145.

8. Brooks, *Reading for the Plot*, 317.

9. Christopher Lehmann-Haupt, review of *Where I'm Calling From*, *Nashville Tennessean*, May 29, 1988.

10. William L. Stull, "Beyond Hoplessville: Another Side of Raymond Carver," *Philological Quarterly* 64 (winter 1985):9.

11. Ibid., 11.

12. Raymond Carver, "On *Where I'm Calling From*," in *No Heroics, Please*, ed. William L. Stull (London: Harvill, 1991), 127.

13. Raymond Carver, *Where Water Comes Together with Other Water* (New York: Random House, 1985), 100.

14. For an insightful discussion of the narrative qualities of "Errand" see: Claudine Verlay, "'Errand'" ou le réalisme de R. Carver dans un bouchon de champagne," *Visions Critiques* 7 (Publications de la Sorbonne Nouvelle).

15. See Tess Gallagher, "European Journal," *Antaeus*, 61 (autumn 1988): 169–70.

16. Gallagher, *Amplitude*, 145, 187, 108–9, resp.

17. See ed. Stull, *No Heroics, Please*, 127.

THE REDEMPTION
OF REMEMBERING

DENIS DONOGHUE'S *WARRENPOINT*

> To John, who died
> —Denis Donoghue, *Warrenpoint*
>
> Everything can be made up . . .
> —Leo Bersani, *The Culture of Redemption*

The culture of redemption structures even the attempts of its own dismantling. In the example of a book of that title the author claims that in the culture of redemption

> [e]verything can be made up, can be made over again, and the
> absolute singularity of human experience—the source of
> both its tragedy and its beauty—is thus dissipated in the triv-
> ializing nobility of redemption through art.[1]

However, the principles of aesthetic redemption are already implicit and secretly at work even in this disavowal. For Bersani can invoke the dissipation of "human experience" only by first redeeming it from history and making it the "source" and reference of "tragedy" and "beauty." Tragedy and beauty, of course, are themselves no products of history, and to invoke them is to invoke precisely the redemptive aesthetic that

203

Bersani would hope to enlist in its self-destruction, so that "the absolute singularity of human experience" would itself become an art.

An aesthetic history, or an aesthetic understanding of time is perhaps inevitable. It is, as I conclude at the end of this book, perhaps impossible to write and not to redeem in writing an order which in time is perpetually dismembered. Wallace Stevens, another aesthete, imagines the redemptive aspect of art in its most doomed encounter with time, "the hooded enemy":

> It is time that beats in the breast and it is time
> That batters against the mind, silent and proud,
> The mind that knows it is destroyed by time.

"Even breathing is the beating of time," but only "in kind," and that small aperture towards metaphor is enough to yield to time "a retardation" and out of the temporary fluttering of its murderous pulse arises, "If we propose," "a form," "platonic," unreal but human.

Such form, Kant or Schiller knew, is arguable only as an ideal in art. History denies it. Bersani's "absolute singularity of human experience" is thus not empirically arguable but an unwitting memory of what Denis Donoghue has recently called "a better life."[2] Why the aesthetic has particular qualities one might consider "better" than those offered by external, historical reality is a question Donoghue asks in *Warrenpoint*[3] with respect to memory. *Warrenpoint* is Donoghue's autobiography of his boyhood in the town of that name, only slightly north of the border of the Republic of Ireland and therefore, I take it, at the site of an exemplary historical intersection, the book might respond to the question we ask of art: can it, must it, redeem history?

Donoghue's book is (only) a memoir, not a work of art, but memory has in common with art that it is to record here, in the manner of poetry, art, or music, "the unofficial sense of history" (124).[4] Yet, like its aesthetic analogues, *Warrenpoint* has no programmatic intention. The book seems, and yet does not seem, particularly keen to remember. It is finally not so much a remembering of the past as a meditation on remembering, and therefore a literal answer to Bersani's charge that "everything can be made up, can be made over again." Implicit in the act of meditation is the question: can it?

As far as history is concerned, particularly the history of "Ire Land"[5] Donoghue's answer is no. He deplores—one feels with altogether too much finality—that "It is pointless to speak of the 'problem' of Northern Ireland if a problem implies a solution. There is no solution. Instead there is a situation—a situation about which, as the history of the past sixty-eight years has shown, little can be done." The last paragraph of *Warrenpoint* concurs. The book concludes with a report from the *Irish Times,* for Thursday, 13 April 1989, of a bombing in Warrenpoint in which a twenty-year-old woman was killed and thirty-four people were injured. Here too, Ireland is a situation, not a problem; little can be done: "Life in the north goes on, in some fashion," is how the essay "Ire Land" closes.

Arguably in these instances Donoghue's position exemplifies Bersani's notion that "[c]laims for the high morality of art may conceal a deep horror of life. And yet nothing perhaps is more frivolous than that horror since it carries within it the conviction that, because of the achievements of culture, the disasters of history somehow do not matter. Everything can be made up. . . ." One cannot immediately see why Donoghue's lifelong claims for "the high morality" of art would *not* confirm Bersani's point. But the last words of *Warrenpoint,* the description of the site of the bombing, are not unequivocal. The passage records that one of the bombings occurred at the site of Donoghue's former home. He adds laconically: "The building . . . was not structurally damaged." The incident, one senses, is quoted with resignation, perhaps with "horror of life," but the site is mentioned with wonder. About wonder, we read elsewhere that it "is the willingness not to draw conclusions from the evidence, or not to draw them immediately."[6] Since the book closes both with the horror of life and the determination not to draw conclusions immediately, it is left in question, for the time being, whether memory accomplishes openings against the closures of history.

Perhaps the test of memory's possible redemptive qualities must be sought in closer relation to the author. *Warrenpoint* is dedicated to Donoghue's brother, who died at the age of fourteen months. In the impossibility of the address, "For John, who died," memory employs itself. It is not, of course, what memory accomplishes, for there is no addressee, but how it behaves itself on the verge of silence. How can memory "be other than . . . history?" (19)—is now the question. How can one reclaim, as Schiller might have asked, from the state the interior state of the fine-tuned soul, how claim from time "The eloquences of light's faculties" and imagine, as Stevens writes, "the speech he cannot speak"?

Such aesthetic concerns are contrasted to seemingly grander, historic observations when Donoghue admits:

> I wonder about the status of things we forget. According to
> my family's history, I was brought to the Eucharistic Con-
> gress in Dublin in 1932. It was in the summer, in Phoenix
> Park, and the Pope celebrated Mass, and McCormack sang
> "Panis Angelicus," and thousands of people came from all
> over Ireland to take part in the ceremonies. I have not the
> least recollection of being present. I was three years and
> seven months old, and the whole episode is blank to me. But
> I remember vividly John's death six months later. The first
> thing I remember was a death in the family. Isn't it strange
> that I developed—if that is the correct way of putting it—the
> power of memory just in time to employ it upon the first
> event worth remembering? (30–31)

The question is rhetorical, with a qualifying pause to ponder the "employment" of memory, and with a sense again of wonder. Donoghue's
qualifying "if that is the correct way of putting it" suspends the conclusion usually drawn from a more deterministic theory claiming that the
incisive event initiates the power of memory and the greater power of
forgetting and suppression. Perhaps the rhetorical form of the question
suspends the answer to the question in what causal relationship memory
stands to event, or whether memory might be held accountable.

The whole passage, with its opening sentence about the status of
forgetting, builds towards the problem of remembering, or rather of remembering as a problem. Such moments are frequently pondered
throughout the book and contrasted with an abundance of dates, even
documentary proof; but the latter suggest only that that is not what is
meant, at all. Here memory, ready to "employ" itself on the death of
John, is belated and fails by half a year to record "The Eucharistic Congress in Dublin" in spite of its attendant splendors. Instead, the "first
event *worth* remembering" (my emphasis)—as if by implication such
value were denied the Eucharistic Congress—is John's death, an event
noted as an incongruity and with an implicit, if muted, hint of guilt and
complaint.

History, so reproachfully charted in the six months between the
Eucharistic Congress and John's death, and so keenly remembered in
the dedication, is irredeemable history, irredeemable because neither
the forgetting nor the remembering will affect it. But the charting, the
guilt, the reproach, or the regret—or other perhaps more appropriate
words of such inward order—constitute an unofficial time, where loss

is entertained in the presence of memory and where memory attempts, one suspects, some form of redemption of John's brief life.

But these suspicions are secular and prove unsupported by Donoghue, who holds to the contrary that "A Christian's conviction impels him to ask, chiefly of his own life: Has it been a valid preparation for the true life to come, when the soul may hope to enjoy the eternal presence of God? The shape is not considered, since the life is to be completed only 'in our next.'" Consequently, few "possibilities" are ascribed to Donoghue's own life, which takes its dejected beginning "with the first moment I remember, my brother's death. . . . The site of my possibility coincided with the end of his" (127–28). Possibility and impossibility, life and death, beginning and end are here, I assume, without intention, linked by the rhetoric of irony and paradox. But these implicit formal closures are opened to an exception: "The site of my possibility coincided with the end of his; except that we believe, as Catholics, that he is in Heaven" (128). Human existence is thus not subject to the aesthetic question: "Had the life a coherent shape, a form, or did it merely break off?" (127). Nor does Donoghue permit himself the satisfactions of well-wrought forms of memory. Instead, by allowing the interventions of exceptions, memory must serve larger purposes than its own form, larger purposes than the past, and larger purposes than those that can be celebrated by thousands of people from all over Ireland.

Like art, memory is the unofficial historian. Both perform a duty to uphold what Emmanuel Levinas calls "an order different from historical time, in which totality is constituted, an order where everything is *pending*, where what is no longer possible historically remains always possible."[7] Levinas's concept of interiority which has appeared repeatedly and assumed an important position in Donoghue's more recent work, would hold the promise of envisioning the arrangements of time and events other than by the "production of the future" (124) or the logic of causality or the temper of chronos. "Other" would be, as Frank Kermode has aptly put it, to humanize time. Such a time, to which memory seems to give us an immediate and often travelled, if mysterious, access (being the oldest muse), is most severely tested against the formidable argument of John's death. But the test yields the ethical dimensions of humanized time. These dimensions do not diminish or shrink in proportion to temporal distance or factual loss, a thing one feels rather than knows when one of the reviewers of *Warrenpoint* comments: "Odd this harping on a person (if a fourteen month-old child can properly be called a person) of whom the memoirist has only the vaguest memories. It is as if this poor, lost mite is here to represent other, greater losses."[8]

Donoghue's book, finally, has no redemptive quality, nothing can be made up, Ireland remains a situation. These are the dimensions of time and matter, inhumanized time in which a fourteen-month-old child hardly amounts to a person. But in these dimensions death and loss, suffering and illness are only charts and statistics, amounting to a diagnosis. About suffering, one might say with Kleinman, they are silent. Memory, like art, always employs itself too late. It can do nothing about the death of John or the bombing at Warrenpoint. Yet memory is free to entertain notions of loss as such, perhaps all the more irredeemable because only imagined and remembered.

As a humanizing of the inhuman, as a calling forth of the human out of suffering and death, memory becomes a prospective of the future, not so much a record as a prophetic speaking.

NOTES

1. Leo Bersani, *The Culture of Redemption* (Cambridge: Harvard University Press, 1990), 22.

2. Denis Donoghue, "Towards a Better Life," in *The Pure Good of Theory* (Oxford: Basil Blackwell, 1992).

3. Denis Donoghue, *Warrenpoint* (New York: Knopf, 1990). All subsequent page references in the text are to this edition.

4. Donoghue derives the concept from Emmanuel Levinas, particularly *Totality and Infinity* (1961), trans. Alphonso Lingis (Pittsburgh: Duquesne University Press, 1969): "Memory recaptures and reverses and suspends what is already accomplished in birth—in nature. . . . By memory I ground myself after the event, retroactively: I assume today what in the absolute past of the origin had no subject to receive it and had therefore the weight of a fatality. By memory I assume and put back into question. Memory realizes impossibility . . ." (56).

5. Donoghue, "Ire Land," *The New Republic* (December 18, 1989):38.

6. Donoghue, *The Pure Good of Theory*, 76.

7. Levinas, 55; see *Warrenpoint*, 124.

8. John Banville, "Portrait of the Critic as a Young Man," review of *Warrenpoint*, *New York Review*, October 15, 1990: 48.

AFTERWORD

Weh spricht: geh!
—German Proverb

"The physical moment tells our knowledge that suffering ought not to be, that things should be different. 'Woe speaks: Go.'"[1] Adorno's formula, "Woe speaks: 'Go,'" is poetically as just in English as it is in the original German. It echoes a fundamental association of suffering with language: the necessity with which the cry needs articulation, how articulation reproaches, denies, wishes away the pain, and yet how language in its sounds and rhythms recalls and repeats the cry. If "Woe" is the inarticulate cry of pain, in the word "Go" the cry of "woe" is given a language. "Go" remembers "woe," "woe" necessitates "go," but "go" also denies "woe." The language emerging from suffering is not only a visceral, immediate bodily reflex, but also the foundation of literature, of elegy and tragedy: ". . . suffering ought not to be . . . things should be different," as Adorno writes. In the word "Go" is implicit the "ought not" and "should be" which are the foundations of culture.

In the same way, as I have suggested in this book, literature contains within itself an inarticulate cry, a pre-linguistic wound. But although it resounds with the echoes of suffering, literature's cause remains without remedy and the literary enterprise therefore infinite, the hermeneutical task endless. While Kleinman's case of the little girl in the burn ward traces this primordial wound beyond the language of therapy to wit's end, we strain to see the same wound behind the Vietnamese woman's hand. But her hand gestures with the same refusal of granting the gaze permission as literature keeps, in its mysterious revelations, the secret of suffering. Were it not for this secret—however unverifiable—would we read in Job's complaints anything but its own eloquence? in his wife's bitter silence anything but blasphemy? in the fierce suffering of Antigone anything but piety? What we learn in the splash of Icarus, in Sylvia Plath's poetry, on the interminable bridge of desire in Tess

Gallagher's poetry, in the material body of Sharon Old's father, is what they will *not* tell us.

Art retains the irreducibility of suffering in its own irreducibility to meaning. Art echoes the autonomy of suffering in its own autonomous form, contains the mute, material experience of suffering in its own artistic materiality. Like suffering, art is gratuitous and purposeless. The hermeneutical task is therefore not a form of mastery but a form of empathy. Contrary to the desires of knowledge to close the unanswerable questions opened by suffering, art keeps knowledge open, makes knowledge itself a wound, and thus art becomes an occasion where our reading, or listening, or looking—if only by empathy—is itself a suffering. Such a hermeneutic is not a form of reason but an admission of the insufficiency of reason in the face of the unreasonableness of suffering and art.

A hermeneutic of empathy often eludes textual verification, as it does most explicitly in the chapters on *Antigone* and on Sylvia Plath. The only verification is in the contours of texture, the way the text awakens suspicion and legitimates hermeneutical curiosity. But even if *Antigone* allegorizes, as I believe, the secrecy of suffering, the act of reading can be transgressive in the same way in which Kleinman's question, "tell me how it is?" could have been transgressive. If the exemplary literary question, which is a question about the secrecy of suffering, can be asked, it can be asked only at wit's end, that is, after other forms of inquiry have failed. If the literary text does not produce such failure, if it does not draw the reader to a final aporia, it is not literature.

In the Opening Remarks of "The Critical Difference" Barbara Johnson writes:

> Literature, it seems to me, is the discourse most preoccupied with the unknown, but not in the sense in which such a statement is usually understood. The 'unknown' is not what lies beyond the limits of knowledge, some unreachable, sacred, ineffable point toward which we vainly yearn.[2]

While I agree with much of this statement, this book attempts to propose suffering as that "unreachable, sacred, ineffable point" radically beyond the limits of knowledge. While Johnson believes the unknown is simply a function of "the oversights and slip-ups that structure our lives," I have here tried to argue that the unknown—while being all these things—is also, or additionally, a fundamental, indeed essential reality: a meaninglessness, a secrecy, a causelessness, against which literature launches its strategies of remembrance and forgetting, avowal and denial.

The present book thus takes issue, though implicitly and only at the very end somewhat more polemically, with a historicized world where everything is constructed, nothing essential. While I maintain that suffering—though not its modes of expression—is an essential reality beyond the historically constructed world, the point of this book is also that one cannot prove such a point in writing a book. If suffering is indubitable certainty, self-presence of existence, fundamental aloneness, the difficult purpose of art is to maintain the paradox of the expression of suffering, to convey certainty through the doubt of language, the indubitable presence of the suffering body through its absence in representation, the unbearable pain in the sharable syntax of narrative. And if art is to articulate precisely *this* paradox, neither can such a proposition, based as it is on a radically unknown, be verified. The positing of suffering as an essential reality, and of art as defined by the paradox of its expression—these assumptions must necessarily remain in question.

NOTES

1. Theodor Adorno, *Negative Dialectics* (1966), trans. E. B. Ashton (New York: The Seabury Press, 1973), 203.

2. Barbara Johnson, *The Critical Difference: Essays in the Contemporary Rhetoric of Reading* (Baltimore: Johns Hopkins University Press, 1980), xii.

INDEX